Route 66

MICHAEL WALLIS

Route 66
THE MOTHER ROAD

75th Anniversary Edition

ST. MARTIN'S GRIFFIN ❧ NEW YORK

To
Ann Wallis
and Ellen Fitzgerald,
Two women who knew the highway's lure,
And to
Suzanne Fitzgerald Wallis,
My constant companion on the Mother Road

The publisher gratefully acknowledges permission to reprint from the following: "Oklahoma Hills" by Jack Guthrie and Woody Guthrie, copyright © 1945 Michael H. Goldsen, Inc., copyright © renewed and assigned 1973 to Michael H. Goldsen, Inc.; "So Long It's Been Good to Know Yuh" ("Dusty Old Dust") by Woody Guthrie, TRO—copyright © 1940 (renewed), 1950 (renewed), and 1963 (renewed) Folkways Music Publishers, New York; *A Guide to Highway 66* by Jack D. Rittenhouse, copyright © 1946, 1989 Jack Rittenhouse; *Route 66 Revisited* by K. Hilleson, copyright © 1985, 1988; *The Grapes of Wrath* by John Steinbeck, copyright © 1939, 1967 (renewed) by John Steinbeck, reprinted by permission of Viking Penguin, a division of Penguin Books USA Inc.: "(Get Your Kicks on) Route 66," words and music by Bobby Troup, copyright © Londontown Music, Inc.

Endpapers: An early promotional map of Route 66 used for the Bunion Derby. Courtesy of Jim Williams, Broken Arrow, Okla./Macoupin County Historical Society, Carlinville, Ill.

Title page: Cadillac Ranch, created in 1974, west of Amarillo, Tex. Photograph by Suzanne Fitzgerald Wallis, 1989.

Contents page: Inside the 66 Cafe in Ash Fork, Ariz. Photograph by Terrence Moore, 1976.

www.stmartins.com

Book design by Glen M. Edelstein and Judith Stagnitto Abbate
Page layout by Susan Hood

Library of Congress Cataloging-in-Publication Data

Wallis, Michael,
   Route 66 : the mother road, 75th anniversary edition / Michael Wallis.
    p cm.
  ISBN 978-0-312-28161-8
  ISBN 0-312-28161-7 (pbk)
West (U.S.)—Description and travel—1981– 2. United
   States Highway 66. I. Title. II. Title: Route sixty-six.
F595.3.W35 1990
917.804′33—dc20   89-77813
           CIP

Anniversary Note:
The Mother Road Turns 75

Route 66—the highway some folks thought was dead and gone—is alive and well and kicking like never before.

This historic ribbon of asphalt and concrete paid its dues through several incarnations since its birth in 1926. In the process it endured the wrath of nature as well as more than its share of human abuse and neglect. The old road (at least a major portion of it) also survived the coming of five interstate highways that tried in vain to take its place. That is why it is only fitting that the date of the Mother Road's anniversary—November 11, 1926—falls on the same date as the birth of the national holiday now known as Veterans Day.

Today's rendition of Route 66 is a grizzled veteran but with the allure and prestige of an aging celebrity. The highway has become part of popular culture, something no other highway can claim. There is a deep, some say even subconscious, reason for the highway's abiding fame. Route 66 runs from Lake Michigan across two-thirds of the continent to the Pacific shore. So does much of our nation's history. In other words, our economy and culture have been making that same journey. Route 66 expresses who we are, where we live, what we do, and whom we can become. I believe it truly is the most famous highway in the world.

Sometime ago, Route 66 reached American icon status and not just because of the physical roadbed or all the historical and cultural treasures that litter its shoulders from Chicago to Santa Monica. This road is much more than remarkable examples of commercial archaeology, diverse natural and fabricated attractions, and gentle curves tailor-made for a purring Harley or a speedy Corvette.

It is also important to remember that Route 66 is people. That is what the road has always been about and why it remains active and relevant to this day. I was inspired to write and publish this book in 1990 after continuing to meet remarkable people along the highway I loved. As a son of Route 66, I grew sick and tired of hearing the road referred to in the past tense. I knew that although the familiar highway shields had vanished and the new interstate highways now bypassed towns, the people of the Mother Road remained. I unabashedly consider this book a love letter and tribute to those people.

I believe the people are what count the most. They motivate all those concerned with the highway's preservation. The human equation of Route 66 inspires the writers, poets, musicians, photographers, and artists who revere the highway in their own work and respect the men and women living and working along the road.

Through good and bad times, the people of the Mother Road remain. They are in Bloomington, Edwardsville, Rolla, Joplin, Riverton, Vinita, Clinton, Shamrock, Vega, Tucumcari, Gallup, Winslow, Needles, Barstow, and all the other towns and cities and wide spots in the road. The people are there. They run convenience stores and souvenir shops. They have refurbished an abandoned home or a forgotten building, turning it into a tearoom, a bed-and-breakfast, or an antique haven. They are still serving up old-fashioned, meat-and-potato meals with homemade rolls and pies, or they have turned to lighter fare for the health conscious traveler. They leave tried-and-true careers behind to bring back to life a historic theater or curio shop or mom-and-pop motel.

No matter how the people make their living, a growing number of them trumpet their services and wares, adding a Route 66 shield to their signage in front of everything from auto salvage yards and photocopy centers to video rental stores and tanning salons.

I find proud people anxious to meet and serve travelers at Fedderson's Pizza Garage, Red Cedar Inn, Boots Motel, Eisler Brothers Store, Lyons Indian Store, The Big Texan, Blue Swallow, Monte Carlo Restaurant, Jack Rabbit Trading Post, La Posada Hotel, the Museum Club, the Goffs School, and Santa Monica Pier. The people of the road make the trip worthwhile.

Each time my wife, Suzanne, and I venture out on Route 66 we always find someone new and original. Our journeys are never stale or boring. We turn over a rock and another genie appears. We round a bend and come across another dreamer or muse or a keeper of magic. We open a door and discover a new friend.

The people keep us going and they keep us coming back for more. They give us choices. They help us realize that although we cannot get along without the big superhighways, it is so good to have the alternative of the old road to turn to when we find time is on our side and we can savor its pleasures. The people of Route 66 stir our passion for the Mother Road and constantly remind us why we prefer this trail of Steinbeck, Guthrie, and Kerouac to the impersonal detached superslabs.

In some places the old highway may only be a service road or paved fragments of original alignments that run off into the weeds. But the very act of finding it is part of the adventure. And along many stretches, the road once known as America's Main Street is free of overwhelming interstate traffic and truly is the best way to go.

It has been a sweet ride for seventy-five glorious years, but I believe the best is yet to come. I trust you will agree after reading this book. This new edition includes the 75th Anniversary update section filled with testimony and images of the unprecedented Route 66 revival.

Happy Anniversary, Route 66! Happy Anniversary to all of you who guard the past, keep the road in the present, and look forward to the future. Job well done. Bravo! Bravo!

MICHAEL WALLIS
Out on Route 66
On the brink of 2001

Contents

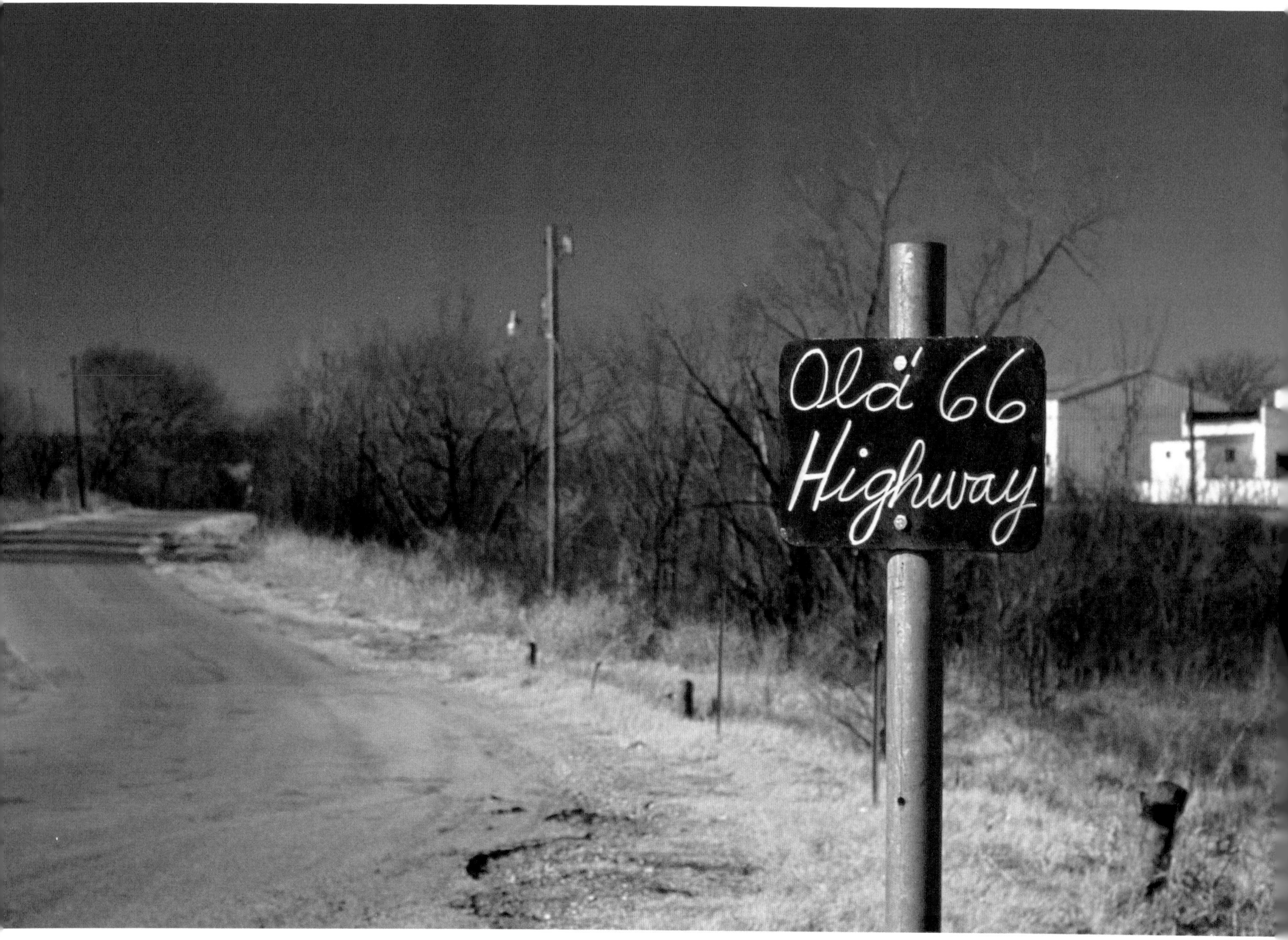
Old 66
Highway

Introduction

"A stop in one of the small towns most anywhere along old Route 66 offers evidence that life begins at the offramp. Away from the superslab, you can still order a piece of pie from the person who baked it, still get your change right from the shop owner, still take a moment to care and to be cared about, a long way from home."

Open-road travelers are made more than born. They are as different from theme-park tourists as anything you can imagine. Tourists rush; travelers mosey. Tourists look for souvenirs; travelers seek out the souvenir makers. Tourists want to see all the right places; travelers simply go into the country.

Travelers are openly romantic about the going itself, the adventurous possibility of it all. Some who are also writers and photographers create images of what they find. Others just take everything to heart, sharing their keepsakes through a love for us all. This book takes both into account. Superbly.

If you are to become a traveler, it helps if your first big trip as a child is a lulu. Mine was. We were California bound—on Route 66.

The first winter day's run south to St. Louis was blurry with snow, and I am embarrassed to recall that my just traded *Flash* and *Green Lantern* comics were more interesting to me than anything passing by our old Buick Roadmaster. So I read and slept mostly.

At the famous Chain of Rocks crossing, which connects Illinois with Missouri, my father slowed to a crawl, waking me to see the icy Mississippi River. Girder shadows slipped over us as we rolled out beyond the minifortresses standing guard in the main channel below. Reaching the far side, I could just make out a federal highway shield: MISSOURI / U.S. 66. WEST.

For a kid who had never traveled more than a few miles from home, that sign and everything it conjured up was a revelation. I believe it was the first time I saw myself in

Tribute to The Mother Road, west of Sapulpa, Okla.

relation to the world instead of the other way around. Highway 66 had my attention.

Soon Missouri's craggy limestone gave way to the round-shouldered hills of Oklahoma. Gray winter land and frozen surfaces turned to boggy red with splashes of green still showing. Even the concrete in the highway took on a strange new pinkish hue. From there it was up onto the high plains of the Texas Panhandle, flat featured and unforgiving. Near sundown each day, most travelers on Route 66 would find a cozy motor court and stay put. We frequently kept going.

At night, out on that old two-lane, it was common to drive for an hour or more without seeing another pair of sealed beams. Rolling along in the darkness for miles without finding an encouraging highway sign, we would sense a feeling of tension creeping into the car. *Were we still on the route? Maybe we should've quit at the last town. How's the fuel? Will we make it? No filling stations way out here.*

Then suddenly, on the rim of the surrounding blackness, some tiny oasis of light would appear: Texola, Shamrock, McLean. Friendly roadside neon, like airport runway lights, guiding us in to a safe night's rest. In the morning: still, cool air, with frost on the windshield. Time enough to appreciate a warm

leather jacket on the way over to a steamy cafe, proverbially said to be the best place in town. Which, often as not, it was.

By the time we reached the rimrock country of New Mexico and Arizona, my consciousness had been altered forever. I didn't think of it that way, of course, but I certainly felt it. Everything seemed connected in some intangible way. I sensed something resonant in the cliff faces, in the sky, in the endless run of highway beneath. Something that seemed to be in me, too . . .

That was back in 1947, and if time has changed the highway, its attraction for me has never diminished. The "innerstate" is safer, easier now, of course. Yet even a brief drive along old Route 66 reminds us of what is missing on the superhighway—and in our lives. On the old road, every rise or dip, every side-road junction, every new direction gives rise to the feeling that we have actually been somewhere, that we are actually getting somewhere. In between, the ever changing roadway helps us regain the experience of *going,* rather than of merely being transported from place to place.

A stop in one of the small towns most anywhere along old Route 66 offers evidence that life begins at the offramp. Away from the superslab, you can still order a piece of pie from the person who baked it, still get your change right from the shop owner, still take a moment to care and to be cared about, a long way from home. *Come far today? Oh, where ya headed? Still got quite a ways to go, then. Well, thanks for stoppin' in. And drive careful. We hear there's some weather up on the ridge. Come see us when you're through this way again.*

So, beyond the sense of history and romance and adventure evoked by the old road, there's something else: a feeling of personal involvement. And that's what *Route 66: The Mother Road* conveys so well.

Michael and Suzanne Wallis are travelers in the fullest sense of the word. And like real travelers, they are of the land and its people, caring deeply for everyone and everything they touch. So it is natural for us to want them to stay awhile. To spin a yarn and share a memory or two before moving on.

On these pages are the sharply etched literary and photographic images of what can be found along that wavy old two-lane. This book then is a keepsake to other travelers who may also, in rediscovering old Route 66, find something of themselves.

—TOM SNYDER
Founder, Route 66 Association
Oxnard, California

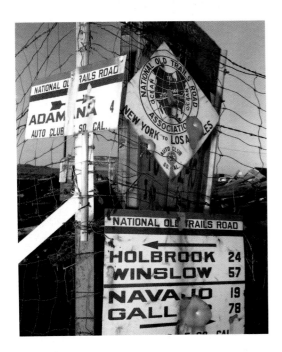

CHAPTER ONE

America's Main Street

"66 is the mother road . . ."
—*John Steinbeck*

oute 66. Just the name is magic.

Route 66. It conjures up all kinds of images. *Route 66.* An artery linking much of the nation.
Route 66. An inspiration to literature, music, drama, art, and a nation of dreamers. *Route 66.* A
highway fashioned from vision and ingenuity. *Route 66.* A broken chain of concrete and asphalt.

Route 66. It has forever meant "going somewhere."

U.S. Route 66, starting at Grant Park in Chicago, reached across more than 2,400 miles,
three time zones, and eight states—Illinois, Missouri, Kansas, Oklahoma, Texas, New Mexico,
Arizona, California—before it dead-ended at Santa Monica Boulevard and Ocean Avenue in Santa
Monica. People like to say the highway started at Lake Michigan and ended in the roaring Pacific.
It was one of the country's first continuous spans of paved highway linking East and West.

Almost everyone in the United States, at one time or another, has traveled at least a stretch
of its length. One of the most famous highways in the world, parts of it have also been known as
the Pontiac Trail, Osage Indian Trail, Wire Road, Postal Highway, Ozark Trail, Grand Canyon

Left: A 1937 stretch of Route 66 near Valentine, Ariz.

Above: Relics marking the Mother Road's antecedents in
eastern Arizona.

Route, National Old Trails Highway, Mormon Trail, and the Will Rogers Highway. John Steinbeck called it "the mother road, the road of flight." Some, like the Okies, knew it as the "glory road." Because it went through the center of so many towns, it became the "Main Street of America."

Route 66 is Steinbeck and Will Rogers and Woody Guthrie and Merle Haggard and Dorothea Lange and Mickey Mantle and Jack Kerouac. It's thousands of waitresses, service station attendants, fry cooks, truckers, grease monkeys, hustlers, state cops, wrecker drivers, and motel clerks. Route 66 is a soldier thumbing home for Christmas; an Okie family still looking for a better life. It's a station wagon filled with kids wanting to know how far it is to Disneyland; a wailing ambulance fleeing a wreck on some lonely curve. It's yesterday, today, and tomorrow. Truly a road of phantoms and dreams, 66 is the romance of traveling the open highway.

It's the free road.

The highway has been a mirror held up to the nation. Route 66 put Americans in touch with other Americans through its necklace of neon lights, Burma Shave signs, curio shops, motor courts, garages, and diners and cafes with big-boned waitresses. Waitresses who served up burgers, plate lunches, and homemade pie. Waitresses with coffeepots welded to their fists. Waitresses with handkerchief corsages pinned on their bosoms. Waitresses, like Steinbeck's Mae, who called everybody "honey," winked at the kids, and yelled at the cook.

Route 66 means a time before America became generic—when motels didn't take reservations, when there were genuine barber shops and drugstores, and doctors made house calls. Movie theaters weren't look-alike boxes in a shopping center. There were no diet soft drinks or imported waters. People drank straight from the tap and sipped iced tea brewed by the sun, or guzzled bottles of cold beer or Coca-Cola or Grape Nehi. America seemed more innocent. Billboards on the highway were legal; hitchhiking was safe. Nobody knew about cholesterol. Summers lasted longer because there were drive-in movies and miniature golf courses and slow-pitch softball games under the lights.

Route 66 was also a highway of flat tires and overheated radiators; motor courts and cars with no air-conditioning; tourist traps with few amenities; treacherous curves, narrow lanes, speed traps, and detour signs.

A thread looping together a giant patchwork of Americana, this fabled road represents much more than just another American highway. Route 66 means motion and excitement. It's the mythology of the open road. Migrants traveled its length; so did desperadoes and vacationers. Few highways provoke such an overwhelming response. When people think of Route 66, they picture a road to adventure.

Route 66 in the decade of the 1920s was the America of Edgar Lee Masters, Sinclair Lewis, and Thorton Wilder. It was the America of garden scarecrows, porch swings, watermelon feasts, lemonade stands, and children sticking their stocking feet out the back window of the family car as

Dad made time on the road.

The highway that spanned two-thirds of the nation was christened in 1926, when the nation was between wars and on the wagon. Calvin Coolidge was president. People across the country, especially in the Bible Belt, were still mulling over the Scopes trial of the previous year. Aimee Semple McPherson, Admiral Richard Byrd, Gertrude Ederle, and the U.S. Marines, landing in Nicaragua to quell a revolt, were also making headlines. Queen Elizabeth II was born that year. So was Fidel Castro. Luther Burbank, the man who developed about one thousand new plant varieties, died on his Santa Rosa, California, farm. Charles Russell, the famed Western artist, also died.

The great Florida land boom was at its zenith. Congress established the Army Air Corps. It was a vintage year for Ferber, Fitzgerald, Hemingway, and O'Neill. Robert Goddard launched the first liquid-fueled rocket, and the St. Louis Cardinals became world champions of baseball on an October afternoon when a right-hander named Grover Cleveland Alexander strolled out of the bullpen in Yankee Stadium and struck out Tony Lazzeri with the bases loaded. That same month much of the nation went into mourning when Rudolph Valentino, the matinee idol who had arrived in America penniless dreaming of a farm in the West, died at the age of thirty-one.

In 1926, Sherwood Anderson had just completed his novel *In Dark Laughter,* which H. L. Mencken characterized as "having the cruel truth of a snapshot." Theodore Dreiser

Top: Cracked Route 66 shield near Albuquerque,
N. Mex.

Left: The Route 66 game inspired by the popular
television series "Route 66" that aired from 1960 to '64.

Right: Cafe door, Twin Arrows, Ariz.

Bottom: U.S. 66 decal.

lumbered out of the Hoosier midlands, writing books that depicted the ordinary lives of commonplace people in America. George Gershwin was the rage. Greta Garbo and Gloria Swanson were big Hollywood stars. Motion pictures were still a year away from finding their voice, and Fred Astaire, dancing with his sister, Adele, had not yet discovered Ginger Rogers. Another Rogers—Will, the cowboy philosopher—was holding court in New York.

It was also in 1926 that Henry Ford changed the life of the nation by lowering the price of motorcars. The growth of the automobile industry and the addition of more drivers put added pressure on state and federal authorities to come up with some better roads. Politicians were made acutely aware that drivers were also voters. At long last, the stage was set to build a transcontinental American highway, which became steeped in the history of the land it crossed. It had been a long time coming.

Americans had desired good roads back in the 1800s, but their interest faded for a while when railroads came along and gave people a rapid and inexpensive way to travel across the country. Following the Civil War, there was a renewed push for road improvements. That effort continued to grow in the twentieth century once inventive geniuses, such as Ford, appeared on the scene and the motorcar made its debut.

Two sharp reverse curves above Goldroad between Kingman and Oatman, Ariz., 1934.

By 1915, as pressure for new highway construction mounted, some states, such as Oklahoma, strengthened their state highway department by establishing a larger highway commission and assigning new duties for the members. Then the federal government passed the Federal Aid Road Act of 1916, which made funds for new highways available to the states. This new act encouraged more cooperation between local and state authorities when it came to choosing routes and building roads. By the end of World War I, the good-roads movement in America was gaining momentum. Still, as of 1920, of the almost 3 million miles of highways in America, the majority were fit only for travel by horse and buggy. Only about 36,000 miles had all-weather surfaces that would accommodate the wear and tear of automobile traffic.

By the 1920s the automobile began to stir the popular imagination. The motorcar was changing the nation, including courtship habits and family life. The auto allowed workers to live outside the city and commute to their jobs. It ended the farmer's isolated life. Most of all, it provided an escape. That meant roads had to be in better shape. To this end, Congress modified the Federal Highway Act in 1921; the new law called for the construction of a system of interconnected interstate highways. The states were warned that if they wanted to stay on the federal revenue teat, they would have to designate up to 7 percent of their roads as national highways. This was the start of the federal highway system.

One of the key forces behind this national plan, and the country's strongest booster of the Chicago–Los Angeles route,

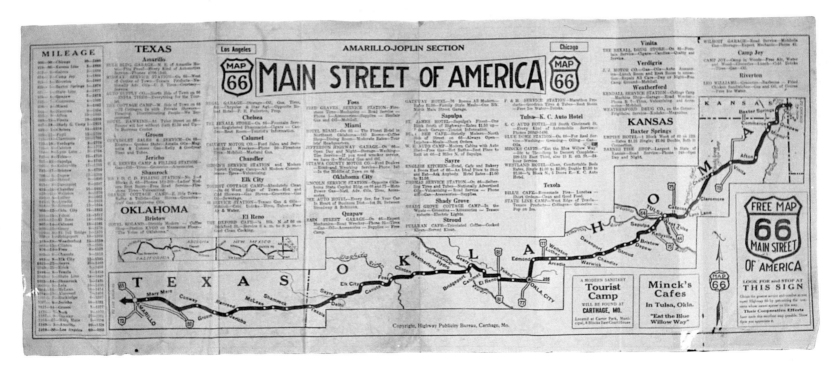

Highway Publicity Bureau's "Main Street of America" vintage map.

Cyrus Stevens Avery, 1927, "The Father of Route 66."

Right. Blading the road through Arizona's Music Mountains, north of Hackberry Wash Bridge, 1934.

was an untiring Oklahoman, Cyrus Stevens Avery, better known as Cy. Without Avery it is doubtful that U.S. 66 would ever have become a reality. As a result, he has become known to thousands of admirers as the "Father of Route 66."

Born in Stevensville, Pennsylvania, in 1871, Avery came to Indian Territory, present-day eastern Oklahoma, when he was in his early teens, growing up on a farm near Spavinaw Creek in the Cherokee Nation.

After graduating from William Jewell College at Liberty, Missouri, he married Essie McClelland. In 1907, the year Oklahoma became a state, Cy and Essie moved to Tulsa, the city that became Avery's home for the rest of his life. He organized a realty firm and a coal company, and he started acquiring oil leases—including some with Harry Sinclair—in the booming Oklahoma oil patch, and demonstrated for several decades a fervent interest in developing major roads and highways for the region.

Shortly after World War I, the Avery family built the Old English Inn and Service Station adjacent to their farm at the junction of Highways 33 and 75, just 7 miles outside Tulsa. The gray fieldstone buildings with red tile roofs were located on what was known as "Avery's Corner," and became a landmark for all Tulsans. Locals and visitors alike enjoyed Sunday dinners of chicken and biscuits or heaping mounds of tasty chicken salad served in the tea room.

Avery was determined to see better highways built, not only for his state but for the nation. In 1921, he was elected president of the Associated Highways Associations of America, with forty-two member associations across the country. His work in this organization had a profound impact on state and national highway legislation. Avery was appointed state highway commissioner of Oklahoma in 1923 and also acted as the first chairman of the new three-member State Highway Commission, which laid out the state highway system, organized a maintenance program, and established a method of installing markers on the highways.

Avery also emerged as a leader of another important highway organization—the American Association of State Highway Officials. It was at the association's 1924 annual meeting in San Francisco that a landmark decision was made regarding the future of federal highways such as Route 66. The highlight of the session came when the membership made a formal request of Secretary of Agriculture Howard M. Gore to

appoint a board, composed of representatives from the Bureau of Public Roads and various state highway officials, to take action concerning the nation's highways. Some highway archivists believe this petition may have been the single most important action in America's twentieth-century highway history. The membership's request was straightforward and to the point:

This Association hereby requests the Secretary of Agriculture, in cooperation with the several states, to underwrite immediately the selection and designation of a comprehensive system of through interstate routes and to devise a comprehensive and uniform scheme for designating such routes in such a manner as to give them a conspicuous place among highways of the country as roads of interstate and national significance.

As a result of this action, the Secretary of Agriculture appointed a twenty-one-member board to confer with the forty-eight state highway departments. The Secretary also appointed Avery, through the Bureau of Better Roads, to act as a consulting highway specialist. Avery's primary task was to lay out and create what would be known as the United States Highway System and prepare for submission and approval a map showing the most important interstate highways in the United States. Avery was ideal for the job. All of his past experience and know-how was brought into play as he and other members of his board studied existing trails and roads to

determine candidates for the federal system.

Beginning in 1925, Avery and the others who wanted to find a way to make travel easier began actual selection of existing state roads for the proposed network. Because of private road clubs that had popped up all around the nation, there were at least 250 marked trails throughout the United States. Many of these road clubs began lobbying and fighting for their trails to be included in the national highway system. Because of Avery's persistence and ability to withstand tough political and regional infighting, the transcontinental highway that passed through Kansas from Chicago and St. Louis and continued west over the National Old Trails was diverted south to what ultimately became known as Route 66. Instead of adopting the traditional northern route, which followed the historic Santa Fe Trail, or the far southern route, which tracked the Butterfield Stage line, Avery was successful in establishing yet a third route. This one ran between the two other routes and roughly corresponded to the old Gold Road from Fort Smith, Arkansas—a route that happened to come directly through Avery's hometown of Tulsa and the state capital, Oklahoma City.

To help avoid confusion, the nation's highway commissioners decided to assign numbers instead of names to the existing roads, with even numerals for highways running east and west, odd numbers for those running north and south. The routes that crossed state lines would be given shield-shaped signs signifying U.S. highways or circular signs identifying them as state roads.

candidates left and found that the number 66 was available. It was accepted, and memos were sent to the state highway departments of the eight states along the route informing them of the proposed highway's name—U.S. Route 66.

Most people, including Cy Avery, liked the way 66 sounded. There was something catchy about 66, and the double sixes were easy to remember.

"We assure you that U.S. 66 will be a road through Oklahoma that the U.S. Government will be proud of," Avery wrote the chief of the Division of Design for the Bureau of Public Roads. The national interstate map showing the rest of Avery's highway system, including all the proposed numbering, was approved by the federal government. On November 11, 1926, a committee of federal and state highway officials met in Pinehurst, North Carolina, and signed off on the interstate routes for all forty-eight states. After two years of planning, bickering, and compromising, it became official —Route 66 was a reality.

The highway would wind out of mighty Chicago and traverse the gently rolling Illinois farmland, where the soil was the color of licorice. In Missouri the road would closely track the old Osage Indian Trail and the Wire Road, and cut across the state in a southwesterly direction. The highway would

It was also decided that main highways would be numbered under 100, with the more important roads designated with zero numbers, such as 40, 50, or 60. As it turned out, the assignment of the route numbers proved to be as controversial as the route selection itself.

Initially, Avery and officials from Missouri and Illinois decided that the Chicago–Los Angeles passage should be called Route 60. Officials from Kentucky and Virginia vehemently objected. They were supporting a proposed highway linking Newport News, Virginia, with Springfield, Missouri, and wanted that highway to carry the number 60.

Both sides dug in and refused to yield. Avery's faction even had U.S. 60 signs in production and 600,000 state highway maps were printed in Missouri that actually showed Route 60 winding through the state.

After months of firing salvos back and forth, both sides grew fearful of congressional intervention, which they believed could wind up scuttling the entire national highway plan. Finally, Avery and his supporters resigned themselves to picking another number for their highway. At a gathering of the Oklahoma, Illinois, and Missouri officials in early 1926, they looked at the list of possible

briefly caress the Kansas prairie before marching across the oil fields and ranchlands of Oklahoma. It would continue through the Texas Panhandle, climb the steep plateaus and mountains of New Mexico and Arizona, and cross the desert of southern California on its way to the Pacific coast.

When the highway became official in 1926, about 800 miles of the route were already paved. The surface of the remaining 1,648 miles was either graded dirt or gravel, bricks covered with asphalt, or, in a few stretches, nothing but wooden planks. It took considerable time for the various state engineers and construction companies along the route to bring the existing roads up to federal standards. As always, local politics and funding problems caused delays. Although paving and road-improvement efforts were started immediately, it would take until 1937 to pave—in most places with concrete or macadam, a surface of broken stone—the

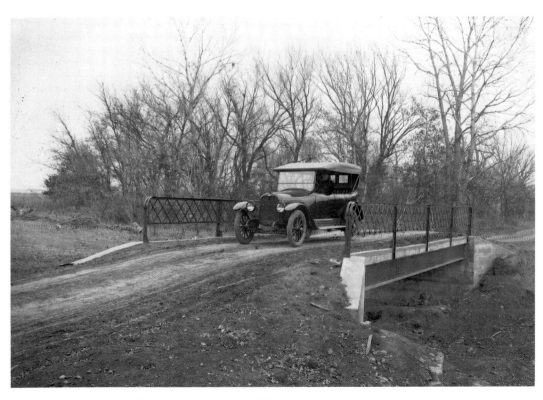

Traveler on state road in northeastern Oklahoma, early 1920s.

A Route 66 Portrait

Bobby Troup

Born: October 18, 1918
Occupation: Songwriter, actor
Residence: Encino, California

"My full name is Robert William Troup, Jr. I was born in Harrisburg, Pennsylvania. My father was an excellent pianist, but I was not a very good pupil and he gave up on me. He died when I was in high school, never knowing I had taught myself how to play.

"I was educated at the Wharton School of the University of Pennsylvania.

entire length of this American highway.

Shortly after the announcement about the creation of U.S. Route 66, Avery and John Woodruff, a Missourian from the Ozark Trails Association, organized the National U.S. 66 Highway Association, with a vice president from each of the eight states on the route. The primary goals of the association were to get the road paved and to let citizens along the route know about the imminence of the new highway. Representatives from Illinois, California, and Arizona failed to show up at the group's first meeting, held in Tulsa on February 4, 1927. But the members from the rest of the Route 66 states, along with a noisy

Above: Construction of early Route 66 roadbed near Tulsa, Okla., early 1920s.

Right: Early highway boosters gather at Tulsa's old Frisco Railroad Depot, circa 1924, Tulsa, Okla.

but supportive delegation from Arkansas, were more than enthusiastic. It was during his keynote address at this meeting that Cy Avery wisely recommended that the association also adopt the name "The Main Street of America" for use on promotional brochures, postcards, and maps.

By April 1927, the state of Missouri had granted the association a charter that spelled out the group's primary mission. "The association is formed to promote the early completion and secure permanent maintenance of U.S. Highway No. 66 between Chicago and Los Angeles, commonly called 'The Main Street of America,' and to encourage the people at large to use the same. . . ."

The official charter also described U.S. 66 as "the shortest and most direct route between the Great Lakes and the Pacific Coast, traversing as it does the prairies of Illinois, the scenic beauties of the Missouri Ozark region, the lead and zinc section of the Joplin-Miami district, the oil fields of Oklahoma and the Texas Panhandle, the south foothills of the Rocky Mountains in New Mexico, the Grand Canyon area, Arizona and Southern California."

Over the next few years, the association began an advertising campaign in national magazines and newspapers. It used billboards along the route to extol the virtues of the fledgling Route 66. Public enthusiasm quickly grew, and requests for information began pouring into the Springfield, Missouri, and Tulsa offices.

One of the most dedicated proponents of the new highway was Lon Scott, the association's clever public relations director. Shortly after he was recruited by Cy Avery to serve as the "promotions man" for the association, Lon Scott trudged up and down Route 66, getting signatures for the petition to charter the organization. "With an association and a national number, the U.S. 66 Highway was about ready to be adorned with markers, signs, placards, and warnings about deep sand traps, soft shoulders, washouts, deep ruts," Scott later wrote of his busy job. "All Southwestern newspapers, from St. Louis to Los Angeles, were generous with any favorable news, such as construction lettings on sections of U.S. 66, and traffic on the route built up fast, and became furious at times when rain and sand and construction barriers caused detours and other troubles. U.S. 66 received so much hell, it had more detours per mile than any other federal route."

But as Scott also noted, "The U.S. 66 boosters didn't flinch. They could see that traffic was growing, that local business all along the route was improving. The vice presidents were pleased and they drove over the route to see and visit each other. . . . Our publicity releases were going out to the newspapers whenever we had something good and important to print about U.S. 66 construction and the towns and cities on the route."

Although history records it otherwise, it was actually Lon Scott who in 1928 first came up with a rather unusual event that attracted considerable publicity for the highway. It was a foot race. To be exact, a 3,422-mile transcontinental foot race from Los Angeles to

In college I was in the dancing chorus of the Mask and Wig Club. I wrote songs, including 'Daddy.' It was recorded by Sammy Kaye and became No. 1 on the Hit Parade for weeks. That got me my start in the music business. I graduated in 1941, and went to work for my favorite of the big-band leaders— Tommy Dorsey. I was frightened when I auditioned for him, but I got the job as music arranger and songwriter. I worked for seventy-five dollars a week until Pearl Harbor Day, when I reported to the Marine Corps. I was in the Pacific Theater and ended up a captain. I served from 1942 until 1946.

"After the [second] war, I came home to pursue my musical career. The family had music stores in Lancaster and Harrisburg that I could have gone into, but I told my mother I had to find out if I had any talent and there were only two places for a songwriter to go—New York or Los Angeles. I picked L.A. I was really determined to go out to Hollywood and make it as a songwriter. My wife at the time was named Cynthia, and we left our two little girls with my mother. She was going to bring them out later on the Superchief. My mother was crying when we took off in our green 1941 Buick convertible.

"We were out on the Pennsylvania Turnpike headed west when we stopped to eat at a Howard Johnson's. Cynthia

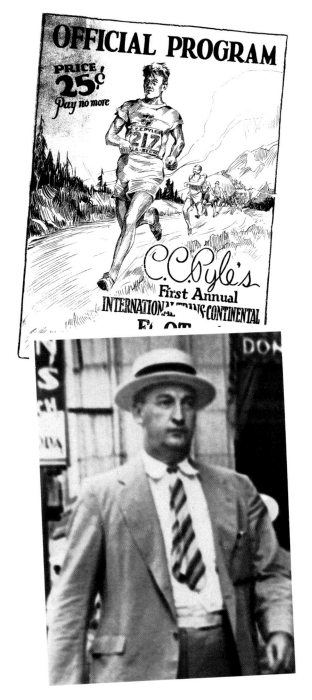

New York. Even in that era of bizarre promotions and fads, when flagpole-sitting, barnstorming, and marathon dances seemed commonplace, the notion of allegedly sane adults shelling out $100 each, in 1928 dollars, for the privilege of racing across the country had to be the most bizarre stunt by far.

The idea for the marathon foot race originated at a U.S. Route 66 civic leaders' dinner in Oklahoma City. According to Scott,

"As the banquet drew to a very happy ending, some waggish booster yelled out loudly, 'What are you going to do next for U.S. 66 publicity?' And quick as a flash somebody else yelled, 'Put on a foot race!' That voice sounded like Alec Singletary, of the Oklahoma City Chamber of Commerce, but I never found out for sure. So many were flabbergasted and so utterly stunned with mirth they were guffawing, 'Foot race, foot race, foot race,' and laughing as they walked out of the banquet hall. There were dozens of them—the finest gentlemen in Oklahoma, Missouri, Kansas, and a few from Texas. Our business, political, and religious leaders, our civic leaders, yes, our best citizens were red in the face from laughing."

Above: Bunion Derby program, 1928.

Left: Early Route 66 publicist Lon Scott, in the late 1940s.

But not everyone present thought the foot race idea was outlandish. "One of the reporters, who was still talking to the guests, came up and commented, 'That foot race idea, you'll want to be sure to dig into that, it's worth a lot to your highway. You'll reap more publicity for your southwest country than any other idea I know.' Another reporter suggested, 'If you're through here, come along with me to the city desk and we'll ask them for ideas.' "

The reporters told Scott if he wanted to hold a Route 66 foot race the man to get was C. C. Pyle, a promoter known around the country as the P. T. Barnum of professional sports. Pyle's initials stood for "Cold Cash" or "Cash and Carry," depending on the audience. The son of a Methodist preacher, Pyle's reputation grew when he convinced University of Illinois football sensation Harold "Red" Grange to turn pro and join the Chicago Bears. "A call was put in for him to one or two sports desks in New York City," wrote Scott. "Neither could find him so they left word for Pyle to call me in the morning at my office in Springfield, where U.S. 66 Highway Association was using space rent free. So the next day C. C. 'Cash and Carry' Pyle called and wanted to know who stirred up the foot race. That's how it all got started."

Although Pyle got all the credit for masterminding the race, it was Lon Scott, the publicist for the Route 66 boosters, who had, of course, first proposed the promotional scheme. The association pledged $60,000 if Pyle would oversee the race. He agreed. Scott was hired to handle publicity. The idea was for the runners to leave Los Angeles, race the length of Route 66 to Chicago, and then turn northeast and head for the finish line in Madison Square Garden in New York. The race winner would be handed $25,000 and all the towns and cities along U.S. 66 would receive publicity that advertising could not create.

Pyle was also certain he would personally make a fortune from the $100 entry fees. He planned to peddle programs along the race route and to receive endorsements from shoe, foot ointment, and suntan lotion manufacturers. Billed throughout the land as "C. C. Pyle's International Trans-Continental Foot Race," reporters stuck their tongues in cheek and quickly dubbed the grueling event the "Bunion Derby."

In the promotional literature that was prepared for the race, Pyle wrote, "Authorities on crowds are unanimous in predicting that with proper local advertising millions of persons can be attracted to various cities and towns along U.S. 66 Highway to witness the titanic struggle between the greatest long distance runners of the entire world." No stranger to hyperbole, Pyle declared that winning the race would be "the most stupendous athletic accomplishment in all history."

On March 4, 1928, 275 runners took their places at the starting line in Los Angeles. "Red" Grange was chosen to ready the contestants and start the race. A crowd of more than 500,000 well-wishers waited. At 3:46 P.M. the famed "Galloping Ghost" set off a bomb and the Bunion Derby began.

The runners had come from across the United States and several foreign nations. Many were true greyhounds—bona fide long-distance runners—with impressive marathon victories to their credit. Of all shapes and sizes, some participants were clad in bibbed overalls and boots, others wore Indian moccasins. A few ran barefooted. One "runner" was an elderly man carrying a cane; another entry toted his ukulele. An out-of-work Hollywood actor took off in a long robe he borrowed from a Biblical movie set. Some runners were accompanied by trainers and even family members and pet dogs. There was a hospital bus and a big bus with sleeping quarters for the press. The serious runners all had one goal—to beat the others and take home the enormous sack of prize money. A doctor monitoring the event predicted that the strain would take at least ten years off the life of anyone who completed the race.

One runner, struck by a hit-and-run driver, miraculously was able to continue, but many others dropped out along the way. A sixty-three-year-old marathoner from England set a fast pace for the first fifteen hours. At the close of the first day, seventy-seven runners had dropped out. A dozen quit the second day, eighteen more on the third. Blisters, heat exhaustion, and fallen arches took their toll.

The trek across the Mojave Desert was especially grueling, an experience shared by Okie migrants a decade later. To add to the difficulties, the first cook hired to feed the runners was fired over a pay dispute. Temperatures were torturous and a

was studying the road map and she said to me, 'Why don't you write a song about Route 40?' I told her that was really kind of silly because pretty soon we were going to be picking up Route 66.

"So we went on and later, out of St. Louis, she leaned over to me and whispered, kind of hesitantly because of my putdown of her first suggestion, 'Get your kicks on Route 66.' I said, 'God, what a marvelous idea for a song! What a great title!' I had a ruler, and I got it out and measured the distances and looked at the scale on the map and figured it was more than two thousand miles from Chicago to L.A. So I started putting the song together in the car. It ended up kind of a musical map of the highway.

"We stopped and saw the Meramec Caverns. We stopped at Claremore, Oklahoma, and saw the Will Rogers Memorial. We hit a big snowstorm near Amarillo that was really very frightening. I got my hair cut in one of those little western towns, and we crossed the desert and mountains. It was a fascinating trip for us.

"When we arrived in Los Angeles, I worked on the song some more, and after about five or six days, I was able to get in and see my real idol, the great Nat 'King' Cole. I played some of my music for him and then I told him I had another song I was just writing—it wasn't quite finished. He said he'd like

replacement chef, fond of mulligan stew, seemed to serve the dish on filthy plates at nearly every meal. The treacherous run to Oatman, the Arizona mountain town, was broken up by a ferryboat ride across the Colorado River, which divides California from Arizona.

Many of the towns along the way balked and refused to pay Pyle their sponsorship fee, and in some areas the huge crowds expected never materialized. Still the runners pressed on. The lead seesawed for several days between two sleek Finns—Willie Kolehmainen and Olli Wanttinen—and an English marathoner from South Africa named Arthur Newton.

About the time the racers reached the heart of the Texas Panhandle, a twenty-year-old named Andrew Hartley Payne, wearing the number *43* on his singlet, and hailing appropriately enough from neighboring Oklahoma, emerged among the race leaders.

A part-Cherokee Indian farm boy who grew up in Foyil, Oklahoma, not far from Claremore, Andy had read about Pyle's cross-country Bunion Derby in a newspaper and was determined to win the race. He immediately started training, first by speed-walking and then running across the rolling pastures of his family's farm. During the first part of the contest, when the runners faced the torrid desert along U.S. 66, Payne paced himself alongside a pair of Hopi Indians, who also had high hopes of taking home the prize money. Lubricated with liniment, the runners arrived at Needles, California, on the Arizona border. Andy, unlike the other runners, didn't

have to fool with the ferry. He was given a canoe ride across the Colorado by some local Indians who heard he was a Cherokee. By the time the runners reached Santa Rosa, New Mexico, accompanied by Pyle and Grange and a small army of reporters, only ninety-three badly sunburned men were still in the race. Andy decided the time had come to turn on his speed. He sensed victory.

As the racers moved across the Panhandle and reached the Oklahoma state line, Andy Payne took the lead for the first time. He became an instant hero not only for Oklahomans but many others along Route 66.

Governor Henry S. Johnston met Andy with a big home-state celebration at the fair grounds when the runners made it to Oklahoma City. As was later the case in Tulsa, motorcycle cops preceded the race leaders past grandstands and cheering crowds on the sidewalks. Andy paused during the festivities to take the speaker's stand and tell his well-wishers, "Hello, home folks. I'm glad to be back. Hope to see you in New York."

There were many other parties and salutes to the lean country boy throughout the state. Rural schools even remotely close to Route 66 were dismissed so everyone could go down to the shoulder of the highway and root for Andy. In Sapulpa, a group of Creek Indians standing along the highway gave the young Cherokee a rousing cheer, and just up the road at Tulsa, while the caravan spent the night on cots in the cool shadows of the Lee School gymnasium, Cy Avery put in a plug for the native son. "We are tremendously lucky to have a young fellow like Andy Payne of

to hear it, so I played 'Get Your Kicks on Route 66.' He loved it! He said it was great, and he wanted to record it right away. I finished the song, and he did just that. On the basis of that song, I was able to go out and buy a house and stay in California. It became a big hit. I never realized when I was putting it together that I was writing about the most famous highway in the world. I just thought I was writing about a road—not a legend. Nat recorded the song and then over the years everyone else did.

"My only disappointment came when they put together the television series *Route 66*. My publisher told me they'd more than likely use my song as a theme. But they didn't. They had Nelson Riddle write the music so they wouldn't have to pay me royalties. I went on to write other songs. I became an actor and appeared in movies and different television series. Cynthia and I divorced, and now I'm married to Julie London, the singer and actress, and we live quietly in Encino. But you know, I still get asked all the time about that song. And years after I wrote it, I'd run into Nat 'King' Cole and he'd tell me the same thing, that out of all his music, out of all the many tunes he recorded, the song that was more requested than any other was 'Get Your Kicks on Route 66.' That always made me feel good."

Tourists in 1937 on a gentle curve on Route 66 near Valentine, Ariz.

Andy Payne, winner of the 1928 Bunion Derby.

Claremore in the race and that he has the stamina to put into the race to win," Avery told a crowd of reporters. The next day, the runners raced toward Claremore, where a white line across the pavement marked the halfway point between Los Angeles and New York. This was Andy Payne's true home country. When he reached the Claremore city limits, a squad of cadets from Oklahoma Military Academy formed a bodyguard around Andy and stayed in running formation with their hero all the way to the white line.

Across Oklahoma and for much of the rest of the race, Andy was pressured by Peter Gavuzzi, an Italian from Southampton,

England, who many predicted would ultimately win the derby. Two years older than Andy, the fleet-footed Gavuzzi was a veteran runner who had already recorded a couple of major marathon victories. The Bunion Derby, in contrast, was Andy Payne's very first race. During the long journey the two men actually became good pals and often ran side by side. In several laps their times were identical. The Gavuzzi-Payne duel continued through Oklahoma, across the corner of Kansas, through Missouri, across the Mississippi River into Illinois and Indiana, and into Ohio where an infected tooth finally caused Gavuzzi to drop out. When the two Hopi Indians reached the humid Midwest, they, too, were forced to give up. The climate and cities proved too much, while Andy Payne just kept on running.

Only 70 brave runners were able to make the Route 66 leg of the race to Chicago. Of the 275 who started, 55 would cross the finish line in New York 87 days after leaving Los Angeles. At the end it was Andy Payne who crossed the finish line first, hours ahead of the remaining runners.

Payne had completed the 3,422.3-mile course in just over 573 hours of actual running time. With $25,000 in prize money, Andy went home to Oklahoma and paid off the mortgage on his parents' farm, and in 1934 went on to become clerk of the state Supreme Court. He was reelected to the post seven times.

A disgruntled C. C. Pyle, whose initials folks now said stood for "Corn and Callus," found himself in the hole. "There has been a

Jack D. Rittenhouse

Charlotte and Jack Rittenhouse

Born: November 15, 1912
Occupation: Writer, editor, rare-book
**   collector**
Residence: Albuquerque, New Mexico

"*I* was born in Kalamazoo, Michigan. My father was an irrigation engineer and his specialty was putting in the huge pumps that were used for irrigation systems out West, so we lived in the Arizona desert during my early years. I

Opposite page: View from Chain of Rocks Park, Riverview Drive, St. Louis, 1947.

A m e r i c a ' s   M a i n   S t r e e t   *17*

lot of talk about how much these boys suffered," lamented Pyle. "There is not one of them who suffered more than I did." The flamboyant promoter placed much of the blame for his financial woes on the association and Lon Scott, who Pyle claimed, spent all of his time and money promoting the highway and not the race itself. But as far as Scott and Cy Avery and the others in the association were concerned, the Bunion Derby was a significant promotional event that greatly bolstered the image of the highway and helped make U.S. Route 66 a household word in America.

"Within a year of its designation, Route

Above: An overburdened flivver in Amarillo, Tex., circa 1941.

Right: Phillips 66 Service Station, 1947, Tulsa, Okla.

66 had entered into the national vocabulary as a special American road," says Arthur Krim, professor of urban geography at Salve Regina College in Newport, Rhode Island. "It is still special. Very special."

Less than three years after the highway was officially opened, the Roaring Twenties lost their force. The economy began to crack, the stock market bottomed, and the nation plunged headlong into the years of the Great Depression. When unprecedented droughts besieged farmers in the Midwest and Southwest, starting in the brutal summer of 1930 and lasting for the next several years, U.S. 66 became the proverbial Dust Bowl highway—a road of flight.

Among those first Okie caravans fleeing to the supposed land of milk and honey in California were vehicles carrying spectators. These folk were also California-bound, but not to find work. They were headed to the tenth modern Olympic Games in Los Angeles, in 1932, where they would cheer for Mildred "Babe" Didrikson, as she established new world records in track and field, and Clarence "Buster" Crabbe, a gold medal winner in swimming before he became Hollywood's Flash Gordon.

But for the poor dirt farmers, whose lives and fields had literally been blown away, there was no time for fun and games on the road. For them, the highway was a migrant's path through a funnel, which they believed would flow into the fertile fields of southern California. Their plight was forever immortalized in John Steinbeck's *The Grapes of Wrath,* the Pulitzer Prize–winning novel of 1939, which told the story of the Joad family and its escape down Route 66 to the promised land.

"Route 66 became more than simply a U.S. federal highway number," says geographer Krim. "It was the symbolic river of the American West in the auto age of the twentieth century. Along its course flowed the American migration from the Midwest to California. In the process, it became an icon of free-spirited independence linking the United States across the mountain divide to the Pacific Ocean."

The grim years of the Depression and the Dust Bowl seemed to last forever. On April 14, 1935, a huge black dust storm blew out of western Kansas, crossed Oklahoma, and moved over the Texas Panhandle. It looked to eyewitnesses like the end of the world. At the time, balladeer Woody Guthrie was living in Pampa, Texas. He spied the ugly clouds descending on the land, went inside his house, and scribbled down the words for a new song.

> So long, it's been good to know yuh,
> So long, it's been good to know yuh,
> So long, it's been good to know yuh,
> This dusty old dust is a-getting my home
> And I've got to be drifting along.

Guthrie's song became an anthem for the down and out, the disenfranchised who traveled west on Route 66 following the sweet scent of orange blossoms to California.

went back East for some time and received an education. I met my wife, Charlotte, in Chicago. She was a Missourian and we were married in St. Louis in 1944. We have three daughters.

"After World War II we were in Los Angeles, and I made my living as an advertising copywriter, writing about oil field equipment. I had driven back and forth on Route 66 probably about six times when I got the idea for the guidebook. I anticipated another big wave going west on 66 after the war. The first real big wave was *The Grapes of Wrath* people. Then during the war it was travel-restricted so people couldn't get up and go like before. But once the war ended I knew there'd be boys from back East who had been stationed in California, and I figured a lot of those fellows would want to return there to live or at least visit. I figured they'd want a guidebook to tell them about the best places to eat and sleep, a book about the worthwhile sights along the way. We got together the WPA Guidebooks for the Route 66 states for some background, and Charlotte helped me by looking up all the altitudes of the various points on the highway. We gathered a bunch of rough data about the road, and then in March of 1946 I was ready to take off. March wasn't necessarily the best month of the year to be traveling, but I happened to be

THRU SCENIC HIGHWAY 66 **NEW MEXICO** *to* **PAINTED DESERT, PETRIFIED FOREST** AND **GRAND CANYON, ARIZ.**

POSTAGE 1½¢ WITHOUT MESSAGE

© BY J. R. WILLIS

Nez by the Log, Petrified Forest

Eventually, the rains did return to the great Southern Plains in the late 1930s. The wind quit blowing and the dust became fertile earth. Then came the century's second war—World War II—and wheat farmers all along Route 66 who had suffered became prosperous once more. Businesses along Route 66 survived wartime gas rationing and the shortage of tires. The highway suddenly turned into a convoy road. Many stretches were filled with jeeps and trucks transporting troops and arms to the many military bases and forts that dotted the length of the

Left: Painted Desert, Petrified Forest, vintage postcard.

Below: Jack Rabbit bumper sticker.

ARIZONA

highway. Bus and train stations in the big cities on the route were crowded with servicemen shuttling between duty posts. Uniformed hitchhikers were scattered up and down Route 66.

Shortly after the war, the road became crowded with shiny vehicles filled with ex-GIs and postwar families on the move. As more automobiles were produced, the traffic count soared. Route 66 became one great big traffic jam. The westward migration surpassed the great numbers of the Dust Bowl era when the highway had been clogged with migrants.

In 1946, in Los Angeles, Jack D. Ritten-

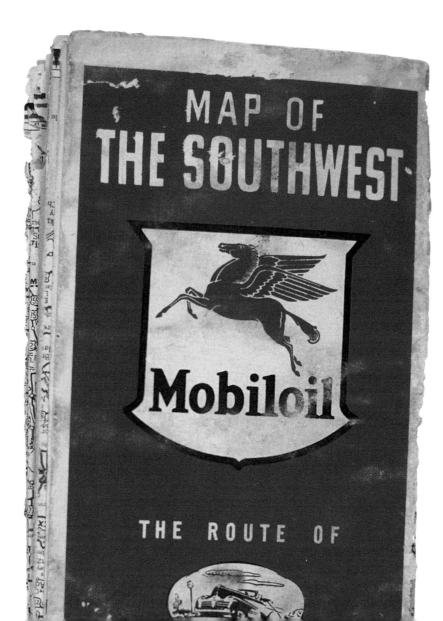

Map of the
Southwest, 1947.

between employers at the time.

"I took off from L.A. and headed east toward Chicago on Route 66. I was driving my 1939 American Bantam, manufactured by the American Bantam Car Co. of Butler, Pennsylvania. The company stopped making Bantams and switched over to what became the prototype for the Army Jeep in about 'forty-one. I sure liked those Bantam cars. They made a Bantam convertible, but I had a two-seat coupe. It was black, and with a full tank of gas it weighed about fourteen hundred pounds. Two men could lift the rear end with little trouble. I was alone on the trip. I had some pencils and note pads and my portable Corona typewriter stashed behind the seat. There was hardly any room in that tiny car. I went pretty slow because I was making a bunch of notes as I went down the highway.

"I drove all day long—from sunrise to sunset. I'd stop for the day when it got so dark I couldn't see to make any notes. I made my notes on yellow pads I kept right beside me on the car seat. There weren't tape recorders then for me to use. In the evening I'd get a room at a tourist court and type my notes from the day while I could still read all my scrawling. I'd mail them back to Charlotte in Los Angeles. If I heard certain things or interesting stories in certain towns, then I'd try to

Main Street of America Highway Association Caravan dedicated Route 66 as "Will Rogers Highway" in 1952. Included in the picture are Lyman Riley (bow tie), Lester Dill (next to Riley), and Jack Cutberth (standing next to the driver's door of Riley's truck).

house published *A Guide Book to Highway 66,* a book that became a Bible for road travelers. For only one buck, travelers could follow Route 66 town by town "over two thousand miles of fascinating highway." Besides listing the best motor courts, cafes, and tourist attractions, Rittenhouse also offered sage advice and road tips:

The entire highway from Chicago to Los Angeles is well paved and passable. War-torn stretches of pavement are being repaired wherever pitted. Snow comes early and lingers late in stretches between Amarillo, Texas, and Kingman, Arizona, so inquire about road conditions ahead at gas stations when driving during November through March.

Be sure you have your auto jack. A short piece of wide, flat board on which to rest the jack in sandy soil is a sweat-preventer. . . . One of those war-surplus foxhole shovels takes little space and may come in very handy. Put new batteries and a new bulb in your flashlight.

Carry a container of drinking water, which becomes a vital necessity as you enter the deserts. For chilly nights and early mornings, you'll find a camp blanket or auto robe useful—and it comes in handy if you find inadequate bedding in a tourist cabin. . . . An auto altimeter and auto compass add to the fun of driving, although they are not essential.

As the growing number of vacationers gassed up their new postwar sedans and thumbed through Rittenhouse's handy guidebook, they

E. J. "Jack" Cutberth, "Mr. 66," 1973.

also heard for the first time "Get Your Kicks on Route 66," Bobby Troup's bluesy pop hit of 1946, which replaced Guthrie's ballads and the folk songs of Pete Seeger, as an ode to the highway. Originally recorded by Nat "King" Cole, the simple tune went on to be immortalized by the Andrews Sisters, Bing Crosby, Chuck Berry, the Rolling Stones, Asleep at the Wheel, Manhattan Transfer, Mel Tormé, Depeche Mode, Michael Martin Murphey, and a host of others. Nothing captured America's love affair with the road more than this song.

find somebody to talk to in order to verify the story. I hit a few steep hills in California and out West that the little car had trouble getting up but I made it. I got through the deserts and when I reached Gallup, New Mexico, there was ice all over the highway. That was some of the worst weather I hit. I ran into snowstorms in other places. In Ash Fork, Arizona, a power line snapped and fell across my car, and a waitress in a cafe in San Jon, New Mexico, dumped a bowl of hot beef stew in my lap. I was lucky that I never did see any real bad accidents. I saw a lot of jackknifed trucks but never anybody in a serious accident. Guess I was lucky.

"I stayed out on the road at least a month. I like the desert country the best. Still do. Charlotte and I were headed west on another trip on Route 66 out of Albuquerque, and were just approaching Laguna Pueblo when we stopped to climb a small mountain—really a good-sized hill or mesa. The road curved right around it and we scrambled up to the top and found some ruins. We knew we weren't the first ones to find the place because there were soda bottle caps on the ground, but still it was the first time we'd ever been near an Indian ruin.

"Anyway, on my research trip I finally came home and put the book together. We called it *A Guide Book to*

"Foothills" oil on canvas (21″ × 168″) by Woody Gwyn.

If you ever plan to motor west
Travel my way, take the highway that's the best.
Get your kicks on Route Sixty-six!
It winds from Chicago to L.A.,
More than two thousand miles all the way.
Get your kicks on Route Sixty-six!
Now you go thru Saint Looey and Joplin, Missouri
And Oklahoma City is mighty pretty;
You'll see Amarillo; Gallup, New Mexico;
Flagstaff, Arizona; Don't forget Winona,
Kingman, Barstow, San Bernardino.
Won't you get hip to this timely tip:
When you make that California trip
Get your kicks on Route Sixty-six!

By 1947 the smoldering embers of the old Highway 66 Association were rekindled by a group of business and civic leaders from the Route 66 states. Jack Cutberth, a barber

from Clinton, Oklahoma, emerged as one of the main forces driving the revived organization, a group that later changed its name to Main Street of America Highway Association. The organization worked hard to upgrade the highway and stimulate business.

In 1952, the members devised another way for attracting more publicity for the highway. Starting at the Chain of Rocks Bridge on the Illinois-Missouri border, a contingent of association members traveled the road to Santa Monica, where they dedicated Route 66 as the "Will Rogers Highway." Along the way, they left bronze markers commemorating the highway, while in small movie theaters, audiences watched *The Will Rogers Story*, starring the cowboy philosopher's son, Will, Jr., in the title role.

In the 1950s, Route 66 was a genuine

celebrity. Families could actually leave their homes in the East and Midwest and drive out to the Grand Canyon or Painted Desert. They could go all the way to the Pacific on a highway that passed through towns where Abe Lincoln practiced law, Jesse James robbed banks, and Will Rogers learned how to twirl a rope. They could cross Mark Twain's great river into lands where outlaws hid in dark caves, and drive through picture-book countrysides where cowpokes still chased dogies into the sunset. Tourists could stop to buy chunks of petrified wood or Ozark curios and sip cups of sweet cider. There were snake pits and caged wild critters and mysterious caverns and real live Indians, sitting like wooden statues, selling rings and bracelets made of turquoise and silver. The lure of the road—especially U.S. Route 66 headed west

—grew even larger in the 1950s when Walt Disney created his kingdom of Disneyland in Anaheim.

But it was in the 1950s that the bright lights of fame and fortune that had shone on the highway for so many years were also beginning to dim. In 1954, President Dwight Eisenhower established a President's Advisory Committee on a National Highway Program. That move signaled the decline of the fabled highway. Ike apparently had been smitten by the efficient German autobahn during his tenure as supreme commander of the Allied Forces during World War II.

The final report from the committee appointed by Eisenhower led to the enactment of the Federal Aid Highway Act of 1956, which spelled out guidelines for a 42,500-mile national interstate highway system. Despite the fact that the old highway was maintained and was divided into four lanes for long sections, it was clear that Route 66 could no longer handle the increasing volume of traffic.

The coming of the interstates was slow and laborious. Construction cost tens of billions of dollars, yet the federal government persisted. A piece of Route 66 was replaced here and there, bypasses were constructed around various towns and cities, and little by little the old highway was turned into a service road for its replacement. All the while, the U.S. Highway 66 Association intervened to prevent total destruction of America's Main Street. In his final battle in the late 1970s,

Highway 66. We printed three thousand copies and sold it for only a dollar. I had a mailing list put together from all the motels and cafes and curio shops I found on the highway. I figured anybody could spend a dollar. There were all sorts of tips in the book, such as 'On the road, don't drink too much liquid, because your kidneys will soon proclaim the strain.' All those books sold. They became collectors' items. Forty-three years later the University of New Mexico reissued my guidebook. People can still use it to find their way along the old road. That makes me feel proud."

the demise of the old highway. *Route 66,* the popular CBS television series of the early 1960s, starring George Maharis and Martin Milner as a pair of highway adventurers in a screaming Corvette, couldn't stop the interstates from coming, either. Even the old-timers from the Main Street of America Association could not prolong the inevitable. Cy Avery, Lon Scott, and Jack Cutberth—Route 66's powerful trinity—were old men by now and were powerless to prevent the decline.

Originally, the national interstate plan was supposed to take about twelve years to complete. It ended up taking more than twice that long. Finally, the last stretch of U.S. Highway 66 was bypassed in 1984, near Williams, Arizona, when a final strip of Route 66 was replaced by a section of Interstate 40. There was a ceremony and speeches and a lot of news coverage.

The bypassing of Route 66 had actually taken not one but five different interstates—Interstate 55 from Chicago to St. Louis; Interstate 44 from St. Louis to Oklahoma City; Interstate 40 from Oklahoma City to Barstow, California; Interstate 15 from Barstow to San Bernardino; and Interstate 10 from San Bernardino to Santa Monica. As one of the old highway's aficionados put it, the opening of the interstates made it possible to drive all the way from Chicago to the Pacific without stopping. The government called that progress.

Thank God, not everyone agreed.

Even as the big Route 66 shields were being auctioned off and the road maps

Cutberth asked that the interstate routes be named I-66, but his request was denied. That designation was instead given to a short stretch of highway connecting Virginia with Washington, D.C.

Beat writer Jack Kerouac's novel *On the Road* was published to enormous acclaim in 1955. The book spoke of "a fast car, a coast to reach, and a woman at the end of the road," but, despite its appeal, it failed to halt

changed, new protectors of the old road gained strength. They remain. They're people from every walk of life who realize that the spirit of the Mother Road cannot be killed. They are people who recognize that Route 66 is reborn every time someone reads *The Grapes of Wrath,* or sees the film, catches a rerun of the '60's television series, or listens to the music of the road. It's resurrected whenever someone pulls off the interstate and drives a stretch of the honest highway that remains.

U.S. Route 66 lives, like an obstinate maverick, in the minds and memories of countless nostalgia buffs, preservationists, historians, 66 diehards, and just plain folks. The old road itself can be found in every one of the eight Route 66 states. It's still there. And in many places the signs are returning; its proud name has been retained. There remain motor courts, gas stations, curio shops, and tourist attractions operating on the edges of the old highway. There are still cafes where the cook in the kitchen baked the pie being offered for lunch. From Illinois to California a Route 66 revival continues, grows larger, and gains momentum. The Mother Road is stronger than ever. The old road has new life.

Route 66. The name is still magic.

Route 66. It will always mean going somewhere.

Opposite page, above: Santa Fe engines, near Amboy, Calif.

Opposite page, below: The Mother Road.

Right: The Snow Cap, Seligman, Ariz.

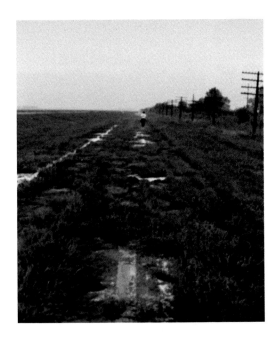

CHAPTER TWO
Illinois

*"The best business you can go into you will
find on your father's farm or in his workshop.
If you have no family or friends to aid you,
and no prospect opened to you there, turn
your face to the great West, and there build
up a home and fortune."*
—Horace Greeley

Left: Grain elevators, Elkhart, Ill.

Above: The Mother Road east of Pontiac, Ill.

The day they took down the Route 66 shield marking the eastern terminus of the Mother Road, the weather was typical for Chicago in winter—bitter cold and wet. There was snow on the ground, and frigid gusts of wind rolled off the lake. In Grant Park, the trees were naked. Foraging pigeons and winos found the park pickings slim. Smelly gray exhaust from the steady flow of traffic on Lake Shore Drive and Michigan Avenue fouled the city air.

On that day, January 17, 1977, the Mother Road was less than two weeks into its fifty-first year. There was no anniversary celebration. No official popped champagne or gave a speech. There were damn few tears.

The American Association of State Highway Officials had decreed that the Route 66 signs should be removed. The old road's time had passed. Signs for Interstate 55—the name for the replacement north-south highway in Illinois—would be erected. New state highway maps already reflected the change of names.

A truck from the Illinois Department of Transportation arrived on the scene, and maintenance men Gus Schultz and John Chesniak got out and surveyed the situation. Both of them wore heavy work clothes, hooded coats, safety vests, and official highway department hard hats. It was an ordinary task —set up a ladder and take down the signs.

Before the two men had time to remove their tools from the truck, a television crew and a *Chicago Sun-Times* photographer appeared. When Charlie McLean and Roy Fonda, operations engineers for the highway department, also drove up and announced they wanted to watch the signs come down, Schultz and Chesniak looked at each other and smiled. This wasn't just a routine job, after all. It was something special.

"The fact that Route 66 had so much prominence across the country couldn't be overlooked," says Charlie McLean, a native Chicagoan who had been born the year after the highway officially opened. "Route 66 in Illinois originally followed State Road 4 from Chicago to East St. Louis. It was the first fully paved highway in Illinois. Taking down those signs that morning marked the end of the old road for us and the beginning of the interstate system. There was simply no need for Route 66 anymore."

Chesniak climbed the ladder leaning against the light standard at the corner of Lake Shore Drive and Jackson Boulevard and unbanded the signs. One at a time he handed them down to Schultz. First came the familiar black and white 66 shield, and then the sign that read END OF ROUTE 66. The entire procedure took only a few minutes.

For a while, Charlie McLean kept the

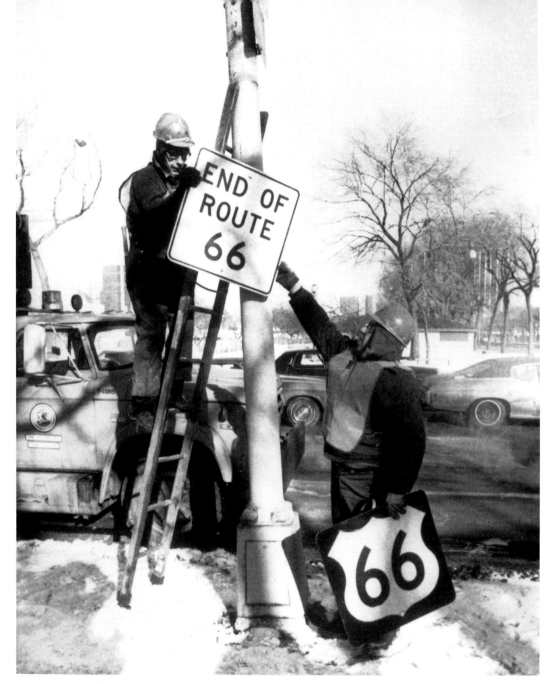

January 17, 1977, Illinois Department of Transportation workers remove Route 66 signs in Grant Park, Chicago, Ill.

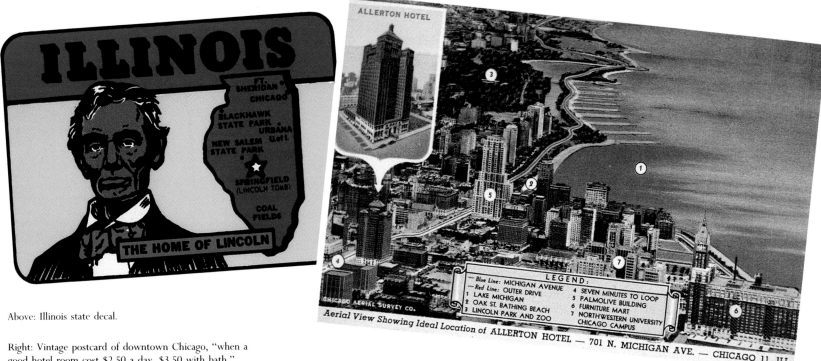

Above: Illinois state decal.

Right: Vintage postcard of downtown Chicago, "when a good hotel room cost $2.50 a day, $3.50 with bath."

Route 66 sign tucked away in his office. Then a big shot with the highway department in Springfield wanted it, so Charlie sent it down there. When that man moved to Washington the sign went too.

"I should have hidden that 66 sign," says McLean. "It was the genuine article, and that was the last anyone saw of it."

By the close of 1977, there were so many requests for the old Route 66 signs from the public that the Illinois Department of Transportation started peddling replica signs. Convicts at the state prison at Pontiac—a

Route 66 town—made the shields. The state sold thousands of the newly minted signs. Many went to nostalgia buffs; some were bought by folks who lived alongside Route 66 and helped build it. The signs served as mementos to remind people of all those years when Route 66 was the main artery in the state, a highway linking Chicago with a series of towns and cities that punctuated the Illinois countryside all the way down to St. Louis on the Mississippi River.

It's fitting that Route 66 started—or ended depending on the direction of travel—

in Chicago. The brawny metropolis on the southwestern shore of Lake Michigan is the archetype of all American cities. For Sarah Bernhardt the city was "the pulse of America." Carl Sandburg dubbed it "Hog Butcher for the World" and "the City of the Big Shoulders."

Chicago is a collection of factories, foundries, and slaughterhouses. It is also still a blend of immigrants—Poles, Germans, Africans, Russians, Mexicans, Jews, Italians, Swedes, Chinese, and Irish. It is a city of neighborhoods, barrios, ghettos, and silk-

stocking districts. Chicago is the birthplace of the skyscraper, the capital of American architecture, a city filled with stately residences, tidy bungalows, crowded flats, elegant hotels, universities, museums, and office buildings.

Chicago is roughhouse politics and legendary tough guys. It's Cermak, Capone, Daley, McCormick, Sullivan, and Wright. It's the Windy City. It's a Brandy Alexander at the Drake Hotel, a slice of cake at the Palmer House, a good night's sleep at the Blackstone. It's Lincoln Park, where people come to cool off on summer nights and find comfort on autumn afternoons. It's a crowded blues joint on the South Side. It's the Loop—that busy island surrounded by the circuits of the elevated train. It's the Wrigley Building in a timeless face-off with the Tribune Tower. It's the Chicago River, Soldier Field, and the Art Institute. It's the shifting colors of the Buckingham Fountain. It's the Bears and the Sox. It's a ride on the El to root for the Cubs.

Studs Terkel said Chicago is "a city of man." The natives claim that if you've never been there, you haven't seen America.

In those early years, before Route 66 was ever conceived, the highways that traversed the state were primitive. The main thoroughfare in Illinois was an unpaved road between Chicago and St. Louis. Following a north–south

direction, this road went by many names— Burlington Way, East St. Louis-Springfield-Chicago Trail, Mississippi Valley Highway, Greater Sheridan Road, and Lone Star Route. One of the most popular names for the road was the Pontiac Trail.

In 1915, when the Pontiac Trail was officially christened and opened to travel, the Goodrich Tire Company saw to it that nameplates were placed on guideposts erected at one-mile intervals. These signs showed the mileage to Chicago and St. Louis and various

towns along the route. The plates bore the name PONTIAC TRAIL and a full-length figure of an Indian holding a map of the state of Illinois.

"The appropriateness of the Indian figure to the name is . . . at once apparent," said an article about the Pontiac Trail that appeared in the August 1915 issue of *Illinois Highways,* a publication of the State Highway Department. "And for this great highway the name is doubly significant, for the famous chief whose name it bears, in the later years of his life,

Construction in 1923 of Route 66 predecessor near Lawndale, Ill.

Chicago train yards, 1930s.

often crossed its course, since near its southern terminus he spent his last years and met his death."

The article explained that the Pontiac Trail was "the shortest route for motor travel between Chicago and St. Louis, with so many large and important towns on its course, and intersecting, as it does, so many important east and west thoroughfares, its rapid development as a highway is easily forecasted. Already it is a well cared for highway, and following, as it does, state aid roads every inch of its length, its permanent improvement will be rapid and certain."

The prediction came true. In 1918, after the defeat of the Germans, a $60 million bond issue was passed for the construction of hard-surfaced roads in Illinois. The Pontiac Trail—this popular north–south route—was at the top of the priority list.

As the predecessor to Route 66, the new highway was designated SBI 4, with the SBI standing for State Bond Issue. The highway was described as "beginning at the intersection of 48th and Ogden Avenue in the town of Cicero, Cook County, and running in a general southwesterly direction to East St. Louis, affording Chicago, Cicero, Berwyn, Williamsville, Springfield, Carlinville, Edwardsville, Granite City, East St. Louis and the intervening communities reasonable connection with each other." Merchants and manufacturers in Chicago and farmers downstate were ecstatic when they heard about the proposed highway.

In constructing this new Illinois thoroughfare, its builders were respectful of

Hardroad Celebration Parade—the 1924 opening of what became Route 66 through Lincoln, Ill.

the past. The route would follow a historic course, tracing the early portage path of Marquette and Joliet during their exploration of the Mississippi 250 years before.

Despite the passage of the bond issue, bureaucracy abounded. For years, only paperwork and drawings piled up. By January 1921, practically no work had been done on the state bond issue system except preliminary planning and reconnaissance surveys. But less than a month later, bids were taken and analyzed. Highway officials found that the

price of an 18-foot concrete pavement averaged approximately $39,000 to $40,000 per mile, including grading and culvert and bridge work. The final plan was approved and work on the new highway proceeded. By 1924, SBI 4 was almost completely paved between Chicago and East St. Louis, and within two more years the entire route in Illinois was completed.

After the last mile of road was paved in Illinois, an inspection was carried out by the American Association of State Highway

Officials, the organization responsible for the approval of all interstate and U.S. route markings. The highway passed muster with flying colors.

In 1927, U.S. 66 signs were posted all along SBI 4 in Illinois, beyond the broad Mississippi River into Missouri, and across the other Route 66 states to California. In 1930, however, Illinois and Kansas, where there was just a 12-mile stretch of Route 66, could boast about being the only states where the highway was paved. It would take until 1937 before U.S. 66 was completely paved from Chicago to Santa Monica.

As traffic on Route 66 in Illinois began to increase, state engineers decided to change the easternmost starting and finishing points. The terminus of the highway was moved from Cicero farther into Chicago to the entrance of Grant Park on Jackson Boulevard. Later, as traffic increased even more, the route started one block north at Adams Street and officially ended at Jackson Boulevard and Lake Shore Drive. The famed Art Institute, guarded by a brace of magnificent bronze lions, was nearby, as was Grant Park, site of the Century of Progress World's Fair of 1933–34, when droves of visitors traveled up and down Route 66 to gawk at the city.

Motorists from the northern and eastern states bound for a western destination would generally slip onto the highway outside of the city to avoid the hubbub of downtown. Those who chose to go to the core of Chicago to begin their journey could find plenty of sustenance at one of the hotels or downtown eateries. Lou Mitchell's on Jackson Boulevard

was always a favorite spot for breakfast or lunch, and a fine choice when it came to fueling up for a long drive. As unpretentious as its name, Lou Mitchell's still offers whipping cream with the coffee; homemade marmalade, mayonnaise, and vanilla ice cream; freshly squeezed orange and grapefruit juice; fluffy omelets; thick slices of toasted Greek bread; and complimentary boxes of Milk Duds for every lady customer.

Contented travelers, with stomachs full and toothpicks in their mouths, left Chicago and motored due west out of the Loop district until they reached Ogden Avenue. This was the city's business route, which cut southwest across the sprawling suburbs of Cicero and Berwyn and then snaked south through the prairies, farms, groves of ancient trees, and coal-mining country of Illinois.

Within a few years the original routing of 66 was moved at various points. From 1926 to 1931, Route 66 followed Illinois Route 4 from Springfield to Staunton. In 1931, the Mother Road was relocated south of Springfield through Litchfield, Mount Olive, and west of Livingston. A decade later Route 66 was relocated from east of Staunton to south of Livingston. During the 1930s and '40s, several towns were bypassed as the highway shifted. Originally, Route 66 passed through the prison town of Joliet, on the Des Plaines River just 35 miles south of Chicago. Then an alternative route was built in 1940, and travelers were faced with a choice when they reached a fork in the road north of Joliet. They could either head to Joliet or take the other route a little further to the west and

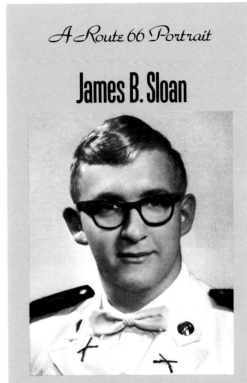

A Route 66 Portrait

James B. Sloan

James Brian Sloan 1963 graduation photograph.

Born: January 5, 1946
Occupation: Photographer
Residence: Morton Grove, Illinois

"*I* grew up a pretty normal kid during the 1950s on the southeast side of Chicago. I remember the music about Route 66 and then later the television show. I can still see those big 66 shields along the highway. But I always had mixed emotions about the road. My parents sent one of my brothers and me

An old stretch of Route 66 serves as a frontage road between Springfield and Litchfield, Ill.

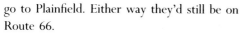

Old Route 66 west of Hamel, Ill.

go to Plainfield. Either way they'd still be on Route 66.

The two roads joined again at Gardner, but just to the north was Braidwood, a town in the coal mining region, where the Rossi family had settled. They were immigrants who had fled the coal mines to launch a successful macaroni factory that became a Braidwood landmark. When the new highway came along, Peter Rossi decided it was his turn to start a new career. The highway was his best bet.

Rossi built a grocery, service station, restaurant, and a pair of motor courts right alongside Route 66. Then, in a grove of trees near the highway, he erected a big wooden dance hall that opened in 1927 and did a thriving business until it was destroyed by fire in 1935. Like others on the highway, Rossi and many of the good citizens of Braidwood made a good living from Route 66 traffic.

After westbound travelers reached Braidwood, they found themselves in the Route 66 groove headed southwest toward St. Louis. The litany of towns and cities they

encountered in Illinois included many named for prairie families, early pioneers, or old Indian warriors and place names. There was Godley, Braceville, Gardner, Dwight, Odell, Cayuga, Pontiac, Ocoya, Chenoa, Lexington, Towanda, Normal, Bloomington, Shirley, Funks Grove, McLean, Atlanta, Lawndale, Lincoln, Broadwell, Elkhart, Williamsville, Sherman, Springfield, Glenarm, Divernon, Farmersville, Waggoner, Litchfield, Mount Olive, Livingston, Staunton, Hamel, Edwardsville, Mitchell, Nameoki, Granite City, Madison, and Venice.

Even by 1957, when Route 66 throughout Illinois had grown from two to four lanes, and after the coming of the new interstate highway system in the 1970s, these country towns that formed the Illinois mining and corn belts persisted. So did the spirit of Route 66. Although some of the highway towns and crossroads shriveled like frosted tomato vines when the interstate appeared, memories and tangible evidence of the old road's glory days remain.

Such memories are there today. All anyone needs to do is look. Most Illinois towns feature more than one Route 66 alignment—the "City 66" route, and one or more bypasses. There are stretches of the old highway surviving either as state highways

Ed Waldmire, inventor of the Cozy Dog (left), and son Bob Waldmire, traveling Route 66 artist (right), Rochester, Ill.

or service roads. There are grain elevators, graveyards, churches, stores, homes, gas stations, cafes, and motels still standing on the shoulders of the highway. There are also dark taverns with pool tables and great jars of pickled pig's feet and hard-boiled eggs sitting on the bar.

There are many remembrances of the old highway at Dwight, Odell, and Cayuga. There are also remnants of 66 in Pontiac. Outside the city limits, the turn-in driveways can still be found. They lead to the site of Dreamland Park—a popular Jazz Age roadhouse like Rossi's dance pavilion—which once flourished on the banks of Rooks Creek before Interstate 55 was schemed. Lilac bushes separate the past and present in Pontiac, but there are traces of the filling stations, hot dog stands, and tourist courts that sprouted among the stately old homes.

Pontiac is also the town where Carmen Rodino lived and worked. An ambitious Italian who first settled in Dwight as a railroad mechanic, Rodino started selling home-grown tomatoes and onions from a pushcart and then a horse-drawn wagon before he moved down the road to Pontiac in the 1920s to peddle vegetables from his truck. In 1926, he built the Rodino Square building on the shoulder of Route 66 and added on to the solid-brick structure a few years later. During the highway's heyday it housed a busy hotel, tavern, and garage. With the help of his six kids, Rodino kept up the garden. The rich Illinois soil—black as asphalt and fertile as a barnyard cat—yielded enough vegetables to feed several generations. Old man Rodino,

to Western Military Academy down in Alton, Illinois, across the river from St. Louis. The only way to get there was to drive down good ol' Route 66. I didn't want to go to military school. Every autumn from 1959 until 1963, Route 66 represented the road to hell for me.

"Traveling down 66 in September meant the summer was over, and I was leaving my pals behind. My father was in the wholesale drug business and he liked to drive big Buicks. The whole family went along for those September rides. The only good part of the trip was that we usually got to see the transport rigs carrying cars to market. We'd get a sneak preview of the new models. Also, my dad made it a point to stretch the trip over two days, and we'd spend a night in Springfield—the capital city. We'd get rooms at the Leland Hotel and eat big steaks at the Black Angus. That was my last meal before going back to the academy. That steak dinner was always very special. The next day we'd get down as far as the cutoff to Alton, and I'd watch Route 66 go on into the sunset out West. That was always very sad. But come June, my dad would be there in his Buick and we'd drive back up 66 to Chicago. We'd pass the slag heaps and strip mines and cornfields. I always wanted to go to the Dixie Truckers Home for a meal, but my father would never stop there.

Funks Grove Country Store and gas pump.

decade after statehood in 1818.

The first Funks who ventured out to the Illinois wilderness came from Ohio and before that, Kentucky. They were drovers, raising cattle and hogs and then herding them to market in Galena and later Chicago. If they couldn't find a suitable buyer, the Funks drove their herds east, sometimes as far as New York. In the years before the Civil War, they ventured into Missouri and Kansas to get cattle. After the railroads were built, the Funks did not have to drive their livestock to market anymore.

One of the Funk boys went to Chicago and established a slaughterhouse, about where the Loop is today. When he died in the 1850s, his youngest brother brought his body home on horseback and buried him near the grove of trees. Some of the Funks fought with the Union during the Civil War, and afterward they returned to farming and raising stock.

The Funks were always making maple syrup, too. In the late 1800s, they started selling it, and pure maple syrup from Funks Grove became big business. They sold their tasty syrup into the new century and during the war years and the Great Depression. They're still tapping maples and selling syrup today—on Route 66.

"Our lives are connected to this old road," says Steve Funk, great-grandson of Isaac Funk, who settled in the grove back in 1825. "They used to say that the whole world went down this highway. Well, they don't anymore. At least not as many. Most folks take the interstate."

Born in 1924, the year the original

always with a smile, sold produce to the housewives of Pontiac until he died in 1968. The building he constructed and named stood until 1989.

Traces of Route 66 will always remain in Pontiac. And in the smaller farm towns— Ocoya, Chenoa, Lexington—that sprang up between Pontiac and the city limit sign for Bloomington. Abraham Lincoln spoke at the political convention in Bloomington in 1856 when the Illinois Republican party was

organized. Folks here still tend to vote the same way today. Besides the usual chatter about politics, weather, and sports scores, the prices of hogs and grain dominate everyday talk along the highway just like always.

A dozen or so miles south of Bloomington on old Route 66, a natural stand of maple trees—some of them centuries old —horns in on the prairie. Called Funks Grove, it's a crossing named for the Funk family who settled these parts less than a

Funk's Grove Pure Maple Sirup [*sic*] Saphouse, 1959, Funks Grove, Ill.

roadway that soon became 66 was first paved through Funks Grove, Steve grew up around the ancient stands of black and sugar maples. He met his wife, Glaida, in Oklahoma, where he trained as a pilot during World War II. After the war, Steve brought his bride back to Funks Grove, where they raised five children and took over the maple syrup operations.

"Our side of the family started making syrup back in pioneer days when they still used wooden spouts and not steel spouts in the trees," says Steve. "My father Lawrence Funk was born here in 1878, and he made syrup right up until he died in a car accident in 1930. I make syrup and now my children are involved in the business." In 1948, Steve Funk was hanging six hundred buckets on the

maples. Forty years later the Funks were hanging four thousand buckets. In that same period of time the price of syrup went from $7 to $29 a gallon.

"Even though we've started a mail order business and we now ship overseas," says Steve, "we've always sold syrup right off the back porch. People know Funks Grove syrup is a sign that spring is just around the corner. We still have regular customers from St. Louis to Chicago."

Like many others up and down the highway, the people at Funks Grove are proud of their ties to Route 66. "We're just a hundred yards from old 66," says Steve. "We'd put signs up for our syrup along the highway. People would see the signs and that would give them a chance to talk about our syrup and think about buying a jar. We had signs at Shirley and some between McLean and Atlanta. Now we have signs up on I-55. But that new highway has never been the same. It's harder to lure folks off the interstate. When you travel the interstate, it's dull. It's straight and boring. It may be a lot safer and you can make better time, but going down Route 66 was fun. It still is."

Admittedly, not everyone had fun on Route 66. When the traffic was thick on the highway, its many twists and curves could also be deadly. There were tales of wrecks with victims so badly mangled that they begged state troopers to shoot them and end their misery. Old-timers claim that near Lincoln, Illinois, car crashes occurred every few hours. On that part of the highway—as was the case for similar stretches in Missouri—the route

"When I graduated from military school in 1963, I went to Europe, North Africa, and Israel, and then I went to De Paul University in downtown Chicago not far from where Route 66 begins and ends in the East. Then I went to Columbia College in Chicago, and then I joined the VISTA program and trained in Oklahoma. I finally got a chance to go west on Route 66.

"After my training I was assigned to Las Vegas, New Mexico, and I went even farther down the highway. I'll never forget being in a 1963 Corvair in Tucumcari and stopping at some classic 66 joint for lunch. It was my first true taste of New Mexican cuisine and I've loved the food and the state ever since. I stayed in New Mexico for a while and worked and went to school. Eventually I returned to Chicago and finished school and worked at different jobs and started a family.

"Now I live in a suburb and own a photography business. I usually take a plane when I travel, but sometimes I drive and find myself on the old highway—on Route 66. The military academy is closed and I haven't been back to the Black Angus for a steak. I became a vegetarian. I've passed the Dixie Truckers Home several times since I was a cadet traveling with my family, but I still haven't stopped. I drive right on by, just like Dad always did. It wouldn't be right to stop now. Might break the spell."

Drivers' 5th Wheel Specials

HAM STEAK - Center cut	4.65
COUNTRY FRIED STEAK Choice beef dipped in egg batter, flour, and grilled	4.95
BABY BEEF LIVER Grilled with onions With 2 slices of bacon, add .70	4.35
PORK CHOP Grilled or broiled	5.05
BAKED FISH Whitefish served in lemon and butter	4.65

Meat Loaf 4.35
Our own special recipe

Above items served with potato, vegetable, salad, hot rolls and butter.

Steaks

All steaks USDA choice

RIB EYE, 8 oz.	7.95
TERIYAKI, 6 oz.	5.25
GROUND STEAK, 8 oz.	4.95

T-Bone, 12 oz. 9.95

All steaks are char-broiled, served with choice of potato, salad or cup of soup, hot roll or biscuit and butter.

Spaghetti

Served with our own special meat sauce, creamy cole slaw, grated Parmesian cheese, hot roll and butter. 4.25
Half order of Spaghetti 2.95

Shrimp Platter

21 pieces or more. Breaded and cooked to a golden brown. A shrimp lovers feast. Served with potato, choice of crisp salad or cup of soup, hot roll and butter. 5.95

Salads

All salads include choice of French, blu cheese, 1000 Island, creamy Italian, or vinegar and oil dressing served with dinner roll or crackers.

CHEF'S SALAD	3.25
TOSSED SALAD	1.25
COLE SLAW (our own recipe)	.75
COTTAGE CHEESE	.75
FRUIT AND COTTAGE CHEESE	1.60
APPLE SAUCE	.75
JELLO (fruit or plain)	.75
SLICED TOMATOES (5 slices)	.95

Chicken

DIXIE BROASTED CHICKEN
Each piece is individually prepared and fried fresh to a crispy golden brown to guarantee that special Dixie flavor.

Chicken Luncheon (2 pieces)	4.50
Chicken Dinner (4 pieces)	5.60

Above chicken orders are served with choice of potato, salad, or cup of soup, hot roll or biscuit and butter.

"CHICKEN EATERS"

Chicken, bread-n-butter	4.25
1/2 Chicken (4 pieces)	7.60
1 Chicken (8 pieces)	

ASK YOUR WAITRESS ABOUT CHICKEN TO GO.

Burgers

All choice ground beef

		With Fries
HAMBURGER	1.30	2.20
1/4 LB. HAMBURGER	1.65	2.55
PATTI MELT	2.60	3.50

With above items add:

Cheese	.20
Lettuce and Tomato	.25
Bacon (2 slices)	.70

Hot Sandwiches

		With Fries
HOT BEEF Thinly sliced top round of beef, served with whipped potatoes and gravy	3.85	
CHICKEN FRIED STEAK Ground choice beef, dipped in egg batter, lightly breaded and grilled	2.40	3.30
GRILLED CHEESE	1.30	2.20
FISH SANDWICH	2.25	3.15
HAM & EGG	2.75	3.65
EGG SANDWICH	1.40	2.30

		With Fries
HOT MEAT LOAF Our own special recipe served with whipped potatoes and gravy	3.55	
RIB EYE STEAK, 5 OZ. Char-broiled	4.50	5.40
REUBEN Tender corned beef, sauerkraut and Swiss cheese grilled on rye bread	3.15	4.05
PORK FRITTER	1.70	2.60
CHICKEN FILET Center cut breast, lightly seasoned, breaded and fried	2.65	3.55
BARBECUE Thinly sliced beef simmered in our own special sauce	1.90	2.80

Deli Sandwiches

		With Fries
HAM	2.25	3.15
TURKEY	2.15	3.05
ROAST BEEF	2.95	3.85

		With Fries
BACON, LETTUCE & TOMATO	2.30	3.20
HAM & CHEESE	2.55	3.45
CORNED BEEF	2.15	3.05

All sandwiches available on white, whole wheat, rye, or bun.

Soup & Sides

All soups and chili made fresh in our kitchen.

	Cup	Bowl
Soup - Chicken Noodle, Potato, Bean, Vegetable	1.20	1.45
Chili	1.45	1.75

Potato: Baked, French fried, hash browns, whipped	.90
Breaded Mushrooms	1.65
Onion Rings	1.55

Desserts

Fruit and Cream Pies 1.00 Prepared daily in our kitchen	
Sundaes	1.50
Ice Cream - 2 dips	1.25
Sherbet - 2 dips	1.50

Beverages

Coffee	.50
Fresh Brewed Decaffeinated	.50
Tea	.50
Milk	.65-.85
Chocolate Milk	.70
Hot Chocolate	.65
Milk Shakes	1.25
Soft Drinks	.50
Soft Drink Refill	.25

---

earned the nickname "Bloody 66." Sometimes it was simply called "the Killer."

But there were also plenty of safe harbors. The Dixie Truckers Home was generally a snug refuge for travelers weary of the highway. Located in McLean, a small community just south of Funks Grove and north of Atlanta, the business was opened in 1928 by J. P. Walters and his son-in-law, John W. Geske. The Dixie has been closed only one day since—in 1965, when the place burned down and operations had to be temporarily moved next door until the building was restored. Walters headed up the business until his death in 1950. Then Geske took over and

Above: Dixie Truckers Home menu, McLean, Ill.

Right: Ernie and Frances Edwards, Pig-Hip Restaurant, Broadwell, Ill.

ran the Dixie until 1982, when his son-in-law, Charles G. Beeler, took the helm. Fourth-generation family members are training in the wings.

The Dixie Truckers Home is considered the first real truck stop in Illinois and probably one of the first on Route 66. It is also one of the best. Even though it's located in the center of a midwestern state, it was called the Dixie in tribute to southern friendliness. The name fits like a lug nut on a new wheel. The Dixie caters to truckers to this day.

Families and couples crowd the lunch counter to slurp coffee and gulp down sandwiches. Truckers have their own special area to sit in and rest their road-weary bones, while grease monkeys pump diesel into the big rigs out front. Broasted chicken is the house specialty, but many a trucker has been fueled with a ham steak or a platter of spaghetti or a plate of fried mush and eggs coaxed onto the fork by a slab of hot corn bread dripping with butter. The Dixie serves no quiche.

Route 66 runs from McLean through the center of Atlanta, across Kickapoo Creek to Lincoln, named for Honest Abe. Lincoln was the site of a big celebration, which included daring aviators and a parade of marching cops from Springfield, when Route 66 became a reality in the 1920s.

Just south of Lincoln is the farm town of Broadwell. Here the famed Pig-Hip Restaurant has served legions of road warriors. Ernie Edwards started the Pig-Hip in 1937 when a pork sandwich cost fifteen cents and a steakburger could be had for a dime. A half-

century later it took two bucks to get a sandwich, but Ernie was still there on Route 66 selling his fare.

"The place has been for sale for years and I've never got a nibble," says Ernie, who outlived two wives and married a third. "I've got ten kids and none of them want any part of this business. I'll just keep it going myself. I'll do it till I die."

In the midst of the rolling prairies, beyond the towns of Broadwell, Elkhart, and Williamsville, looms Springfield with its striking capitol building. It was selected as the capital of Illinois in 1837, the same year that the city's most celebrated citizen became a resident. Lincoln lived in Springfield until 1861 when he departed for the White House. "To this place, and the kindness of these people, I owe everything," Lincoln said about Springfield. The city remains a monument to the prairie lawyer. Lincoln sites, bronze plaques, and public shrines abound, including the only home he ever owned and the tomb in Oak Ridge Cemetery where Lincoln's remains were interred following his assassination.

There's a monument of a different sort on Route 66 below Springfield. It comes after the quiet farm towns of Divernon, Farmersville, and Waggoner, just a few miles west of a little burg called Raymond. It isn't a tribute to Abraham Lincoln. It's a marble statue of the Virgin Mary on the edge of a cornfield. The statue is less than 50 feet from one of the versions of Route 66, now a frontage road for the interstate. Folks up and down 66 know the statue as "Our Lady of the Highways."

Laura and Jeff Meyer

Born: Laura—January 4, 1958
Jeff—December 25, 1955
Occupations: Laura—Grocery cashier,
Roadologist
*Jeff—Grocery stock
clerk, Roadologist*
Residence: Rolling Meadows, Illinois

LAURA: "I was born and raised in Berwyn. That's a Chicago suburb on Route 66. I went to school in Cicero. That's another suburb on Route 66. But I didn't know anything about the highway when I was growing up. My family never really traveled very much. A trip to the Wisconsin Dells was a big

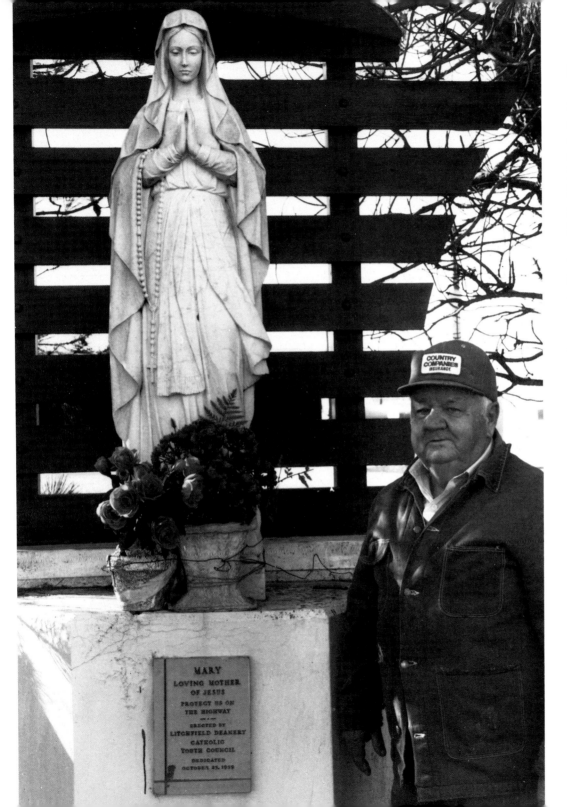

Some call her the "Queen of the Road."

At night, lights shine on the statue. She stands on a concrete pedestal, protected by an alcove of wood and brick and surrounded by evergreens and hollyhocks. A priest helped lay the cobblestone walk leading to the site. She has been there—gazing at the old road, her hands in perpetual prayer—since 1959 when a group of local farm kids from Saint Raymond's parish raised the money to create the shrine.

"My oldest daughter, Loretta, was one of the youngsters from the church who got the money together to put up the statue," says Francis Marten. "They wanted a project to do. I told them they could put it up on my land."

After the boys and girls raised the $400 needed to buy the Carrara marble statue and ship it from Italy, they came up with another $500 for the concrete, lumber, and lights to create the grotto. Marten kept his word and donated a plot of land on the highway.

At the dedication ceremony a couple of priests came out and blessed the statue and some locals stood around and prayed and sang songs. They put a plaque below the statue that says,

MARY

LOVING MOTHER OF JESUS

PROTECT US ON THE HIGHWAY

Then Marten let the kids tack up a dozen hand-painted placards spelling out the Hail Mary, phrase by phrase in the style of Burma Shave signs, on successive fenceposts for about a half-mile along the highway.

After the shrine was erected, there were

Francis Marten and "Our Lady of the Highways" west of Raymond, Ill.

pilgrimages. People would meet up the road and walk to the statue, saying the rosary. They'd stand around the shrine and sing hymns and afterward have a little something to eat. The kids would also come every year to paint, rake up dead leaves, and keep the place looking nice. But after about five or six years the pilgrimages and attention stopped.

"Most of the kids got married and moved away," says Marten. "So my wife, Ruth, and me took over. We kept up the shrine and paid the light bill and trimmed the evergreens and kept fresh flowers at the foot of the statue."

When Interstate 55 came through, the government tried to make Marten take down the Hail Mary signs. But he didn't budge. He knew that the signs were four inches inside his property line, and there wasn't a damned thing anybody could do about it. The signs stayed put.

After his wife died, Marten cared for the shrine by himself. When he goes, some of his eight grown children who maintain the family farm will continue to look after the "Queen of the Road." That pleases Francis Marten.

"Folks don't stop here as much as they used to," says Marten. "Some can't stop, so they send me a card saying they saw it. A few send money for flowers or to help with the upkeep. I'm retired from farming and I just enjoy sitting at my house watching folks come to see the shrine. I'll look after it as long as I live and then my kids will carry on. The shrine will always be here for the highway travelers."

Shrine pilgrims headed southwest toward St. Louis can count on getting a hot meal or cold drink in Litchfield at the Ariston Cafe. In 1924, Pete Adam opened the original Ariston in Carlinville, on what became the first version of Route 66. Several years later, Adam moved his family and business to Litchfield, and on a blustery March day in 1931, he reopened the cafe, billing it as "the most up-to-date restaurant between St. Louis and Chicago." In 1935, yet another Litchfield Ariston was built between the second and third versions of Route 66. It's there today. Highway veterans think the cafe, still owned and operated by the Adam family, will always be the best the old road has to offer in Illinois. After all, Hubert Humphrey ate there. So did Jimmy Dorsey. He sat at the counter in his shirtsleeves on his way to play big-band music at the nearby town of Benld, an original Route 66 town. If Dorsey was smart, he had the pork chops.

Besides the Ariston, there were other popular highway stops in Litchfield, including the Harlow Service Station, Annex Cafe, Sky View Drive-in Theatre, Skinny's Cafe, Blue Danube, Varner Brothers Motel, and The Overhead, a Route 66 restaurant known for serving a specialty called Chicken in the Basket.

Route 66 is sometimes difficult to find in this part of the country. The highway signs may be gone and some of the bypassed towns have undergone major face-lifts, but the pavement is still there, as are the holdouts from the past trying to stay alive. Edwardsville, settled in 1813 and hometown of at least eight Illinois governors, survived the interstate

deal for us. I learned about travel and about Route 66 after I met Jeff. We starting getting out on the road. We still do—every chance we get."

JEFF: "I'm from Rolling Meadows, a suburb north of Chicago. I started working for a local grocery chain in 1973, the year before I graduated from high school. I've worked for them ever since. In 1982, I was picking up some extra money scalping concert tickets. I spotted an ad in the paper for someone who wanted to see an Elton John concert. It was Laura's ad. That's how we met. We talked for hours on the phone, and I ended up taking her to the concert. We had great seats in the tenth row. Six months later we were engaged, and then we got married in June 1984. After that, we hit the road whenever we could get away. I was used to travel. I went all over the place with my parents when I was a kid. I was one of six children and my folks would load us all up and we'd be off on a trip somewhere. When I was out on my own I really started getting into Route 66. I tried to stay off all the interstates and explored 66 in my 1977 Buick Regal. Traveling that old highway raised my consciousness."

LAURA: "We're both Capricorns. We're supposed to be incompatible. But we're not. We love going down Route 66. Heading down the old highway is so exciting. It's as though we're experiencing

The ARISTON
"A BETTER PLACE TO EA[T]
JUNCTIONS U.S. 66 and
ROUTE 16
Litchfield, Illinois

bypass. Traditional neighborhoods and shops tied to the old highway never got word about the supposed demise of Route 66. It's always been business as usual.

Some highway dwellers like the Funks, with their maple syrup business, and Francis Marten, the keeper of the highway shrine, are lucky. They have plenty of family to keep their contributions to Route 66 alive. Others aren't so fortunate.

The Soulsbys at Mount Olive, above Edwardsville and about 50 miles northwest of St. Louis, don't have anyone willing to carry on with what they helped build on the old highway. Russell and Ola Soulsby—a brother and sister team—started working at their father's Shell service station at the same time Route 66 was created. Nobody else has ever run the place. Russell and Ola are Route 66 originals. When they're gone, there will be no one to take their place,

Neon sign, Litchfield, Ill.

Opposite page: The Artison, 1937, Litchfield, Ill.

and Soulsby's Service will disappear.

"I've got three sons, but they've scattered all over and have good jobs," says Russell, uttering a very typical complaint of many other elderly shopkeepers and vendors along the national route. "They're not coming back here. When we quit, we'll just lock the door and that will be it."

Russell was born in 1910, Ola in 1912, and another sister, Velma, in 1914. All three worked at the gas station alongside their parents.

"Our father, William Henry Soulsby, knew they had surveyed for the highway and so we broke ground in 1926, and then we watched them lay the pavement," says Russell. "I was going to high school at the time. For all these years we've sold gasoline on what was the original Route 66."

The cream-colored building with red trim looks the same; only the pumps have changed through the years. Inside, Russell keeps records on the same rolltop desk his father bought secondhand when he opened the business. Russell became a widower in 1970, and Ola never married. Their sister Velma died in 1976, yet Russell and Ola decided to keep the station open.

"We used to sell ice cream and sandwiches our mother made," says Russell. "We had very busy times here. We even had a slot machine during the thirties. It was bolted to the counter, but somebody came in during broad daylight and pried it loose and took it. Now we sell lottery tickets. Everyone still wants to be a millionaire overnight. Nothing's changed that way."

American history firsthand. It's never boring. Before, I had only heard old road stories. My dad talked about how he had gone out to California on Route 66 when he was a young man during the highway's prime years. He had a lot of stories about the road. Now we have our own Route 66 stories. We have a great collection of Route 66 junk, too. And postcards and photographs and old maps. We even have a personalized license plate on our car that says LOVES 66. We're part of the effort to revive interest in the highway and let people know there's more to life than driving down the interstate."

JEFF: "Route 66 is America's past that's never died. So much of the old highway is still there. In Illinois alone we take the old road almost all the way from Chicago to St. Louis. Probably ninety percent of the road's original bed is still in place. Most of the little towns along the way are in business. Entire sections of the highway are out there. They might have taken away the old signs and they might have bypassed some places, but I believe there will always be a Route 66. You can feel it."

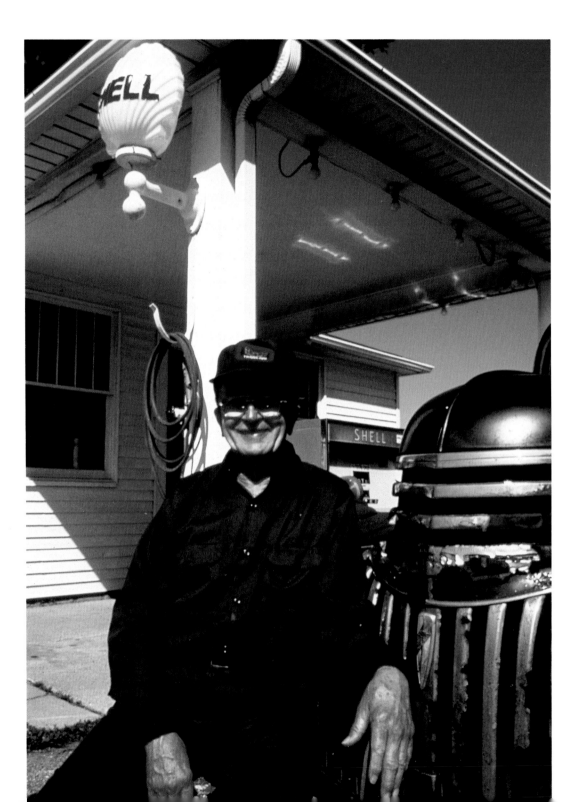

"Our work ties us down, but we like our life here. Even after the interstate came and things slowed down. Once in a while someone gets off I-55 and buys our gas. The interstate may have cut us off, but we kept steady customers. They'll stick with us always. See, we try to satisfy the public. We pump the gas ourselves and clean every windshield."

For decades, Soulsby Service was open seven days a week. Then Russell and Ola decided to rest on Sundays. They believe the Sabbath is a good day for remembering the way things used to be.

"My father played in a string band every Saturday night and when we were kids we always went along," said Russell. "He played mandolin and guitar. He was real good. Sometimes his band would play until daylight and us kids would find a place to sleep."

Later Russell played clarinet and sax in another dance band called the Melodians, which played sweet music 50 miles in either direction on Route 66. After he served a hitch in the navy during World War II, Russell came back to Mount Olive to resume his place in the band and work at the family gas station.

Most Saturday nights, Ola can be found at her home next door to Soulsby Service. Two blocks away at his own house, Russell spiffs up and slips on his fancy shoes. It's his night to howl, for it's time to go dancing. Russell knows that dancing keeps him young. "I don't go to the doctor or take pills.

Russell Soulsby, Soulsby Service Station, Mount Olive, Ill.

Instead, I take prize ribbons with my dancing. That's my secret."

The moon, looking like a huge slice of pockmarked cheese, appears for the evening. Russell gets in his car, picks up his regular dance partner, and motors to Springfield or Benld or Sherman or Litchfield. He may drive south on the old road to Livingston, Hamel, or Edwardsville. He goes anywhere he can step out on the floor and ballroom dance. When Russell Soulsby drives the old road—Route 66—he's young again. The night is full of magic, and the moonlight shines on the cracked pavement and shows the way.

And just for a moment—from Mitchell and Granite City and Madison, sleeping near the Mississippi River across from St. Louis, all the way to the bright lights of Chicago—the whispers of a thousand ghosts along the Mother Road can be heard.

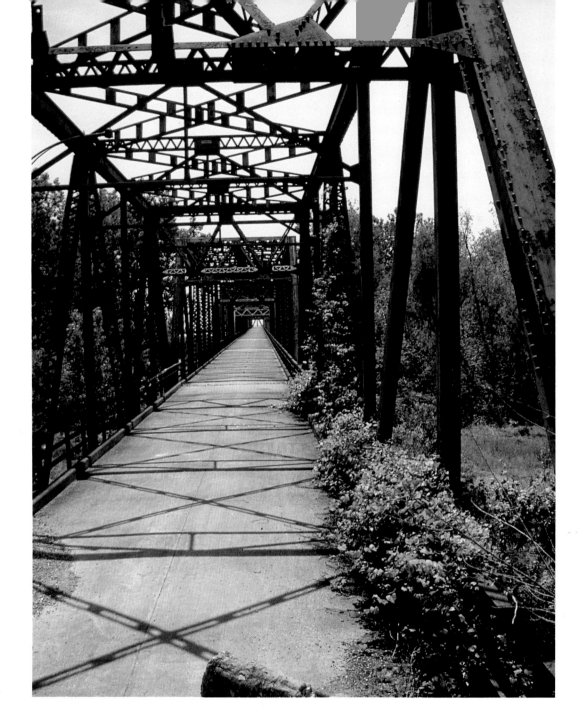

East end, Chain of Rocks Bridge, near Mitchell, Ill.

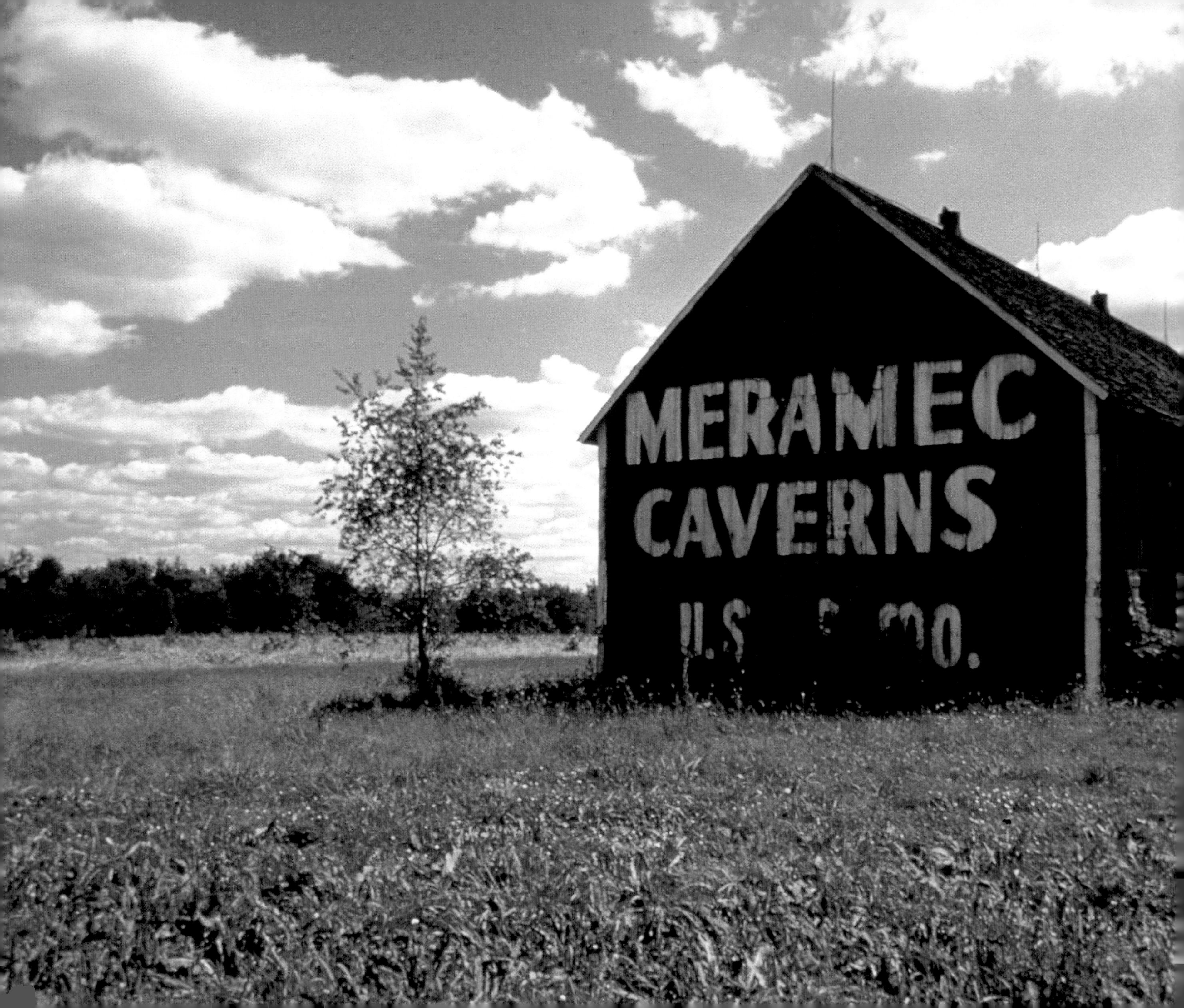
MERAMEC
CAVERNS

CHAPTER THREE
Missouri

*"I come from a state that raises corn and cotton
and cockleburs and Democrats, and frothy
eloquence neither convinces nor satisfies me.
I am from Missouri. You have got to show me."*
—Willard Duncan Vandiver
U.S. Rep. from Missouri

Left: Old barn on Missouri's Mother Road.

Above: Sky Chief pumps, Conway, Mo.

igh summer in St. Louis. Sprinklers soak scorched lawns, overworked air conditioners bellow and snort, and beer sales are way up. The city pants in relief when the sun starts its disappearing act and a Saturday afternoon bows to twilight shade.

Down on Chippewa Street, one of the aliases Route 66 once used as it meandered through this old river city on its way to the Ozarks, folks are stacked up ten deep at the rows of windows at Ted Drewes Frozen Custard stand. Every age, sex, race, and nationality is in line. The mix of people supports the notion that Missouri is a microcosm of the nation. All of America is in this one place.

Most of the crowd wears the uniform of the day—shorts, T-shirts, sandals, and suntans. A few are barefoot. One couple, dressed to the nines, has just left a wedding reception. Others come straight from Busch Stadium, where they witnessed their beloved Cardinals clobber the Cubs. Some are Cubbie fans from Illinois, nursing their wounds and anxious to drown their sorrows in extra-thick milkshakes before they slink across the Mississippi River bridges a dozen miles away.

There are also bona fide tourists standing in the lines. They have heard about the good ice cream served at Ted Drewes. Before selecting a motel for the night, they desert Interstate 44 and return to the old route to treat themselves to something special.

Inside the white frame building trimmed with wooden icicles, a bevy of teenagers in dandelion-yellow Ted Drewes visors and shirts are working feverishly. They are taking orders and dispensing frozen custard, sundaes, malts, shakes, cones, sodas, floats, splits, and the ever popular extra-thick "concretes," as fast as their hands permit.

"God, this is wonderful," moans a young mother, balancing her baby son in one arm, as she eats a cone of French vanilla. While the creamy concoction slides down her throat, she offers the cone to the baby. The boy needs no coaxing. Ted Drewes's custard is better than mother's milk. Within minutes, their grinning faces have smeary white mustaches. Melting ambrosia dribbles down their shirts. Under the soft neon glow, mother and child glide into ice-cream nirvana.

Standing in the cool shadows where the great freezers purr, Ted Drewes—the Custard King himself—watches like an amused cat.

Above left: Missouri state decal.

Above right: Early Ted Drewes Frozen Custard stand, 1930, St. Louis, Mo.

Left: "St. Louis Finest Since 1929," Ted Drewes neon sign, St. Louis, Mo.

"I'm into inspiration," says Drewes. "When I talk to my workers about dealing with the public, I ask them not to use cute little phrases like 'Have a nice day.' Instead, I tell them to just be themselves. All they need to do is smile and say thanks. I inspire them to be natural."

The object at Ted Drewes is to let the ice cream do the talking. That's one of Drewes's secrets. Another is spirit.

"Gotta have passion for what you do. That's a must ingredient. I like ice cream. I think about it all the time. I have a passion for it. There's nothing wrong with that. People claim it isn't good to take your work home. I say that's a bunch of bullshit. That's the trouble with this country. People stopped taking their work home. They pamper themselves. Passion's the key. Without passion for your work, there's nothing."

Ted Drewes has been passionate about ice cream all his life. He was born in 1928, the year after Route 66 became official in Missouri and the year before his dad, Ted Drewes, Sr., launched the family business. The first St. Louis location didn't pan out, but in 1931, Drewes opened another stand on South Grand Avenue, just a few blocks off Gravois, another name for U.S. 66 in the city. Within a decade, the Drewes family's successful custard stand on Chippewa was in operation. Over the years, not only did the Drewes clan become synonymous with frozen custard in St. Louis, their custard dynasty evolved into an urban Route 66 legend.

Drewes met and courted his wife, Dottie, when she was working as a carhop and

he was learning the ice-cream business from his dad. Ted and Dottie married in 1950. He was twenty-one, she was eighteen. They raised two daughters on frozen custard and literally weaned their grandkids on the stuff. One of the Dreweses' sons-in-law, Travis Dillon, turned out to be a top store manager, just like Ted's big sister, Margie Aussieker, who started working at the stands when she was only twelve.

The two custard stands close for a couple of months every winter, but generations of St. Louisans have selected a Christmas tree from the pine and fir forests that appear each winter in the Ted Drewes parking lots.

Still, ice cream is the mainstay. And, just like the maple sap that rises up at Funks Grove on Route 66 in Illinois, a sure harbinger of spring in Missouri is when the workers at Ted Drewes throw open the shutters and dip into that first batch of ice cream.

Despite countless offers from business parties, the notion of franchising is sacrilegious to Drewes and his family. "We'll keep things going the same as always," says Drewes. "We're not interested in mediocrity and that's what comes when you get into an absentee ownership situation. Our product has evolved. It's better because the equipment has improved. But you can't improve on good service. That has to come from within your people. And you can't improve on location either. That's why we're staying put."

The Chippewa Street stand has been expanded over the years, but any remodeling had to blend with the original building. That

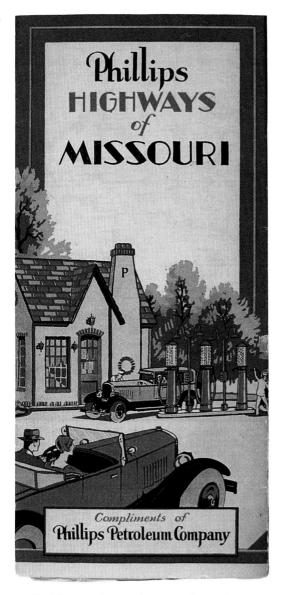

Phillips
HIGHWAYS
of
MISSOURI

Compliments of
Phillips Petroleum Company

Early Phillips Petroleum Highway map, late 1920s.

was a must. "It's heritage we're talking about here. We're part of history. We're a Route 66 institution. That has to be retained. That means something to us."

Like some of the other classic Route 66 establishments, the chances are good that Ted Drewes custard stands will be dishing out cones and floats when most of the franchise joints have long vanished.

Throughout the 300-mile course of the old highway in Missouri are other Route 66 treasures that have survived time and the wrecking ball. They can be found from the banks of the Mississippi, where Route 66 enters the state from the east, all along the highway to the Kansas border.

St. Louis, the largest of the Route 66 cities between Chicago and Los Angeles, has always been proud of its connection to the old highway. Founded by Pierre Laclede in 1763 as a fur trading center, the city is strategically located midway between the headwaters of the Mississippi and the river's mouth at the Gulf of Mexico. After the Louisiana Purchase extended the boundary of the nation to the Rocky Mountains in 1803, all travel to new frontiers began in the city. People said, "The world passes through St. Louis." It was considered a major destination. St. Louis was an open door to the virgin West, as symbolized by the stainless steel Gateway Arch built in the mid-1960s—an ageless monument soaring 630 feet into the heavens, near the

cobblestone levee where slaves once unloaded bales of cotton and riverboat gamblers plied their trade.

Route 66 entered St. Louis several ways. The original route reached from Venice, Illinois, across the Mississippi on the McKinley Bridge. The route then made its way through the city to Manchester Road and went west on Manchester passing through a series of suburban villages to the town of Gray Summit. About 1934 the main route switched and Route 66 entered Missouri via the Municipal Free Bridge (later named the MacArthur Bridge), which opened in 1917 and spanned the Mississippi at East St. Louis, Illinois. The route continued to 12th Street and then to Gravois Avenue, went west to Chippewa, became Watson Road, and finally departed St. Louis to cut across the state.

By the late 1930s, in order to detour travelers around the railroad and warehouse traffic, the Route 66 river crossing shifted to the Chain of Rocks Bridge, first opened to traffic in 1929 as the sixth vehicular bridge in the St. Louis area. Travelers not planning to stop in St. Louis were smart to use this bridge. They could follow the highway as it skirted the northern edge of St. Louis, turned south near Lambert Field, and continued down the west side of the city through the suburb of Kirkwood until the pavement reconnected with the city version of Route 66 about 26 miles from Chain of Rocks.

A $2.5 million two-lane toll bridge, the Chain of Rocks crossing linked north St. Louis and the town of Mitchell on the Illinois shore. The bridge had a roadway 40 feet wide, 10

feet wider than the Municipal Bridge, and shortened the distance between St. Louis and Edwardsville, while avoiding the congested downtown area. Sponsors pointed out that the bridge "will provide a more attractive entrance to St. Louis for tourists, and put them on broad boulevards instead of narrow streets." The river crossing also became known for the bend in the middle of the bridge.

On the Missouri side was the popular Chain of Rocks Amusement Park, offering a picnic grove, rides, swimming, skating, dancing, and softball diamonds. It was perched on an overlook called Riverview Park that had once been proposed as a site for the Louisiana Purchase Exposition—the storied 1904 World's Fair that introduced, among other things, iced tea, hot dogs, and ice-cream cones to the nation. Chain of Rocks was "one of the prettiest spots" in the city, according to a 1917 *St. Louis Globe-Democrat* story, which said that "a day at the Chain, or Riverview, as it is often called, will help any neurotic, hypochondriac, or life-wearied one. It will act the same as an anti-blues serum injected into your blood and will help you to understand poetry."

The parents of Walter Lewis McKee, a young worker from Victoria, Missouri, who lost his life in 1929 when the bridge was being built, came to Chain of Rocks for years each Memorial Day and placed a floral wreath on the bridge.

On summer afternoons, below the well-used Route 66 crossing, shrill whistles from the calliope of the S.S. *Admiral* could be heard up and down the river. The *Admiral,* an all-

West end, Chain of Rocks Bridge, near St. Louis, Mo.

steel excursion luxury liner with five mammoth decks, became a fixture on the riverfront. It was popular with natives and visitors to St. Louis and was billed as the world's largest inland steamer. On summer evenings, couples sipped cold beer and danced in air-conditioned comfort as the big ship churned through muddy waters beneath a canopy of stars and moonlight.

During the late 1970s and early 1980s, the steamer's hull was damaged and the excursion ship became snarled in financial difficulties. It ended up moored at the downtown levee alongside renovated sidewheelers and a floating McDonald's restaurant. The S.S. *Admiral* stopped cruising the river and the sound of its calliope could no longer be heard at Chain of Rocks. No matter—Chain of Rocks was already history. In 1977, after a half century of accommodating the public and thousands of Route 66 travelers, Chain of Rocks Park was closed. The nearby Chain of Rocks Bridge was already abandoned, and down river, the old MacArthur Bridge was also closed to traffic in 1981. New bridges and a maze of replacement highways and interstate loops made the well-worn routes into St. Louis obsolete.

Even after the advent of Interstate 44 and the disappearance of some of the haunts that date the old road, enough Route 66 standbys persevere in Missouri to keep the highway alive in people's hearts and minds.

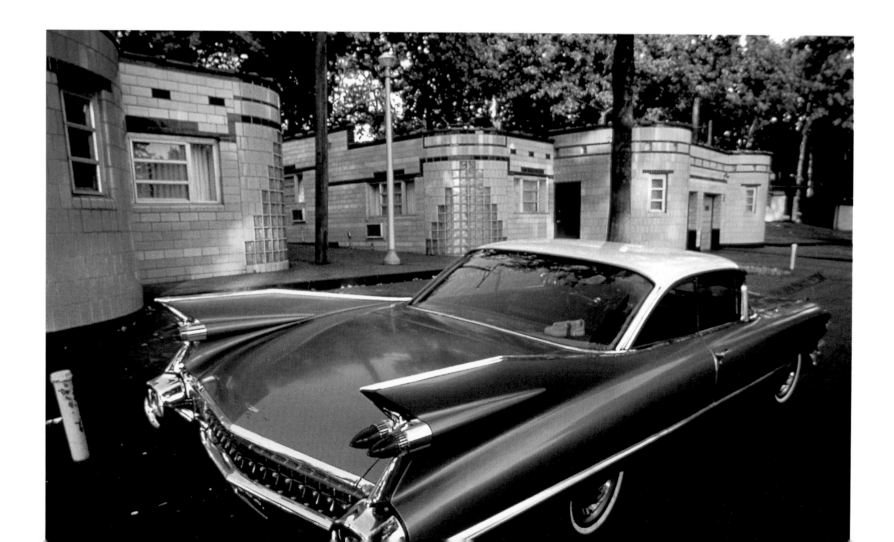

The Coral Court is an especially noteworthy survivor. An Art Deco motor court on Watson Road in the village of Marlborough, Coral Court is just a mile southwest of the St. Louis city limits. Built in 1941 in the Streamline Moderne style, with rounded buff-color exterior tile walls, glass-block windows, lintels and parapets of red tile, the Coral Court did a booming trade on old U.S. Route 66, the highway that carried more out-of-state traffic than any other thoroughfare in Missouri. In those glorious post–World War II years, when motorists resumed highway travel in record numbers, every unit at Coral Court was booked solid often weeks in advance.

For those headed to Chicago, the Coral Court was a pleasant respite before tangling with St. Louis traffic and the long drive upstate through Illinois. Westbound travelers would also seek a night's rest in one of the clean and cozy rooms before continuing their journey through the Ozarks to the Southwest.

The Coral Court was popular with families who picnicked on the eight and a half acres of pin oak–shaded grounds and splashed in the ice-cold swimming pool. Adjoining garages, which allowed guests to enter their quarters in complete privacy, also made the motor court a hit with couples interested in an illicit rendezvous or with smooth-talking salesmen who had gotten lucky for the night. For many guests, the Coral Court was the proverbial "no-tell motel," but with a definite touch of class.

In 1953, a desperado named Carl Austin Hall holed up in the Coral Court with two

1959 Cadillac Coupe de Ville at the Coral Court, St. Louis, Mo.

Right: Big Boy, St. Louis, Mo.

Below: "In sight, it must be right," Steak 'n' Shake neon sign, St. Louis, Mo.

whores the night before he was arrested for the kidnapping and murder of the six-year-old son of a wealthy Kansas City auto dealer. Hall eventually died in the gas chamber, but only half of the $600,000 ransom was recovered, prompting tales that the other half of the loot might be stashed away in one of the hollow tile walls of Coral Court.

By the late 1960s, as more and more travelers opted for the new Interstate 44, the flourishing tourist trade on Route 66 in St. Louis decreased. Restaurants, auto repair shops, taverns, and motels suffered. Some closed their doors and sold out. Despite the loss of business and occasional threats from the owners to sell the property to a shopping mall developer, the Coral Court remained as a tarnished gem of the road. Petitions calling for the safekeeping of the motor court were circulated and a Coral Court Preservation Society was formed. The motor court, with its racy reputation, was a romantic symbol of a bygone era. A night at Coral Court on old Route 66 became a coveted anniversary or wedding gift and was even auctioned at fund raisers.

"The absence of visible parked cars enhanced the surreal beauty of the Coral Court and set it in sharp contrast to the average motel," wrote Esley Hamilton, an

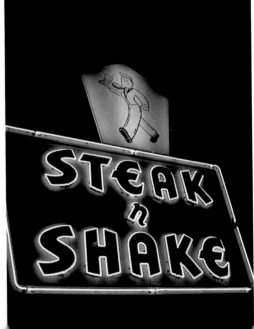

Drive-in theatre on Route 66, St. Louis, Mo.

architectural historian with the St. Louis County Department of Parks and Recreation. "The green of the lawns, the black of the pavement, the yellow and red of the tiles, and the blue of the sky combine to lift the spirits of any lover of America's commercial archaeology."

Not far from the Coral Court are other reminders of Route 66, such as the Wayside Motel and La Casa Grande Motel with its flashing neon signs. There is also the "66" Park In Theatre, built in 1948 on Watson Road (a.k.a. Route 66) in suburban Crestwood.

The "66" drive-in provided patrons with free pony rides, sliding boards, a merry-go-round, and a Ferris wheel. Before the entire world was air-conditioned, the Park In advertised "cool breezes." The concession stand was a busy place, and even had baby-bottle warmers on hand. A pair of frisky bear cubs entertained early arrivals. And, in the days when the price of admission was per person and not by carload, attentive gatekeepers kept an eye open for dragging rear bumpers and cars with only a lone nervous driver—sure signs that some stowaways were perspiring in the trunk.

During the '50s and '60s, weekend crowds, including parents with pajama-clad kids, jammed into the "66" Park In. Caravans of teenage lovers, more interested in the back seat of their Chevy than the action on the big screen, knew the "66" as the "passion pit." Sometimes on summer nights, the cars, trucks, campers, and even school buses stood bumper to bumper for blocks. Situated on a chunk of choice real estate, the "66" managed to stay

open for more than forty years, a period in which more than half of the nation's drive-in movie theaters closed.

A few miles to the west, Watson Road merges with Route 66's replacement. It is soon apparent that I-44 has erased short portions of the old highway in Missouri. Still, most of Route 66 was not destroyed. Beyond the city, long segments of 66 are left, running parallel to the interstate, serving as frontage road, or as a business loop through country towns. Sometimes it wanders off into the trees, or else turns into a county or state road.

It's not difficult to locate the Mother Road in Missouri. All that's needed is a state map and the willingness to take some time. Like the interstate, Route 66 crossed the state diagonally from St. Louis to the high plains southwest of Springfield. As it made its way through the Ozarks, the highway followed a stage-line route established by the federal government twenty years before the Civil War. This route was roughly the same as the Great Osage Trail, one of the major Indian paths that crisscrossed the state. During the Civil War, the path turned into an important military road, used by both Union and Confederate troops. About that time, the U.S. government put in a telegraph line along the road with key stations at St. Louis, Rolla, Lebanon, and Springfield. The route became known far and wide as the "Old Wire Road," and Rebel soldiers took great pains to keep the wires cut. Years after the war had ended, the weathered poles stood wireless and tilting, like ghostly gray totems. Eventually the poles disappeared, but some of the towns along the

A Route 66 Portrait

Lyman Riley

Lyman Riley and wife, Velma, 1954.

Born: May 13, 1918
Occupation: Retired "caveologist"
Residence: Leasburg, Missouri

"*I* was born and raised in Little Sioux, Iowa, at the mouth of the Sioux River. After high school, I went to Graceland College and became a high school teacher. During the summer I went down to Texas and worked for an oil company. I was hitching my way home to Iowa when I got loaded on Choctaw beer up in Oklahoma and wound up broke in Sullivan, Missouri, on Route 66. That's when I met Lester Dill.

Old Wire Road between St. Louis and Springfield prospered. They became prominent Route 66 stops when the highway was paved through the state during the 1920s.

Heading west out of St. Louis on Interstate 44, travelers can find lengthy sections of the old highway. Near the sprawling Chrysler plant with its acres of new cars is a scattering of drab motels, sterile truck stops, and franchise restaurants that look as if they came out of a cookie cutter. But a few of the old places—vintage motels, gaudy fireworks stands, and genuine filling stations—cling to the remnants of the old road.

For the first 30 miles west of St. Louis, the highway is bordered by the Henry Shaw Gardenway, a section that was planted in native trees and shrubs before World War II to honor the gentleman who in 1858 founded the Missouri Botanical Gardens in St. Louis. Saplings, which matured into dense stands of hickory, oak, hawthorn, redbud, and dogwood, blanket the rolling terrain on either side of the pavement. During the cold months the stark white sycamore branches resemble arms raised in surrender. Tall grass, the color of a lion's mane, bends in the winter breeze. A path was carved for the roadway through limestone formations here, and near one of the interstate exits is a wolf research center, where the endangered animals live and breed. The evening howls of wild wolves in the sanctuary echo across thickets of sumac and evergreen

and over the wooded hills that give travelers a hint of the rugged Ozark terrain to be found just down the road.

Continuing west, the Meramec River comes into view. Rising in south central Missouri and winding northwestward to the Mississippi, the Meramec, despite a tendency to overflow its banks, has always been one of the state's popular recreational streams. The impersonal interstate rushes across the Meramec, paying no homage to the cultural memories that linger on each side. Once this was the site of Sylvan Beach, a privately operated amusement and recreational park with free picnic grounds and softball diamonds. The riverside was lined with cabins built on stilts to keep them high and dry of spring floods.

Nearby, a slapdash settlement called Times Beach was spawned in 1925 as the result of a subscription promotional scheme hyped by the *St. Louis Times.* Winners were presented with 20-by-100-foot housing lots and soon a rough-and-tumble blue-collar community sprouted on the muddy riverbanks. In the 1970s, an oil mixture was sprayed on the roads in Times Beach to keep the dust down. Later it was discovered the mixture contained dioxin, a dangerous herbicide chemically related to Agent Orange. By 1982 the entire area was found to be contaminated. The town was declared off limits to its own inhabitants. People moved away and the old Highway 66 river bridge was permanently closed. Only concrete foundations, deserted house trailers, faded billboards, and shattered dreams remained. Times Beach, the town

created by a gimmick, ceased to exist.

Only a few miles up the highway from Times Beach and a half-hour southwest of St. Louis, the Route 66 community of Eureka managed to avoid extinction. A trading center already well established before the Civil War, Eureka evaded death-due-to-bypass because its business district was so close to the interstate. Long yellow buses haul farm kids to the brick high school sitting just over the frontage road that has attracted gas stations, convenience stores, strip shopping centers, and every franchise restaurant imaginable. Many of the small businesses depend on the visitors drawn to the nearby Six Flags Over Mid-America, a theme park where every year thousands of visitors submit themselves to a monstrous roller coaster called "The Screamin' Eagle," or one of a hundred other thrill rides, variety shows, and attractions.

At the exit for Six Flags, travelers can leave I-44 and take the Mother Road simply by following Allenton Road under the interstate and turning west. For decades the intersection of Route 66 and Allenton has been guarded by a Henry Shaw Gardenway building that served as a school bus stop. Vines cover the shutters, and inside are thick wooden benches. Built of limestone and heavy timbers, the sturdy building was made to last forever.

Going west, the old route is plainly marked Highway 66 as it runs parallel to the railroad tracks. High rock bluffs on the other side of the road keep the interstate out of sight and mind. Dead ahead is the town of Pacific, but first the highway passes motels, liquor stores, and gas stations that once made a decent living from road customers. At a vacant motel called the Beacon, the doors of what were once described as "16 modern, inviting, tastefully decorated cottages" stand wide open. The lawn furniture is twisted and broken, and blank windows stare across the highway at the railroad tracks. A forgotten treehouse out front droops from a limb. Flanking the highway, handmade signs tacked to fence posts urge motorists to buy rabbits, goats, eggs, barrels, firewood, manure, or nightcrawlers—plump earthworms capable of tempting wily sunfish onto a hook.

After passing a grassy prison yard surrounded by a high Cyclone fence and coils of barbed concertina wire, the Pacific city limit sign comes into view. It was at this spot, on October 2, 1864, that Confederate raiders paused after burning bridges, depots, and eating houses in the railroad town. On the bluff directly above the highway is a scenic overview named Jensen Point in honor of Lars Peter Jensen, a Dane who became the first president of the Henry Shaw Gardenway Association and for eighteen years managed the Missouri Botanical Garden Arboretum. Stone stairs cut in the steep hillside by Civilian Conservation Corps workers in 1939 vanished with time. The large pavilion built on the natural rock ledge at the summit was made from the same batch of stone and timbers as the school bus stop down the highway. Beneath the open pavilion, covered with a shake shingle roof, thousands of names and initials have been carved in the great beams.

Below Jensen Point a string of traffic scurries along Route 66. Double yellow strips run down the center of the highway, the road's surface cracked and patched with asphalt. Frisco freight, Burlington Northern, and Union Pacific cars trundle down the tracks next to the old road. In the distance, one can see trucks rumbling from quarries and silica mines tunneled into the steep sandstone bluffs.

In the town of Pacific, the highway broadens to four lanes and takes the name Osage Street. Shops, doctors' offices, car dealers, drugstores, and brick bungalows are clustered on the edge of the road. A corrugated metal Quonset hut is home for a cafe called DJ's—for Delisa and Joye. Inside the cafe, there's a gumball machine and jukebox, a bulletin board covered with business cards and notices, and—next to the toothpick dispenser at the cash register—a decorated tin can for diners' spare change to save a local child from a fatal disease. A trucker whose rig sits idling out front gobbles down a platter of bacon and eggs. He eyeballs a crumpled newspaper and, without looking up, chats with two old men wearing red vinyl caps, plaid flannel shirts, and overalls. At the pickup window rest unsliced pies piled high with stiff meringue.

West of Pacific, U.S. 66 climbs slowly from the valley. The village of Gray Summit is off to the right on the far side of I-44. On the left, just past the Galaxy Fireworks Stand, with its red, white, and blue banners, is the entrance to the Missouri Botanical Garden Arboretum and Nature Preserve. Surrounded

"He was running Meramec Caverns, and I eventually went to work for him. I became his right-hand man. Never did go back to Iowa. I lived in a tent for about a year and then I met a girl going through the cave and married her the next week. Her name was Velma Benson and her folks operated a motel and restaurant called Benson's Tourist City on a Highway 66 curve in St. Clair, Missouri. We were married on February 23, 1939, and have been married ever since. I served in the navy during World War II. In 1941 one of our daughters was born, and in '48 the other daughter came along.

"In 1946, we moved down to Onondaga Cave. Les Dill and I managed it for a while. Then we became partners and bought Onondaga and I stayed there until I retired in 1967. I did everything at the cave—bumper signs, cleaned lanterns, guided, the whole bit. At night when everyone left, we fixed up the cave and did repairs. In the summertime it would get very hot down along the river. I recall 118-degree days. I'd have the boys putting out the bumper signs be sure to tell people not to leave their dogs in the car. We'd have the dogs tied to the bumper and get them some water. I had tools so I could get into any car on the lot. I hate to admit this, but it was me who originated the stick-on type of bumper signs. That was about

by a low stone wall and groves of pine and spruce, the Arboretum, created from abandoned farmlands in the 1920s, has been designated as a National Environmental Education Landmark. Inside the gate, the visitors' center, with a sea-green slate roof, was built in 1936 of the same Bedford, Indiana limestone as the Allenton Road school bus stop and the Jensen Point pavilion overlooking Route 66 at Pacific. Located on the Ozark Plateau—the remnants of an ancient mountain range—the Arboretum's natural landscape and managed plant collections cover 4 square miles on both sides of the Meramec River.

Separating the Arboretum and Route 66 from the interstate is the Diamonds Restaurant. It boasts table service as well as a cafeteria line and thousands of cheap Ozark curios. Continuing west, the two-lane road proceeds past the Gardenway Motel and moseys by the Brush Creek Cemetery. Sandwiched between Route 66 and Interstate 44 in a timeless limbo, the graveyard is the final abode for many of the good citizens who settled this part of the country. Some of the graves are from the late 1800s, others are newer. Soldiers are buried here—men who sailed to Cuba for the Spanish-American War, battled in the trenches of France, fought on Pacific islands, experienced the Tet Offensive. Plastic geraniums and poinsettias adorn some headstones and there are homemade wooden crosses next to large slabs with psalms chiseled in the granite. One resting place is marked with a concrete block painted black. There are rows of nameless infants and plots filled with generations of farm families.

Honeysuckle twists around a rusted barbed wire fence separating the cemetery from a thicket of persimmon, black oak, and honey locust, once called the Confederate Pintree because its large thorns were used to pin together the tattered uniforms of Rebel soldiers. The graves on the sloping grass face east. There is a fine view of the trucks and cars speeding in both directions on the distant interstate. On the far side of the cemetery, the view is of the old road where traffic is sparse and moves slower.

Near the junction of State Highway 100, Route 66 crosses over the interstate, winds through the countryside, and becomes known as County Road AT for a stretch. This is the domain of the Tri-County Truck Stop—once the original Diamonds restaurant, which billed itself as "The Old Reliable Eating Place." A favorite stopping point for auto and bus travelers before there was ever a Route 66, the first Diamonds was destroyed in 1948 by a spectacular fire that was so intense troopers had to stop Highway 66 traffic in both direction for thirty minutes. The owners rebuilt the restaurant, and many years later moved the Diamonds farther east, across the

Scenic overview at Jensen Point, circa 1940, Pacific, Mo.

"Scenic Missouri" vintage postcard.

highway from the Shaw Arboretum. Although the interstate bypassed the site of the original Diamonds and the building stood vacant for years, the business was eventually renamed and resurrected. Truckers and others who value greasy cheeseburgers and hot coffee available twenty-four hours a day continue to make their way to the Tri-County for fuel and a meal, or maybe a fresh cigar and a few minutes on one of the pinball machines near the truckers' lounge.

The bulletin board just outside the truck stop's front door is covered with signs for benefit chili suppers, chicken and dumpling dinners, and turkey shoots. Several posters seek information about missing girls. Most of them include brief physical descriptions, including any scars or birthmarks, and there is usually a smiling photo from the yearbook. One sales notice pinned to the board, with a photo of a white horse grazing in a pasture, says: "Mare for sale. $275. Very gentle for child or woman. Has very own personality and shoes on front. Will ride like the wind, only if asked."

West of the Tri-County, the curving

1950. Before that we could only tie them on. We called those signs a badge of honor. We told folks if they had on a bumper sign from our cave, the state patrol would leave them alone because they'd realize they were tourists, spending money. Public relations was the key. I would make dates with all the waitresses and guys working at service stations up and down the highway. Then I'd drive out and pick them and their spouses up and haul them all back for a day at the cave. If they were too far away for me to get, I'd buy their gas. From then on those people would tell everybody they met about Onondaga Cave. Then we had our signs up too— from Springfield, Illinois, to Oklahoma City. I really loved the cave business. It was my life.

"Route 66 was very important to us, too, so I got involved with the Route 66 Association. You had the side streets and all that, but the major attractions were all on 66—the land of Lincoln, the caves, the oil wells, the cowboys and Indians, the Grand Canyon and Petrified Forest, Santa Monica beach. Route 66 really was the 'Main Street of America.' I was elected president of the newly organized Route 66 Association in Missouri a few years after the war.

"I was the common denominator on the road for a number of years. All the businesses along Highway 66, from

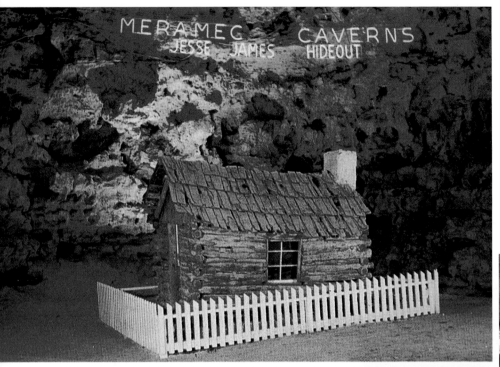

highway descends into the Bourbeuse River Valley, where at one time Route 66 motorists crossed the green waters of the Bourbeuse on twin steel and concrete bridges. Nearby is St. Clair, settled in 1843 and named Traveler's Repose, until the locals grew weary of their town being mistaken for a pioneer cemetery. The pavement continues to follow the route of the Old Wire Road through the town. Practically every house has a front-porch swing ideal for watching traffic pass in review

Above: Moonshiner's Cabin, Meramec Caverns, circa 1955, Stanton, Mo.

Right: Les Dill, Meramec Caverns, circa 1940, Stanton, Mo.

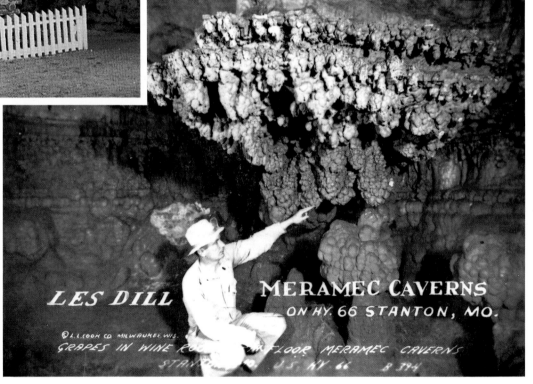

on summer nights. Front yards are decorated with ceramic deer, windmills, wagon wheels, and whiskey barrels cut in half to hold bumper crops of marigolds and petunias and irises the color of root beer. Here, kids still peddle Kool-Aid from stands, swap baseball cards, and put captured lightning bugs in jars with holes punched in the lid. Like every Route 66 town worth its salt in Missouri, St. Clair has a ballpark, a National Guard armory, and churches with steeples.

Back out on the interstate, for many miles in both directions, travelers encounter colorful billboards extolling the finer points of one of the most famous Route 66 tourist attractions —Meramec Caverns.

**GREATEST SHOW UNDER THE EARTH—
MERAMEC CAVERNS**

**WORLD'S ONLY FIVE STORY WONDER—
MERAMEC CAVERNS**

**TOURS EVERY 30 MINUTES—
MERAMEC CAVERNS**

JESSE JAMES HIDEOUT—MERAMEC CAVERNS

**SCENIC RIVERFRONT CAMPING—
MERAMEC CAVERNS**

**MISSOURI'S BURIED TREASURE—
MERAMEC CAVERNS**

Located a little more than 3 miles off Route 66, down a twisting road that leads from the town of Stanton to the Meramec River, the vast caverns were commercially developed in the 1930s by Lester B. Dill, an ingenious Missouri farm boy with the flair of P.T. Barnum. "I have put more people underground and brought them out alive than anyone else," Dill liked to brag. No one could dispute his claim.

Born in 1898, the second of nine children, Dill was only six years old when he and his father, Thomas Benton Dill, first ventured into Fisher's Cave, across the Meramec from the family farm. By the time he was ten, Les, armed with a kerosene lamp and some candles, was earning small change by taking city slickers from St. Louis on guided cave tours. Through the years, Dill continued to explore the many caves in the Meramec valley. Later, Les and his bride, Mary, followed the oil boom in Oklahoma, dabbled in Florida real estate for a short time, and moved to St. Louis, where Les worked as a carpenter. In 1928, when his father was appointed the first superintendent of the newly created Meramec State Park—the site of Fisher's Cave—Les came back to the Meramec valley. He signed a contract with the state and launched his cave-guiding business, complete with homemade food and souvenirs.

A few years later, when the state contract expired, and with the nation caught in the grip of the Great Depression, Les searched for a cave of his own to develop. He finally decided to lease Salt Petre Cave just a few miles downstream from the park.

Chicago to California, knew me because I was putting out cave folders in the motels. Later I was a director of the national organization. Make no bones about it, our main purpose was to get more business on the highway. We were money grubbers. If Route 66 was anything, it was commercial. We were getting hundreds of people every day through the caves in these parts, but we were always ready for more.

"Not many people will admit it, but between St. Clair and St. James on old Highway 66 in Missouri was the red light district of America's Main Street. That was before the Second World War. I recall at Rose's place there were five working girls, and there were trap doors to get bootleg liquor into each bedroom. A fella named Monk got fifteen years for white slavery. He was handing out coupons to truckers that said for every hundred gallons of gas, they got themselves a girl. Businessmen and truckers stopped at some of those ol' tourist courts a lot. We called them 'whoopie cabins' back then. There were also bunko games all up and down the highway. They were usually behind the scenes at the snake pits or roadside zoos, where they had taught chickens to ring bells and play the piano—anything to get folks to stop. That was a come-on. They wanted to get people in there to bet two bits on a shell game. They

Right: Wagon Wheel Motel, Cuba, Mo.

Below: Gordon Moreland waits for customers at the Blinne Filling Station, circa 1935, St. James, Mo.

Hernando de Soto was said to have visited the huge cave in 1542, and a couple of hundred years later, it was probed by French miner Jacques Renault. During the 1800s, the cave was used by saltpeter miners for storage and shelter. Legend has it that escaped slaves were sheltered there as they made their way north via the Underground Railroad. There were tales that outlaws, including the legendary Jesse James gang, found refuge in the caverns and may even have left some of their booty buried there.

The legends about the cave were important to Dill, but of equal significance was the cave's proximity to U.S. 66, the nation's ribbon of commerce. Dill knew if he got the word out, lots of tourists would come calling. He renamed his new attraction Meramec Caverns and opened for business on Decoration Day, 1933. By the end of that first day, a total of six visitors had paid forty cents for the privilege of following Les Dill through the damp passages. Dill wasn't dismayed. He eventually bought the property and put almost every cent he earned into improving and promoting the caverns.

Throughout the bleak Depression years, tourist traffic was sparse, so Dill hosted big public dances in the spacious cave. The entire Dill clan, including the children, worked day and night. For the first three years, they lived in a tent. They battled treacherous ice on the steep road between the caverns and Route 66 during the winter months, and in the spring they built rock dikes and dredged the river channel to combat floods that could turn the parking lot into a lake and engulf the cave entrance. During the sweltering summer, before the parking lot was constructed, visitors parked their automobiles inside the cave with the windows rolled down. When they left, they'd roll up the windows and for a few miles they'd drive down Route 66 in cool comfort.

The visitors would also have a Meramec Caverns sign tied to their bumper. School kids hired by Dill saw to it that a sign was plastered on the front bumper of each and every vehicle parked outside the cave. Later the job became easier when adhesive was developed for the backs of the bumper signs. In 1940, while he was exploring an unknown part of the cave, Dill uncovered some rusty guns and an old chest, which he claimed had belonged to none other than the infamous Jesse James. Immediately the phrase JESSE JAMES HIDEOUT was added to the bumper signs.

Besides the millions of bumper stickers and promotional folders distributed to passing motorists, Dill promoted Meramec Caverns by posting signs, mostly painted on barns, along highways in as many as forty states. Dill and his crew scoured the countryside, especially along Route 66, searching for just the right barn for one of his eye-catching signs. To entice the farmers who owned the barns, Dill handed out watches, pints of whiskey, or free passes to the caverns. If he encountered a widow who had a barn he coveted, there was always an ample supply of boxed chocolates in the back of his truck.

During World War II, when gas rationing hit, Dill went down Highway 66 to Fort Leonard Wood, a large basic training camp, and convinced the army to convoy troops to the caverns for maneuvers. Hundreds of soldiers bivouacked in the river bottom and marched into the mouth of the big cave in full battle dress. Every night, Dill threw dances for the GIs in the cave and gave special rates to anybody in uniform.

Francena, one of the Dill daughters, even married one of the soldiers—Rudy Turilli, a handsome Italian from New York. After the always tried to get tourists when they were headed west. Coming out of Chicago and Detroit and St. Louis, the people were flush with money. Going back home they were broke.

"In 1952 we decided to rededicate the entire highway. The 66 Association got behind it and we formed a caravan and went through every town announcing that we were calling the route the Will Rogers Highway. It brought some great national publicity. We were all in western dress and had Will Rogers, Jr., and some other folks along. I got Ford Motor Company to give us some cars to use and we had them all painted up. We went all the way to Santa Monica on Route 66."

war, he became general manager of the cave and handled much of the promotion and publicity. It was Turilli who, in 1949, stumbled across J. Frank Dalton, a one-hundred-year-old man living in Oklahoma. Dalton raised some eyebrows when he proclaimed that he was the real Jesse James, and that the man who was shot in 1882 was actually Charlie Bigelow. Turilli brought the old man to live in a cabin near the entrance to the cave, and reporters and photographers from across the nation journeyed to Meramec Caverns to visit him. The old-timer told wonderful yarns, showed off his old pistol, and occasionally fired it when he got upset. There was no way to calculate the publicity value of J. Frank Dalton, who died three days shy of his 104th birthday during a visit to Texas in 1951.

About that same time, Meramec Caverns became known as the "safest bomb shelter in the world," when Dill offered the cave to the government as a haven from atomic blasts. "I'm a hundred times safer in my cave than when I try to cross Michigan Avenue," Dill told reporters in Chicago. In the postwar years, thousands of Route 66 tourists made it a point to spend some time at Meramec Caverns. Celebrities from Lassie to Kate Smith and Pearl Bailey toured the "world's only five-story cave."

Lester Dill never missed an opportunity to promote his beloved caverns. When the

"Headquarters for Gifts of the Ozarks," Newburg, Mo.

cost of marriage licenses in Missouri jumped from $2.05 to $2.55 in 1961, Dill responded by announcing that "any couple that will agree to be married in Meramec Caverns this month will be given a free wedding, including the fees of the minister or justice of the peace, and a wedding dinner." Thirty-two couples made the trek on Highway 66 to tie the knot underground.

Toasted on network television shows and by the press as "America's Number One Cave Man," Les Dill died in 1980. Despite the passing of the dynamo who made Meramec Caverns a household word, the cave remains in family hands and continues to draw big crowds from Interstate 44.

"I'm very proud of both my grandparents for all the blood, sweat, tears, and money they poured into this place," says Les Turilli, who eventually took over management of Meramec Caverns following the death of his father, Rudy Turilli. "We've upgraded the building and the facilities, but the tour guides use the same basic script. And out on the highways, those signs are still bringing people to us. We have signs in about ten states now. We have fifty-eight barns and forty-eight billboards."

Like many others who worked at the caverns, Les Turilli started out as a bumper-sign boy when he was ten years old. "I'll never forget one Fourth of July—I put on 427 bumper signs all by myself. At the time that was a record for one person. Was my grandfather ever proud. He took the whole family out for steak dinners at Wurzburger's, a good cafe not far from Highway 66 that's

A Route 66 Portrait

Anne Remington

"Bobbie Anne" Remington and her parents, Annabelle and Bob O'Connell near Devil's Elbow, 1943.

Born: April 5, 1941
Occupation: Health professional
Residence: Beverly Hills, California

"*I* was born Roberta Anne O'Connell in Springfield, Missouri. My family and friends called me Bobbie Anne. My mother's aunt and uncle were Slim Wilson, a left-handed fiddler, and Aunt Martha. She owned Aunt Martha's Pancake House and the Corn Crib Cafe in Springfield, and her son was Speedy

gone now. He bragged on me all through the meal and then he slipped me a twenty under the table. I was making forty cents an hour then. That twenty dollars was almost a week's wages."

Back on Route 66 at Stanton is the Jesse James Wax Museum, where Francena Turilli honors the memory of her husband, Rudy, as well as the mysterious J. Frank Dalton, the man who claimed to be Jesse James. Inside are life-size wax figures of Jesse and other outlaws, some of their personal belongings including enough guns to arm several posses, and one of the best-stocked souvenir shops on the highway. Francena, who started dealing with tourists when she was a little girl at her father's cave, sells admission tickets, gives her best Jesse James spiel, and runs the cash register without missing a beat.

"Sometimes it was very bad on old Highway 66," recalls Francena. "It was narrow and there were no shoulders. On a weekend or holiday the traffic was thick and you couldn't pass. There were an awful lot of accidents. That's the old road right out there in front of the museum. Now we get people coming here from off the interstate. Most of them don't know this was Highway 66."

South of Stanton, the old highway remains on the south side of the interstate all the way through to Sullivan, where George Hearst, the father of publishing czar William Randolph Hearst, was born. A few miles away, the town

of Bourbon still uses the name "Old Hwy. 66" for its main street. The pavement curves below the water tower and passes backyards, where damp wash flaps from clotheslines and children swing on old tires tied to the branches of shade trees. The highway continues into the countryside past the cutoff to Leasburg, just above Onondaga Cave. Formerly owned by Les Dill and Lyman Riley, Onondaga was considered one of the country's most spectacular caves because of its gigantic rock formations, cavernous rooms, and huge stalactites and stalagmites. Another of the area's major tourist draws, Onondaga became a state park and a registered national landmark shortly after Dill's death.

At Cuba, once an important Route 66 town just down the pike from the road leading to Onondaga, the memories of the old highway are sweet. For decades Cuba boasted it was the home of the Midway, a restaurant and garage with a car showroom, which was typical of the businesses that thrived on Highway 66 before Interstate 44 was constructed. Allyne Earls leased the Midway for ten years and finally bought the building in 1944. She put in twenty-four bedrooms and four bathrooms on the second floor and expanded the restaurant into the garage area. By the time she finished remodeling there were thirty-six persons on staff. During World War II, the rooms were filled with Fort Leonard Wood soldiers and their wives. As many as six hundred soldiers a day were fed at the Midway restaurant. A sizzling T-bone steak, fries, vegetable, and salad set a customer back only $1.20. If money was scarce, a

Hill Cemetery, east of Bourbon, Mo.

hamburger was just twelve cents. For thirty-eight years, Midway was open twenty-four hours a day. When Allyne finally sold the place in the 1970s and the new owner asked for the keys, she couldn't find them. The doors to the Midway had never been locked.

At Cuba, the old highway becomes county road all the way through Rosati and into St. James. The town of Rosati was started by Italian grape farmers, and St. James still hosts an annual grape festival. Along this stretch each September, grape stands that used to dot the side of Route 66 now grace the shoulders of the interstate, but not nearly as many. Truckers looking for a break from institutional interstate food still grind their big rigs to a halt on I-44 and buy sacks of grapes and jugs of fresh juice.

Just a few miles down the highway from St. James lies the Mule Trading Post, a well-known Route 66 tourist stop. Just ahead is the educational center named Rolla, home of a branch of the University of Missouri.

Jim Foote Service Station, circa 1955, St. James, Mo.

When the concrete two-lane Route 66 was completed in Missouri in 1931, the towns-people in Rolla commemorated the event with a public celebration. Here the highlands of the Ozarks merge with the time-worn Springfield plateau of southwestern Missouri. Travelers find substantial sections of Highway 66 between Rolla and Springfield. The old road remains through many of the towns and hamlets—Martin Springs, Doolittle, Newburg, Hooker, and others.

This was an important stretch of the Mother Road. Just two miles west of the Rolla city limits, Martin Springs was used for watering horses and livestock long before Route 66 came along. By the time the old highway was created, a store was built, and nearby, on the site of a pioneer cabin, one of the first truck stops in the nation—The Old Homestead—opened in 1925. Three years later W. D. and Lynna Aaron built a radiator shop next door, and for many years the

Haworth, a guitarist. They were known as the Goodwill Family, a group that played country and gospel music for years on KWTO's 'Ozark Jubilee' in Springfield. That's where Red Foley and Tennessee Ernie Ford and a bunch of others performed. None of my family had any formal musical training, but they could play guitars and fiddles and sing and yodel with the best of them. My mother sang with them until she met my dad.

"My dad couldn't get into the service during World War II, so when I was about a year old, we moved near St. Robert on Highway 66 close to Fort Leonard Wood, where he was a civilian maintenance man at the base laundry and also ran the movie projector for the German prisoners of war. Some of those men gave him a wooden cabinet they made. It weighed a ton and through the years we always referred to it as the 'German prisoner cabinet.' Housing was scarce then, so for a while we had to live in a one-room cabin. My mother called it a shanty. The row of cabins was along Highway 66, west of Waynesville. Later we moved into post housing. They were two-story barracks. Early condo, I guess.

"After the war my father bought the Oakwood Service Station in St. Robert, and we lived in a converted liquor store. It had four rooms and there was a gravel drive and it was right by

Aarons operated the only wrecker service in the area. Lynna served light lunches and kept a few groceries to sell, and when business picked up, she helped handle the gas pumps out front. A mile west was Club 66, opened in 1938, which twice burned to the ground.

Along this busy part of the old highway, M. L. Pierce opened a salvage yard around 1940. Poe's Truck Stop was ready for its first customers in 1953, and Lou Hargis took the wraps off his skating rink during World War II. Hargis was the second mayor of Doolittle, a town named in honor of General Jimmy Doolittle, the World War II flying hero who flew his own airplane to the dedication ceremonies the citizens of Doolittle hosted on October 10, 1946, on the eastbound lane of Highway 66.

Al Cook was Doolittle's first mayor, and he opened a gas station in 1945. Directly across the old highway, Malone's Service Station—built in 1941 and purchased by Dan Malone in 1953—survived the coming of the interstate. Almost forty years later Dan's brother Pat was still pumping gasoline, and other Route 66 businesses and relics of the old highway still remain. Doolittle won't sever its ties to the Mother Road.

"I was born in Rolla, grew up in Doolittle, and I rode my bike up and down Route 66," says Kim Corder, son of J. L. "Jake" Corder, the man who organized the town's volunteer fire department and a former fire chief at Fort Leonard Wood.

"Most of my childhood memories are within a few feet of the old highway. The old-timers would tell me stories about the Old

Wire Trail, and I'd stop at Malone's Service Station or go to Towell's Store to get a drink. That place was built in 1928, and Ike and Edna Towell added wooden cabins which rented for a dollar a night. For fifty cents more, the guests got supper. There was another grocery and filling station called Joe's Place, and there was the T & T Cafe and Vernelle's Motel and Restaurant. We used to pick blackberries along Route 66 and we got a dollar a gallon at the local restaurants."

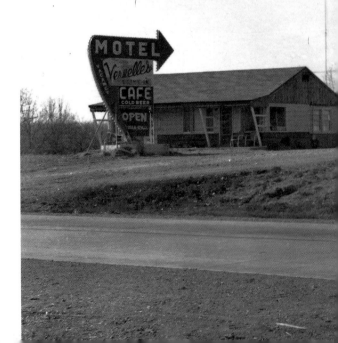

Left: Inside the T & T Cafe, circa 1955, Doolittle, Mo.

Below: Vernelle's, 1958, west of Rolla, Mo.

Highway 66, on the strip where all the clubs and joints were located. Some of those places were notorious and there were lots of floozies. My mother hated it. I can recall making trips with my folks back to Springfield to see relatives. My dad was always picking up hitchhiking GIs. They were plentiful back then. I also remember shopping trips to Lebanon and seeing wildflowers and barns and the old Eden Rock Resort and Devil's Elbow. My parents would stop at a little place on the way and get me a Grapette to drink. When I was five we moved back to Springfield and soon after that my brother was born.

"That's when Daddy hit the road, selling wholesale auto parts. He drove a red truck with shelves in the back, and he'd go to different garages starting at Strafford and all up Highway 66 as far as St. James. He also visited the little towns off 66—Iberia, Dixon, Crocker, Richland, and some others. My daddy worked very hard for his sales commission and he provided a good living. He loved his job and his customers.

"Unlike my mother and me, he had no fear of 'Bloody 66,' as people called it. He knew every curve and crack in the road. He'd leave at the crack of dawn on Monday and not come home until Friday night. He'd reload his truck on Saturday. Every Monday morning his mother would call and warn him about

Continuing on, the 66 highway curls around Devil's Elbow. This was the last section of old 66 pavement in Missouri to be replaced by I-44 in 1981. At this location on the road a group of tourist cabins and resort cottages once sprouted. Legend has it lumberjacks gave Devils Elbow its name because of the inevitable logjams they found in the bend of the Big Piney River.

The route twists through St. Robert and Waynesville—home of Fort Leonard Wood. It scoots by Buckhorn, Laquey, and Hazelgreen, at one time another popular fishing resort and tourist stop, and continues on toward Sleeper. In the summer, great beds of wild sweet pea, Queen Anne's lace, and clover line both sides of the road. The old highway bends southwest once more through Lebanon, the largest town between Rolla and Springfield and the site of the popular Munger Moss Motel. Lebanon was also the home of the renowned Nelson Hotel and Dream Village, a tourist attraction that was conceived and built shortly after the creation of Route 66 by Arthur Truman Nelson, an outspoken proponent for good roads in Missouri. Dubbed "Nelsonville" by the locals, the complex included a filling station, restaurant, and cottages. It was billed by gushing newspaper writers of the day as "the best known spot on Highway 66 between Chicago and Los Angeles." The Nelson dream ended decades later when Route 66 yielded to Interstate 44 and the tourist traffic patterns changed.

Sheldon "Red" Chaney, "the world's first drive-through window," Springfield, Mo.

After Lebanon, the road pushes on to the towns of Phillipsburg, Conway, Niangua Junction, Marshfield, Northview, and Strafford. At the end of this run through southwestern Missouri is Springfield, the "Queen City of the Ozarks." Springfield was the terminal point of the Old Wire Road and the site of the Civil War battle of Wilson's Creek, where on August 10, 1861, 2,500 men died. In 1865, "Wild Bill" Hickok shot and killed Dave Tutt over a gambling debt on the town square. Hickok hired a future Missouri governor as his legal counsel and got off the hook. Later, he ran for town marshal but came in second.

Springfield grew in time to be the third largest city in Missouri and a favorite jumping-off point to the Ozark playgrounds. Route 66, and eventually Interstate 44, brought carloads of visitors to spend the night, eat a few meals, and get some gas. The old road entered Springfield and spawned scores of service stations and garages. As was the case in several of the larger cities on the route, the course of Highway 66 in Springfield changed several times as the city grew and new bypasses were constructed to ease downtown congestion. At various times, Kearney, Glenstone, and other city streets served as Route 66 in Springfield. St. Louis and College Streets continued as the U.S. 66 Business Loop until 1960 when the Chestnut Street Trafficway was given that designation. By 1967, Interstate 44 was completed north of Springfield and a few years

the bad weather that was coming and tell him that he ought to stay home. But he never did. He always went. There'd be ice storms and deep snow and hard rains, but he'd go out on Highway 66 and sell those parts. He saw a lot of wrecks on the highway and started carrying a camera. We had a bunch of home movies of mangled cars. One time he witnessed a fatality on Highway 66 in his rearview mirror and had to go to court to testify. I'd pray every night to God to please bring him home to me.

"Daddy carried his wallet on a chain, like most truckers do, and he'd leave us some money. But by the end of the week, we'd be out. Mother would be gathering soda bottles for spare change and we'd be having corn bread and gravy for dinner. But Fridays were always good because Daddy came back. We were like the families waiting for a ship to return from sea. Every Friday evening, we waited at the corner and watched for that red truck to come into view. He'd have stories about his trip and the customers. Once, he brought me a puppy. One night in the early fifties, my mom and I were waiting at the corner for Daddy and we saw a silver object shaped like a cigar in the sky. We thought it was a UFO. I remember it vividly. My dad thought we were loony.

"The big treat on Friday nights was for Dad to take us to dinner at Gus

WELCOME! TO CAMPBELL "66"

Above left: Early Campbell "66" Express trailer, circa 1930, Springfield, Mo.

Above right: 1950s drawing by Snortin' Norton's creator, William Boyd, circa 1953.

Right: Big City girls visit Springfield, Mo.

Country musicians from KWTO radio, circa 1950, Springfield, Mo.

later the old 66 markings were dropped altogether.

During the heyday years of Route 66, there were many fine tourist courts in Springfield, including the Cordova, Black's, Lone Star, DeLuxe, Lone Pine, Mack's, Ozark, Rail Haven, Snow White, and Otto's. The down-home chophouses, which catered to tourists, were also top drawer. Some of those motor courts and cafes survived the coming of the interstate, but many were lost in the process as virtually every American motel

chain and franchise restaurant came to town.

There was a time when Springfield managed without all those look-alike restaurants smelling of disinfectant and lacking in character. Springfield was the site where Sheldon Chaney, better known as Red, and his wife, Julia, opened what was probably the world's first hamburger stand with a drive-through service window. The year was 1947. The location was Business Route 66, and the Chaneys found that travelers and locals in a hurry liked hollering their orders into the

Otto's on St. Louis Street in Springfield. There were red booths and chrome trim on the tables and nice tile floors and lots of families gathered there. The food was great. They served steaks, fried chicken, and my very favorite—hot roast beef sandwich on white bread. In the late fifties, my dad got rid of the truck and started hauling the car parts in an old bus. When times were tough, folks would trade things for the auto parts. He traded for televisions and radios, motor scooters, the hull of a twenty-five-foot boat, which he made into a cabin cruiser, and a 1950 Studebaker convertible that he gave to me. He had a recorder, too, and he'd sing and my mother would play the piano and they'd record some music. When Dad was on the road, Mom would play those songs and she'd cry.

"Finally, Dad came off the road in the early 1960s, and he went to work for an electric co-op. My parents are gone now. My mother died in 1972, and Daddy passed on in 1980. My brother lives in Malibu, and I live in Beverly Hills. I'm a long way from Springfield, but I'm still close to the highway. I live a block from Santa Monica Boulevard. That's the name Highway 66 went by here. The highway ends only a few miles from my house. I still have my memories—bitter and sweet—of Highway 66 and I know it's there. You just have to know how to find it."

kitchen through an open window. Named Red's Giant Hamburg, the restaurant's abbreviated spelling of the word *hamburger* was Red's own fault. He didn't measure the sign before it was erected, so it had to be spelled HAMBURG because he couldn't fit in the ER. That really didn't matter to Red or his faithful customers. What counted were the beef patties sizzling on the grill, the homemade root beer, the dill pickles, and the Skoal tobacco can filled with chili powder that Red brought to those diners who wanted some spice in their lives. The interstate

highway failed to knock Red's Giant Hamburg out of commission; the food and service were just too good. It finally closed in the mid-1980s when Red decided to retire. Red Chaney quit with his apron on.

About the same time that Red was flipping his last burger, another Route 66 institution based in Springfield—Campbell 66 Express—also closed. Founded by Frank Campbell, the Campbell 66 Express trucks hauled all types of cargo on U.S. 66 and other highways in twenty-two states for more than sixty-five years. Travelers smiled and waved

whenever they spied the Campbell trailers bearing the company's familiar symbol— Snortin' Norton, a galloping camel with his tongue flapping in the breeze and a big red 66 on his side. The hard-working beast's motto, HUMPIN' TO PLEASE, was also painted on each trailer. Bill Boyd, the chief camel painter, created close to twelve thousand images of Snortin' Norton during a forty-year career. In 1986, Campbell 66 Express filed for bankruptcy. The trucks and trailers were sold and painted over. Snortin' Norton sadly disappeared.

Proceeding west from Springfield, the old route follows Missouri 266, just above the interstate, through Halltown, a favorite haunt for antique hunters. At that point, to avoid Kansas and to connect with the Will Rogers Turnpike in Oklahoma, Route 66 (now I-44) dips to the south toward Joplin. But Missouri 96 takes up the old route through Heatonville, Albatross, Phelps, Rescue, Plew, Avilla, and on into Carthage, the picturesque hometown of Belle Starr, the notorious outlaw and "Bandit Queen." Carthage was also a major intersecting point where stagecoaches made connections with the main line.

Beyond Carthage comes Carterville and Webb City. The old road goes south and finally there's Joplin—the last stop in Missouri. Situated in the southwest corner of Missouri, Joplin once called itself "The Gateway to the Ozarks," a slogan city boosters

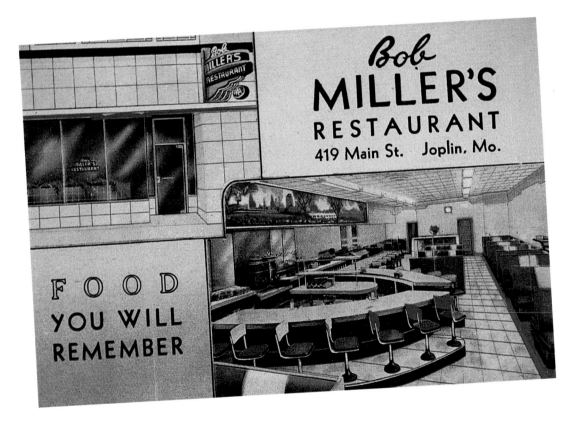

"Steaks, Fried Chicken, Salads, and Best in Pastries," vintage postcard, Joplin, Mo.

later changed to "The Crossroads of America."

Founded in 1840, the city is near the center of a region that was considered the greatest zinc-producing area in the world. Once lined with saloons, dance halls, and gambling rooms, Main Street was part of the path of Route 66 through the heart of the city. The notorious House of Lords, a haven on Main Street offering fine cuisine, gambling, and "soiled doves," is long gone. A park took its place. None of the twenty downtown hotels or the eight downtown movie houses is in operation. A long string of motels and franchise restaurants located in strip centers east of the city is the main attraction. Main Street survives because of some taverns, cafes, doughnut and butcher shops, and other small specialty businesses that have refused to move to distant shopping malls.

When Kansas was bone-dry, Joplin was the last-chance watering hole for travelers heading west. Highway 66 followed Main Street downtown to 7th Street, and then went west to Kansas. Motorists not interested in sailing down the interstate can still go that old route. Driving west out of Joplin on 7th Street, travelers pass Dolly's Chili House, Bill's Hamburgers, the Tophat Diner, Dutch Village Motel, Schifferdecker Park, and Dixie Lee's Dine & Dance Bar. All of them soon fade in the rearview mirror. Route 66 heads across the Kansas border.

After traipsing across hundreds of miles of mid-American countryside, the Mother Road works up the courage to wander into the buffer lands on the edge of the Great American West.

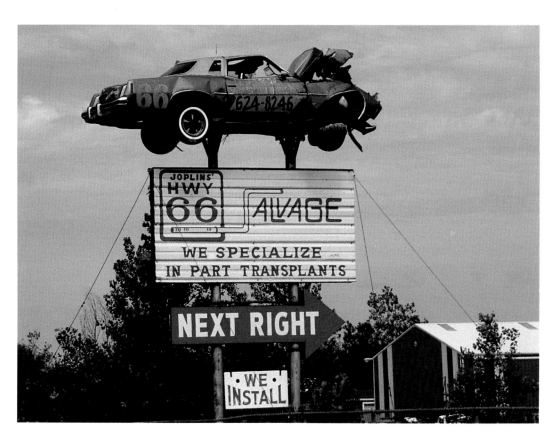

Salvage yard west of Joplin, Mo.

CHAPTER FOUR

Kansas

"There's no place like home."
—Dorothy

West of Joplin, past the Black Cat Body Shop and the acres of discarded vehicles at the Highway 66 Salvage yard, straddling the border of Missouri and Kansas, stands a sign on a newer spur of the old highway. It reads:

OLD ROUTE 66

NEXT RIGHT

Those who make the turn don't regret it. This is a piece of original U.S. 66—a 2-mile strip of unimproved two-lane with no curb and little shoulder. The center stripes have faded away. Still, some highway travelers know they're moving through what was once some of the best lead and zinc mining country in the world. The road passes the old Eagle-Picher Company smelter, at one time a great producer of lead. Steep mounds of chert, or chat—waste from the mines—are piled in the distant fields and along the railroad tracks. The highway goes through the heart of

Left: Route 66 east of Galena, Kans.

Above: Kansas highway sign.

Galena, turns west for a couple of miles and crosses the Spring River, heads 9 miles south to Baxter Springs, and then, after just 2 more miles, crosses yet another state boundary and makes its debut in Oklahoma.

This short Kansas stretch of Highway 66, just like the long route through Illinois, was completely paved by 1929. At that time, Missouri was less than two-thirds concreted. Oklahoma was only a quarter hard-surfaced, the people of the Texas Panhandle hadn't even thought about laying concrete, and only about 64 miles of the remaining 1,221-plus miles of Route 66 from New Mexico to Arizona and California were paved.

Kansas may have accounted for only a dozen miles of Route 66—a brief section of the route that sliced off the southeast corner of the state—but the highway was a source of pride to the rugged miners, farmers, and small town merchants. It brought the rest of the nation through their territory.

Valuable raw minerals were discovered in this region where Kansas, Missouri, and Oklahoma touch. Mining operations got underway in the late 1800s, and in the twentieth century, there were several boom towns straddling the three-state territory. During the busy years of the world wars, the Tri-State district, as it was called, became a major producer of zinc and lead ores. In due course those mines, like the highway that cut through the area, gave out.

By the early 1960s, Kansas, with just its short leg of highway, had the dubious distinction of being the only Route 66 state to be completely bypassed. A few miles to the south, on the Missouri-Oklahoma border, Interstate 44 connected with the new Will Rogers Turnpike, a much faster route for travelers scurrying east and west. The detour of Kansas received little attention. The name 66 was retained as a state highway, and life quietly went on.

Out on that link of Kansas Highway 66, there is today none of the violence that erupted there during the turbulent 1930s. In 1935, after John L. Lewis, the powerful union chief of the United Mine Workers, had called a labor strike, a mob of angry miners blocked U.S. 66 in front of the Eagle-Picher smelter and sprayed bullets and rocks on cars that failed to heed their commands. The striking miners attacked carloads of scabs returning to their homes in Missouri after they had worked in the Kansas and Oklahoma mining field. Sheriff's deputies were forced to detour the Highway 66 traffic, and it finally took a downpour of cold rain to quiet the bloody situation. Martial law was declared by Kansas Governor Alf Landon, who one year later would run on the Republican ticket for president against the incumbent, Franklin D. Roosevelt. Landon dispatched National Guard troops, armed with fixed bayonets and machine guns, to nearby Galena in order to quell the riot. Nerves remained frayed for years and labor unrest continued. On April 11, 1937, nine men were gunned down in Galena in front of the headquarters of the International Mine, Mill and Smelter Workers

Kansas state decal.

Union, a CIO affiliate, after four thousand tri-state lead and zinc miners wielding pick handles demonstrated against CIO organization efforts.

There is no marker or monument on the road outside Galena. There is nothing left to commemorate the blood that was shed on the highway. The pitted surface of the road is scarred only from years of use. Flowing into Galena, the old route is quiet except for a few passing cars and trucks. The pavement rises into a gentle curve over a bridge and enters the town as Front Street, then makes a sharp left-hand turn near a cluster of catalpa trees and becomes Main Street. After several blocks, the highway turns right and continues its jaunt as Kansas 66. Along Main Street are barber shops, drugstores, taverns, and cafes intermingled with many old deserted brick buildings. Once a rip-roaring mining town complete with what were called "haunts of dissipation and vice," there exists not a sign of the swindlers, gamblers, and black-hearted whores who made easy pickings of miners' hard-earned wages. They vanished long ago as did the miners, who rest in the cemeteries strung along the highway west of town.

Through the years, Galena shrank from a town with a thriving population of close to 15,000 to less than 4,000. Named after a type of lead ore that often contains silver, Galena is today a good example of a small American town that should be placed on an endangered species list.

At the Galena Museum, which was fashioned out of an old train depot and moved to the edge of the highway, local citizens view treasures from the town's glory days when their ancestors worked the mines or made a living from the thousands of Highway 66 motorists. Inside the museum are newspapers with bold headlines about the labor violence, stacks of high school annuals, battered miners' helmets and lunch buckets, extensive mineral collections, and photographs of men and women from long ago. A yellowed newspaper clipping dated September 18, 1951, tells of the daring rescue of seventeen-year-old Gene McCumber from an old mine shaft called Pigeon Cave on West Fifth Street. The injured boy was saved by Howard Litch, a member of the volunteer fire department. Litch, a local garage owner, climbed inside a mining bucket that was lowered into the shaft by his own wrecker boom.

When they surfaced, the youth was whisked by ambulance to a hospital in Joplin. The clipping is tacked to a wall, and nearby are carbide lamps, pickaxes, and glass display cases holding invaluable souvenirs of people's lives—antique toys, picture albums, and the Nazi flag a local soldier brought home from the war. Each week more items are donated. The museum is Galena's attic, a comfortable place to rummage through memories on a rainy afternoon. It houses the town's "silver" that remained after the "lead" was discarded.

Leaving Galena, the state highway signs —an image of bright yellow Kansas sunflowers with black 66s in the center—point the way across the Spring River to the historic town of Baxter Springs, founded in 1858.

Just north of what was to become the Oklahoma border, the town site of Baxter

Howard Litch

Born: July 17, 1906
Occupation: Museum director, retired garage owner, mechanic, and fireman
Residence: Galena, Kansas

"My father was Tom Litch. He came from Arkansas and settled in Galena, Kansas. This is where he met my mother. Her name was Gladys. They got married, and I was born and raised here in Galena. I was an only child. My mother died in 1907 of tuberculosis and me and my dad boarded. We lived in kind of a rough section. Just a road separated us and a wild place folks around here called Hell's Half-Acre.

"My dad was a miner, and later he worked in a jig room at the mill where they crumbled rock and cleaned ore. He was paid twelve dollars a week, and that was enough for our clothes, our food and keep, and a roof over our heads. I went to school until I was sixteen, and then I talked Dad into letting me quit so I could work as an automobile mechanic.

"I was a mechanic for fifty years on what became known as Highway 66. I started out working for the Ford agency. Then, in 1936, I opened my own business. I went with a girl for eight years, but I didn't marry her until my father died in 1935. I had to care for him. My wife was born in a mining camp north of here called Badger, and she was a bookkeeper at the garage. Her name is Ruby Gladys Litch. Her middle name's the same as my mother's first name. We never had any children, but she had a son and daughter from her first marriage. That man died. My wife changed my life for the better in a lot of ways. I like to say I've had an angel around me all these years. My business was named Howard Litch Garage and it was in a building that had been an old livery stable right up on Main Street, which was Highway 66 in this town. I sure did work on a bunch of those

Springs already existed on the Black Dog Trail opened in 1803 by Chief Black Dog and his band of Osage Indians. Some years later, John J. Baxter came along and settled in these parts. An imposing six-foot, seven-inch man, who usually had a pair of navy Colts strapped around his waist, Baxter operated an inn and general store. Dying with his boots on in a

gun battle near his cabin in 1859, he did not live to see the town named for him.

Four years later, in 1863, the Baxter Springs Massacre took place. Just six weeks after they laid waste to the Kansas town of Lawrence, Confederate guerrilla raiders, led by the notorious William Quantrill, attacked and massacred a small Union force under the

Marsh Rainbow Arch Bridge, built in 1922 over Spring River, dismantled in 1986, Riverton, Kans.

command of General James G. Blunt on the prairie outside Baxter Springs. Only the general and a handful of his troops survived the attack to recall this chapter of the "Bloody Kansas" story.

Baxter Springs was incorporated as a city in 1868 and became known as "the first cowtown in Kansas," the terminus of the famed Shawnee Trail. Texas cattlemen drove large herds of longhorns northeast across the Red River and up through Indian Territory. They crossed the Arkansas River and continued northeast following an old established military road into the frontier town on the southern border of Kansas.

At Baxter Springs, large corrals and collecting pens were built so the cattle could be fattened before they were driven or shipped to Kansas City. Jingling spurs and snorting mustangs became familiar sounds on the town streets, as swarms of dusty Texas drovers—generally wearing broad-rimmed hats and high-top boots—rode into Baxter Springs. They quickly looked for something to quench their thirst after spending as many as 110 days on the trail. There was a saloon on nearly every corner in the business district of Baxter Springs. Public hangings, gunfights, and bawdy-house brawls were common occurrences.

With the completion of the Missouri River, Fort Scott and Gulf Railroad through Baxter Springs, even more people poured into the shipping center. Fortunately, besides the desperadoes, gamblers, and misfits, came plenty of merchants, traders, and ranchers. When the longhorn cattle drives shifted westward, the town endured hard times.

For many years, Baxter Springs earned a reputation as a resort when it was discovered that the spring from which the town took part of its name possessed curative powers. A park was laid out on Military Avenue near the bathhouses. It became the promenade for the town's young couples, and visitors came to Baxter Springs from across the country to drink the healing waters. During the summer and autumn months a silver cornet band serenaded the bathers from a fancy pagoda in the park. The discovery of rich deposits of lead and zinc just across the Missouri line also helped Baxter Springs thrive economically and attracted more residents. The mining operations grew and reached into southeast Kansas and the northeast corner of Oklahoma. In its day, Baxter Springs was one of the prominent cities in the tri-state district, but once the lucrative mining operations arrived, the dependence on the mineral springs disappeared. The bathers stopped

Sign on Main Street, Galena, Kans.

Route 66 cars. We did everything.

"I stayed open all the time except for a couple years during World War II. I joined the army in 'forty-three and served as a motor mechanic. I got out because of my age in 'forty-five and went back to my garage. Edward Beyer, one of my boys at the garage, was a soldier and swiped the Nazi flag from Hitler's hideout in Austria, called the Eagle's Nest. He brought it back to Galena. Business was real steady when we got back. I had good equipment and a twenty-four-hour wrecker service.

"Traffic was heavy through here in the forties and fifties. Route 66 ran right down Main Street past my garage and turned the corner. I always got a kick out of those tourists. While one of my men would be working on their car, I'd take them over to see Pigeon Cave, an old mine near town. At Highway 66's peak, I had five mechanics, two body men, and a colored boy who greased cars and fixed tires. One mechanic worked for me for twenty-two years. I was with the volunteer fire department for forty-six years, and we'd use my wrecker for rescue work out on the road or if somebody went down a mine shaft. I helped pull a boy out of a mine one time.

"I retired in 1974. My stepson is a mail carrier and my stepdaughter and her family run my auto parts store just across Main Street from my old garage. When I sold the garage, the man who bought it said he was going to leave my sign up on the building. It's still there—Howard Litch Garage. This town was good to me. I always had a lot of business so I wanted to do something for the town. That's why I got involved with the Galena Museum. We moved to this spot in 1984. The old train depot this museum is in came right down Main Street and turned the corner and settled right here on Highway 66. I was saving things to put in it for years. We've got that Hitler flag that Ed brought home. He died up at the Veteran's Hospital in Kansas City in 1980, and this flag's here in his memory. We've also got quite a collection of minerals and mining tools and photographs. I had some trouble, but I finally got ahold of a pair of Route 66 shields. I really wanted those old highway signs. They belong here. We've got a lot of history in this town and that highway out there was a big part of it."

coming to town and the silver cornet serenades stopped.

The town that had all the makings of another Dodge City settled down into a respectable burg with tree-shaded streets, churches, and social clubs. For many years, Baxter Springs drew more national attention through Soldier Reunion Week, when Union veterans of the Civil War gathered there from all parts of the nation. Naturally, as the veterans began dying off, so did the reunions.

During the several decades when Route 66 was the main highway through the area, Baxter Springs was served by five major truck lines and was used by one big freight company as a division point and maintenance shop for eight states.

It was also during those busy years of the late 1940s that Mickey Mantle got his start in organized baseball. The kid from down the highway in Commerce, Oklahoma, played for three years with the Baxter Springs Whiz Kids prior to signing with the New York Yankees.

Driving into Baxter Springs on the old road, the town has changed little since those years when Mantle was swatting home runs down at the ball park. Across from the high school, a marker honors the memory of those who died in the Baxter Springs Massacre. It reads:

**THE BLOOD THAT FLOWED IN KANSAS
BEFORE AND DURING
THE CIVIL WAR NOURISHED THE TWIN TREES
OF LIBERTY AND UNION**

At the city limits, there is still a big sign welcoming visitors to the "First Cow Town In Kansas," and 66 plows right through the business district on Military Avenue just as it did back in the late 1920s.

Those riotous Texas cowboys rode off into the sunset long ago, but thirsty folks still find cold suds at Shirley's Place ("Where Good Friends Meet"), Bill Buck's Palace, or the Silver Buckle Bar. Customers at Milo's Drugstore settle for tamer beverages and look over newspapers, boxes of chocolates, and tobacco, while their prescriptions are being filled.

At Bill Murphey's on Military Avenue, charbroiled steaks are cheap enough for a hitchhiker to afford. The building that houses Murphey's was previously a bank. One May afternoon in 1876, Jesse James and Cole Younger rode into town, tied their horses to a corn crib, and walked into the bank. They asked the cashier to change a five-dollar bill. When the cashier turned his back, James and Younger pulled their guns and "withdrew" $2,900. The outlaws jumped on their waiting horses and made a run to Indian Territory to the south. A posse was soon organized and the chase was on. About 7 miles south of Baxter Springs, in what is now Oklahoma, the bandits stopped at a blacksmith shop to get their horses shod. They realized they were being chased and when the posse came riding by, James and Younger waylaid their pursuers. They disarmed the posse and broke their guns on some rocks. Then the posse was ordered to return to Kansas. Not a single shot was fired during the entire episode and not a person was injured.

Just down the street from Murphey's Restaurant, the words "Furniture" and "Undertaking" are fast fading from the brick front of another downtown building that became a flea market filled with the town's discarded junk—mostly all lead and little silver.

But on warm spring evenings, when kids are pulling ball gloves out of their closet and choosing up sides, the whole mighty roar of those glory years—when trucks were "haulin' ass" out of town and the young Mick was just starting to flex his muscles—comes rushing back. For an instant, the town and the highway don't seem old at all.

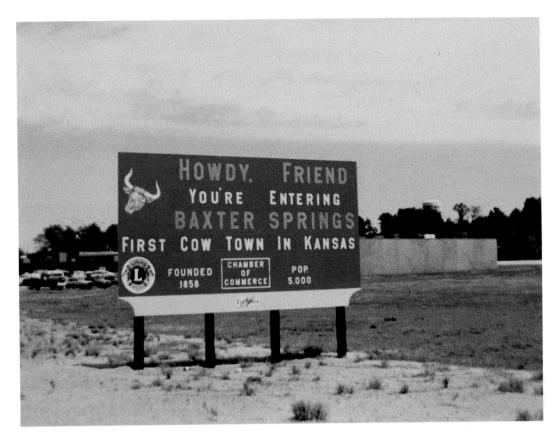

City limits, Baxter Springs, Kans.

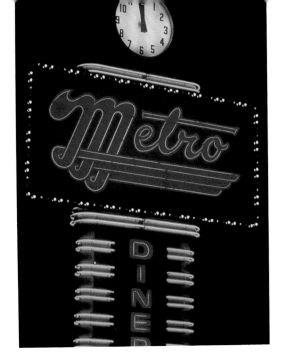

CHAPTER FIVE

Oklahoma

"Many months have come and gone
Since I wandered from my home
In the Oklahoma hills where I was born.
Though a page of life has turned
And a lesson I have learned
Yet I feel like in those hills I still belong."
—Woody Guthrie

The man aimed his automobile down the old highway connecting Tulsa and Oklahoma City. He didn't consider taking the turnpike. Not for a moment. He would never do that. He was too old and time had become holy for him. Time was something he treasured. He knew the turnpike was a faster way to go, but it wouldn't make the best use of his time. The "free road," as some folks still called it, was the way to go. It was a road of character and memories, both bitter and sweet.

As he drove in and out of towns along the way and passed farms, fields, and crossed creeks, he saw that many things were still the same. The drive made the old man feel young again, but with the patience and honesty that come with age. Traveling the old road did that for him. It gave him the best of both worlds—past and present.

He paused for coffee and pie in Bristow, and near Little Deep Fork Creek, he pulled his car off the road and picked a handful of wildflowers. Their scent filled the car, and the old man remembered his wife and how she looked when she was a girl. He said her name out

Left: A section of Route 66 near Depew, Okla.

Above: Midnight at Metro, Tulsa, Okla.

Left: Billboard near Elk City, Okla.

Above: Oklahoma state decal.

Below: Nightfall at the Metro Diner, Tulsa, Okla.

loud, just to hear it, and he hummed her favorite song as he drove down the road.

After he passed through Arcadia and Edmond, the busy traffic of Oklahoma City loomed ahead. He turned the car around and drove back to Tulsa. He stuck to the free road, and he hummed the song, and some others he could recall, most of the way back. He switched off the air conditioner and rolled down the windows. Summer air rushed through the car. That night the old man ate a big supper at a cafe he liked, and he went to bed and dreamed—of being a boy in the Canadian River bottoms before he moved to the city, of his wedding day, and of other times that only returned to him in sleep.

When he opened his eyes the next morning, the first thing the old man saw was the jar filled with flowers, wildflowers from the edge of the ghost road—from Route 66.

Nowhere is Route 66 more at home than in Oklahoma, where the pavement follows the contours of the land as though it had always been there. In Oklahoma, the West and East collide on Route 66, and the state becomes the crossroads for America's Main Street.

In a way, Route 66 was born in Oklahoma—home of Cyrus Avery, Lon Scott, Andy Payne, Jack Cutberth, Will Rogers, and so many others who inspired the growth of the highway. In 1926, when word of the new U.S. Route 66 got out, Oklahoma was celebrating its nineteenth anniversary as a state, and Woody Guthrie, then a scrawny fourteen-year-old, had already outgrown those Oklahoma hills where he was born.

Route 66 was big news in Oklahoma. All along the highway, which linked the industrial states of the East with the golden plains of the West, Oklahomans watched a new culture emerge complete with hitchhikers, Burma Shave signs, and neon lights. It took several more years to connect the bits and pieces, but before too long the highway reached across the land, racing through time and history, following old trails blazed by explorers and adventurers.

The path through Oklahoma emerged from the trails worn in the prairie, and slashed through tangles of blackjack and mesquite. The highway begins its descent into northeastern Oklahoma at the Kansas line and slashes southwest through old Indian Territory, past Tulsa and Oklahoma City, the state's two largest cities, and then proceeds westward to the Texas Panhandle.

In the 1930s, Route 66 became the road of desperation described so poignantly by John Steinbeck in *The Grapes of Wrath.* As the brutal Dust Bowl years arrived, many of those Oklahoma refugees, or Okies, struck out on Route 66 in single cars or caravans, carrying all their furniture, kids, hopes, and dreams with them.

Sometimes only humor kept folks sane. According to the common folk wisdom, a car with three mattresses strapped to its roof meant a family of rich Okies; two mattresses meant mediocre wealth; and a lone mattress meant the Okies inside were dirt poor. Some officials estimated that as many as a third of a million Okies—or 15 percent of the population—fled the choking dust storms and took Route 66 to California.

Those tragic years of the Great Depression and the Dust Bowl left deep scars on the land and emotional wounds on the people along the highway. In the early 1930s the rain stopped and did not come again for years. The timing was horrendous—the century's worst drought arrived to accompany the century's worst Depression. In 1925, wheat sold for $1.16 a bushel; in 1931, the price dropped to thirty-three cents. Banks foreclosed, and families moved on.

Parts of Oklahoma, Kansas, Texas, New Mexico, and several midwestern states looked like the landscape of the moon. Years of drought and outdated farming methods turned the land into a desert of sand and pale dirt. The sky was a choking sea of dust. Giant dark dust clouds swept away the topsoil. Folks wrapped wet neckerchiefs around their faces and crammed newspapers and pages ripped from catalogs under the doors and around the windows to keep the powder-fine dust from

U.S. 66, Lincoln County, Okla.

seeping in. It did little good. Dust covered everything and coated the lungs of people and livestock. Some dust storms lasted seventy-two hours straight with no letup. Schools closed, and cars, trucks, and trains sat still. People died from dust pneumonia. Flocks of geese, blinded by the swirling storms, crashed to the ground. Cattle by the thousands died of thirst. Derricks were used no longer to drill for oil, but water. Route 66 became a road of safe passage to what the Dust Bowlers prayed would be a better way of life.

Steinbeck described the highway this way:

> Highway 66 is the main migrant road. 66—the long concrete path across the country, waving gently up and down on the map, from the Mississippi to Bakersfield—over the red lands and the gray lands, twisting up into the mountains, crossing the Divide and down into the bright and terrible desert, and across the desert to the mountains again, and into the rich California valleys.

> 66 is the path of a people in flight, refugees from the dust and shrinking land, from the thunder of tractors and shrinking ownership, from the desert's slow northward invasion, from the twisting winds that howl up out of Texas, from the floods that bring no richness to the land and steal what richness is there. From all of these the people are in flight, and they come into 66 from the tributary side roads, from the wagon tracks and the rutted country roads. 66 is the mother road, the road of flight.

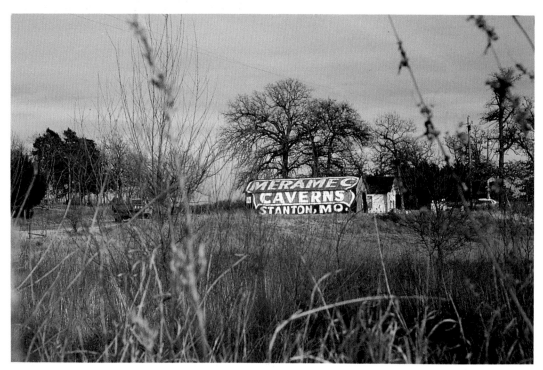

Old barn on Oklahoma's Mother Road, west of Chandler, Okla.

For many Oklahomans, any memories of the Dust Bowl era—including Steinbeck's prose and Guthrie's ballads—are best forgotten. Many of them are apt to wince at the mere mention of the word *Okie*. To them, the words *Okie, Dust Bowl,* and *Route 66* are phrases from the past. Interdispersal loops, cloverleafs, turnpikes, and interstates are much preferable.

"Everybody always talks about Okies—those folks who packed it all in and went on down the road," says an old farmer who left Oklahoma only long enough to serve a hitch in the army. "I'd like to know about the ones who stayed and spit in the dust and stuck it

out. They were the tough ones. They were the real Oklahomans. Or the ones who did leave and built new lives. Some of them even came back. What about them? There's nothing wrong with being called an Okie. That should be a name of pride, not a brand of shame."

Besides serving as an escape route for the migrants, Route 66 in Oklahoma carried more than its fair share of vagabonds and poets, servicemen heading to and from war, truckloads of commerce, and, of course, an endless stream of tourists. It was this wave of tourists headed to the Painted Desert or the Grand Canyon that helped romanticize Route

66. They motored along listening to a series of warblers croon about "getting their kicks" on the highway. In the post–World War II years, Route 66 became the nation's most popular highway. It was the evocative symbol of freedom, fun, and escape. Americans took to it in droves.

The route was heavily traveled all year long, but the main season was summer when the schools let out. On some portions of Route 66 in Oklahoma during those busy summer months, traffic was so thick it was difficult to cross the road. Highway towns in Oklahoma thrived on the revenue.

At the height of its popularity, Route 66, especially in Oklahoma, signaled the age of the hamburger stand, filling station, and the motor court with refrigerated air. Tourists got no wake-up calls because there were no telephones in the cabins. But most desk clerks worth their salt had a stash of alarm clocks behind the counter to lend their customers. The tourists tried to stop at the cafes where they spied the trucks, knowing well that the legions of truckers hauling oranges and beefsteak always dined where the gravy was the tastiest and the biscuits were the lightest. These authentic cafes can still be found in

Above: Aviatrix models in front of an early Phillips 66 filling station in Oklahoma, circa 1927.

Right: Boots Adams (left) and Frank Phillips (right) in 1939 with the Phillips 66 Highway Hostesses, who cruised the highways providing assistance to motorists and inspected rest rooms for cleanliness.

Oklahoma. They still turn out homemade pies, thick hand-patted burgers, real milkshakes, and there's nothing instant, except the service.

In Oklahoma, there are still garish postcards to buy and joints where patrons are serenaded by jukebox tunes. There are still people who consider time important. They take time to chat with a trucker or waitress. Take time to watch a hawk sail across the summer sky. Take time to pull off the road for a skinny-dip in a shady creek.

Even though folks are singing new songs and driving new highways and the old road has been nudged aside by the interstate, America's Main Street in Oklahoma continues as a vital frontage road, a business loop, an alternative for those people who aren't particularly anxious to go lickety-split. Remnants of the proud highway can be found from one end of the state to the other.

Route 66 also cuts directly through the prime marketing territory of the Phillips Petroleum Company, founded in 1917 by oil tycoon Frank Phillips. Coincidentally, almost every major midwestern city on the Phillips Petroleum marketing list happened to be located on the highway. Eager to find a suitable name for the new gasoline, Phillips finally settled the question of the company trademark on the eve of an executive committee meeting in Bartlesville, Oklahoma, in 1927. Returning to Bartlesville from Oklahoma City, John Kane, one of Phillips Petroleum's top executives, was in a company car driven by Salty Sawtell. The tank was filled with the company's new gasoline. As the men sped toward Tulsa on Route 66, Kane

noticed how fast they were traveling.

"This car goes like sixty with our new gas," said Kane.

"Sixty nothing," answered Sawtell. "We're doing sixty-six!"

The men looked at each other and grinned. Going 66 on Route 66. That was the sign they were looking for. They already knew the new fuel was in the gravity range of 66, an especially high gravity mark. Now that they'd had this experience on the new Oklahoma highway, it seemed that 66 was destined to be the name. When Kane reported the news to Frank Phillips, it was all the colorful oil tycoon needed to hear. Before long Phillips 66 gasoline was selling across America. Although the original Phillips logo started out on disk-shaped signs, the company by 1930 was using the familiar six-pointed shield that resembled the national highway signs. The Phillips Petroleum shield has been altered somewhat during the years, but Phillips 66 signs still dot much of the old road and many of the interstates and turnpikes.

"Oklahoma is where it's at as far as Route 66 goes," says Terrence Moore, a southwestern photographer raised in a California orange grove right beside Route 66. "I've traveled and photographed the length of the old highway most of my life. I've found that Oklahoma is the central state on the route and the heart of the road. Then there are the connections—*The Grapes of Wrath*, Phillips 66, the Will Rogers name—that link the road geographically and historically to the state. But the main thing is that Route 66 in Oklahoma means you are in the West.

Especially when you get past Oklahoma City and the sky opens up. Then you know you've arrived. That's a spiritual connection."

Out of his many trips down the Mother Road, one particularly sticks in Moore's mind. "I was a kid hitching to California and I found myself on Route 66 at El Reno, Oklahoma. I can recall that precise moment very well. I felt like I was really home. It was so simple. I only stood there for a moment, and then somebody stopped and I rode all the way into L.A. But that single moment, there in El Reno, has never left me. It was just me all alone on Route 66. That's an entirely different feeling than being on the interstate. When you're on 66 you're in another time, another place."

The long surviving stretches of Oklahoma's Route 66 recall those other times. The old road that remains takes people back to the days before freeways, shopping malls, and designer clothes. Out on the open highway, along the old route—the free road —are towns where the only men wearing neckties are bankers and undertakers. These are places where lunch is called dinner, and what city folks call dinner is supper. Towns where people sit on the front porch in the evening and have conversations. Where they put up screens on the windows in the springtime and leave their keys in the ignition overnight. Towns where the biggest fear is a renegade tornado. Towns that will always consider Route 66 to be the "Queen of Highways."

For those unhurried motorists who choose to visit these places and leave the turnpikes and interstates, traveling the old road can be a potent tonic. Part of the route passes through an area of Oklahoma visited by Washington Irving in 1832, when the territory was still a virgin wilderness and the early American essayist was gathering material for *A Tour of the Prairies.* Going east to west on Route 66 in Oklahoma, the towns and cities and forgotten crossroads have one thing in common besides the water tower covered with senior-class graffiti—they are all united by the Mother Road.

The old highway quietly enters the northeastern corner of Oklahoma, a region that was once the center of some of the richest lead and zinc mining in the nation. Originally, this main road that linked the Oklahoma-Kansas border to Oklahoma City was called State Highway 7. In 1926, the government changed the name to U.S. Route 66. Initially just a wagon trail, the road had been graded by teams of mules and paved in some sections in the early 1920s. Much of Route 66 through eastern Oklahoma was constructed by widening State Highway 7, or in some instances straightening out curves. By the early 1930s at least 85 percent of U.S. 66 in Oklahoma was concreted.

Four miles south of the Kansas border, the first Oklahoma town on U.S. 66 is Quapaw, named after the tribe which moved to Indian Territory in 1833. The town was founded in 1897 on land those Indians once owned. During the mining boom years around the turn of the century many Indians became wealthy by leasing their allotments to the mining companies. Just 6 miles east of Quapaw on the bank of the Spring River is Devil's Promenade, a huge stone bluff where the Quapaws commemorated the return of Indian soldiers from the world wars, built council fires, and danced in elaborate costumes.

After Quapaw comes Commerce, a mining town that got its start in 1913. It is best remembered as the boyhood home of Yankee slugger Mickey Mantle, whose father worked as a shoveler for the Eagle-Picher Zinc and Lead Company.

"The Depression for us lasted longer than for most people," says Mantle. "During that time, we lived in Spavinaw, Oklahoma, and I think my dad was working for about fifty cents a week. His dad was a butcher, and that's the way we ate—from my grandfather. Later, my dad got a chance to move up to the lead mines in Commerce and Picher. We never realized we were poor, I don't think. You go back up there now and look at the places where we lived, and you can't believe it. It really looks like a slum."

Like most boys in that country, Mantle grew up climbing the giant piles of spent ore called chat, rooting for the St. Louis Cardinals, and playing pickup games of baseball on a cleared field near the town's abandoned mine shafts.

"We made our own ballparks," says Mantle, "and we made our own baseballs out of that black tape you put around water pipes. We always had gloves, and we could make

A Route 66 Portrait

Will Rogers, Jr.

Born: October 20, 1911
Occupation: Retired newspaper
*   publisher, actor, public servant*
Residence: Tubac, Arizona

"*I* was the oldest child born to Will and Betty Rogers. I was born in New York City. My father was with the Ziegfeld Follies at the time and our family had an apartment overlooking

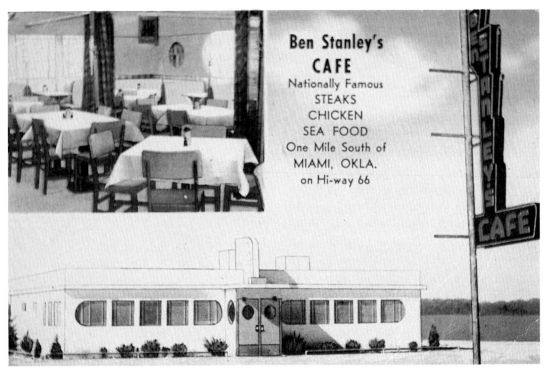

"We Don't Fool You, We Feed You" vintage postcard, Miami, Okla.

our own bats from broomsticks or whatever. So we made our own entertainment. All we had to do was play ball."

Nowadays, Mickey Mantle Boulevard runs through Commerce, a town where there are still good cafes serving the public and local kids playing sandlot games before it gets too dark to see the ball.

Only 3 miles south of Commerce is Miami, pronounced *My-am-ah* in Oklahoma, and an important area trade center. Named for the small Indian tribe living on the site in the nineteenth century, Miami bears no

resemblance to the more exotic Florida city of the same name. Some old motor courts and restaurants that serve broasted chicken endure as does the remarkable Coleman Theater, a restored Route 66 treasure at the corner of First and Main in the center of Miami's downtown business district. A Spanish Colonial revival masterpiece covered with stucco and intricate terra cotta gargoyles, the Coleman first opened its doors in 1929 and was immediately showcased as one of the most beautiful theaters in the Southwest. Will Rogers and many other notables made

the Hudson River near Grant's Tomb. About 1919, my dad signed a contract with Sam Goldwyn and began appearing in silent pictures out in California. He sent for the rest of the family to join him and we took the train across country.

"The rail followed close to what eventually became Route 66. I'll never forget that trip out West. It was very hot and my mother would get some ice and dampen cloths to keep our faces cool. When we finally reached Needles, California, on the edge of the Mojave Desert, the railroad workers all went on strike. The trains couldn't move in either direction. We were stuck in Needles. It was midsummer and the temperature was well over 110 degrees. My father heard about all of the trouble and he jumped in a car back in Los Angeles and raced all by himself out to Needles and rescued us. He drove up and we took off for the coast on that old road made of wooden planks that reached across the desert. We first had a home in Beverly Hills, and then we moved to the ranch that overlooked Santa Monica and the Pacific Ocean. I went to Beverly Hills High School and was a swimmer, debater, and edited the school paper.

"Then I went to Stanford University. I was a swimmer there and captained the polo team. I also

Coleman Theater, built in 1929, Miami, Okla.

appearances at the Coleman, and everyone who grew up in Miami had an emotional attachment to the theater as well as to the highway that continues to serve as the city's main street.

As travelers leave Miami behind, they cross the Neosho River that flows into Oklahoma from Kansas and meanders southward for 164 miles until it joins the Arkansas River at Muskogee. Soon after passing a tiny settlement named Narcissa, the once thriving farm and railroad center of

Afton appears on the highway. Founded in 1886, the town was named for Afton Aires, the daughter of a railroad surveyor who named the girl after the Afton River in his native Scotland.

In this part of Oklahoma, near Miami and Afton, there are good examples of the original one-lane concrete route with curbs. The short piece of Route 66 from Miami to Afton was the last part of the old road to be paved in the state. The paved road was finished in the autumn of 1937 and was marked by a celebration, which included Governor E. W. Marland cutting a fancy silk ribbon. Many years before, when the runners in C. C. Pyle's famed Bunion Derby came streaking through town, a crowd of more than 2,500 gathered along the sides of Route 66 in Afton to cheer for Andy Payne, the Oklahoman who would ultimately win the contest. Afterward, onlookers could spoon down a bowl of fiery chili and crackers for only fifteen cents, or slip into a pie shop for a slice with fresh coffee for just two dimes.

Prices have changed in Afton. But after a heated game of horseshoes, hungry men can march right down to the Rocket Drive-In—across the highway from the Rest Haven Motel and just down a piece from the old Palmer Hotel—and eat their fill of pork tenderloin sandwiches, Rocket burgers, and deep-fried onion rings. Afton is also the closest town to the famous Afton Buffalo Ranch where, since 1953, tourists from across the country have stopped to see bison in their pens. There's a trading post, a restaurant serving barbecue sandwiches, fries, sundaes,

and—for the courageous—buffalo burgers. A patch of grass called the "Dog's Restroom" is patrolled by noisy turkeys and peacocks. A small army of house cats lurks in the shadows of the buildings, waiting for tourists to pitch the last bite of their buffalo burger at a garbage barrel and miss.

A few miles down the highway comes Vinita, an old railroad town founded in 1871 and named for Vinnie Ream, the sculptor who created the life-size statue of Abraham Lincoln in the nation's capital. Vinita hosted a big celebration in August 1933, when the paving of Route 66 was completed in the area. Will Rogers, who attended secondary school in Vinita, telegraphed his friend Earl Walker, the cashier at First National Bank, with congratulations.

"Ain't it wonderful to go from Vinita to Chelsea and not have to go by Coffeyville or Muskogee?" Rogers wired. Vinita became the site of the Will Rogers Memorial Rodeo, held each August. The famous Oklahoman was planning to attend that very first rodeo in 1935, when he was killed with Wiley Post in a plane crash near Point Barrow, Alaska. Vinita was also one of Cy Avery's early homes before he moved to Tulsa and started pushing for the creation of Route 66.

West of Vinita, the old road passes through White Oak, and then Chelsea, where the first producing oil well in Oklahoma was completed in 1889, and once the home of Sallie McSpadden, sister of Will Rogers. Gene Autry, the famous Singing Cowboy, also worked at the Frisco depot in Chelsea for a time. Next there's Bushyhead, named for an

continued my debating and newspaper work. I majored in philosophy and graduated with the class of 1935. My father was killed that year. I met my wife, Collier Connell, while I was at Stanford. She was an amazing woman, an unusual person. She came from El Paso and moved to Los Angeles, where her mother had a restaurant called Mother O'Leary's Home Cafe. Collier worked in the restaurant during the Depression and her family was flat broke. She really wanted to get an education, but there wasn't any money. A man named Shorty Harris ate at the cafe quite a lot and he heard Collier talking and he could tell she was an educated young woman. He had a gold mine in Death Valley and one day he asked Collier if she wanted to go there and be his camp cook. She said she didn't want that job, but she'd do anything else. So she went to Death Valley and worked in the Skeleton Mine. Mostly, she drove a truck. Harris was quite a flamboyant character and when he sold that mine he gave Collier a thousand-dollar grubstake so she could go to college.

"She applied to Stanford, which was a tough place for women to get into back then, but she sailed on in and got her education and met me. We were married in Las Vegas, Nevada, on May 26, 1941. The war was very much underway in Europe and the day after

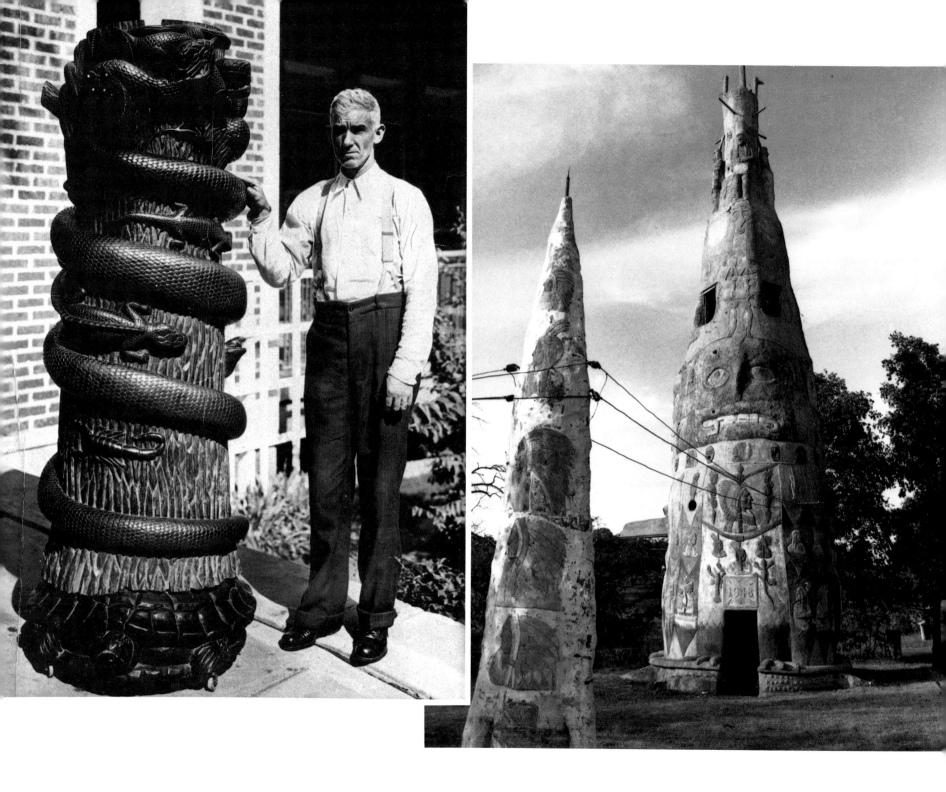

old chief of the Cherokee Nation; Foyil, a farming hamlet close to Bunion Derby winner Andy Payne's family farm and also the site of "the world's largest totem pole," a 90-foot tall concrete monument built by Ed Galloway; Sequoyah, a coal-loading settlement on the railroad and now nothing more than a memory; and Claremore, the seat of Rogers County, named in honor of Clem Rogers, father of Will.

The town of Claremore was named for the Osage chief, Clermont or Clermos, and became a busy trading center. The old stage route from Vinita to Albuquerque passed through the settlement. A bloody battle between Osage and Cherokee warriors also took place near the town site, but many years later it was Will Rogers, born "half-way between Claremore and Oologah before there was a town at either place," who brought Claremore its fame. As Rogers liked to explain, he claimed Claremore over Oologah because "nobody but an Indian could pronounce Oologah."

Claremore was also the home of Lynn Riggs, the author of the play *Green Grow the Lilacs,* from which came the classic American musical *Oklahoma!* The simple love story set in early Oklahoma is based on Riggs's play, with music by Richard Rodgers and lyrics by Oscar Hammerstein. It premiered in 1943 and was one of the longest-running musicals in Broadway history.

Far left: Ed Galloway, totem pole creator, circa 1935, Foyil, Okla.

Near left: The World's Largest Totem Pole, circa 1955, Foyil, Okla.

Nonetheless, Will Rogers—at least his name and spirit—dominates the town of Claremore. Oklahoma honors its most famous citizen at the Will Rogers Memorial, located about a mile west of Route 66 on a twenty-acre site Rogers once owned. Rogers, his wife Betty, and an infant son are buried at the Memorial, and there are also collections of his personal belongings, keepsakes, and mementos. In the main entrance stands a duplicate of Jo Davidson's familiar bronze of the cowboy humorist. The original resides in the national Capitol.

Route 66 winds past the motels, restaurants, and highway businesses of Claremore. Back out into the countryside, it moves along the edges of pecan groves and across the Kerr-McClellan Arkansas River Navigation System. The old highway then crosses the twin steel bridges spanning the sluggish Verdigris River. On the other side of the crossing waits the town of Catoosa.

Just past the WELCOME TO CATOOSA sign on the highway is a once popular tourist stop that has fallen into decay. It was a swimming hole and the ideal spot on a scorching summer afternoon. There aren't any swimmers in sight anymore. Floating in the murky pond is a large fading blue whale. Sunbathers used to rest on its back and kids dove from its big gaping mouth frozen in a perpetual smile. The wooden docks along the banks are slowly rotting and no one goes near the round picnic tables. A marooned ark surrounded by weeds bakes in the sun. Long ago, children's birthday groups and tourists armed with cameras came here to gawk at snakes and alligators housed

our wedding, President Roosevelt issued a proclamation declaring that a state of unlimited national emergency existed. We left Las Vegas and picked up Route 66 and we drove to New York in our new Packard car. That was our honeymoon, out on the open road. As we drove down Route 66 through Oklahoma and Kansas and Missouri, we listened to the war reports on the radio. We usually liked to camp out, but on that trip we stayed in motor courts all the way across the country. We spent at least one night in Claremore. I remember very clearly as we approached New York, Hitler's troops were advancing across Europe.

"I had been in the newspaper business before the war, publishing the *Beverly Hills Citizen,* and I'd covered the Spanish Civil War in the late 1930s. Then, in 1942, I was elected to Congress from California. I resigned from Congress in 1944 to reenter the army and serve overseas. We landed in France a month after D-Day, and my unit was one of the reconnaissance platoons that raced toward the German border with General Patton. We fought at the Battle of the Bulge and I was wounded at the battle of the Ruhr.

"After the war I was a newspaper editor again and lost a hard battle for Congress. In 1948, I was the campaign manager for Harry Truman in southern

in the Animal Reptile Kingdom (A.R.K.) and Catoosa Alligator Ranch. Now honeysuckle covers the vacant buildings and climbs the fence surrounding the property. Visitors are clearly no longer welcome. One sign says KEEP OUT OR EAT LEAD. Another sign puts it this way:

DANGER
DON'T MESS AROUND
DO NOT ENTER
KEEP OUT
YOU MAY BE
SHOT

Just across the road—called State Highway 66 along this stretch—are the remains of the Chief Wolf Robe Trading Post, which once sold its share of Indian crafts and silver jewelry. Chief Wolf Robe Hunt, a full-blooded Acoma Indian, was known as a skilled painter and silversmith. Between the old trading post building and the highway is a plaque that commemorates the former site of Fort Spunky, used during the Civil War, and a relay station on the old Star Mail route between St. Louis and California. After the Civil War, Catoosa was founded as a post office by John Gunter Schrimsher, an uncle of Will Rogers.

The name Catoosa comes from nearby

Catoos Hill just west of town. It is said that the word derives from an Indian expression meaning "Here live the People of the Light," and that the "People of the Light" gathered on the summit of the hill. Lookout Mountain, an old Indian vantage point is also nearby. During the wild days of the cattle drives, Catoosa was a rip-roaring gathering place for cowboys who had delivered their stock to market and were anxious for a Saturday night celebration. Used as a shipping point, Catoosa in recent decades has become known for the nearby Port of Catoosa, perched on the 440-mile-long Arkansas River Navigation System.

Past Catoosa, the old road blends with the interstate and rolls into the outskirts of Tulsa, the second largest city in the state. Before the interstate and turnpikes were built through Oklahoma, the old highway proceeded farther south of Catoosa. It then turned sharply west and ran straight into Tulsa on either Admiral Place or 11th Street, both of which were Route 66 loops through Tulsa at one time or another.

Travelers can still take those early business routes. They can go south out of Catoosa on 193rd E. Avenue, past clusters of gas stations, auto parts shops, trailer parks, and fast-food franchises. After crossing below the interstate, they have the option of turning west on either Admiral Place or 11th Street. As they move toward the city, both roads pass through mixed rural and industrial areas before entering business and residential districts.

Pauline Puroff remembers old Route 66 winding its way into Tulsa, particularly the hot July afternoon in 1932 when she and her husband, John, and their six-week-old son first arrived in the city. A Chicago native, Pauline quit her job wrapping candy bars at a downtown factory, and John, a Bulgarian immigrant, left the printing plant where he worked on Chicago's West Side after they received a letter from his parents asking the young couple to move to a plot of land they were farming outside of Tulsa.

"We were going to become truck farmers," recalls Pauline. "I had no idea what our life would be like. I was a city girl and had never been near a farm. I didn't even know for sure where eggs came from. But the Depression was on and we felt we could better our lives."

They packed enough food to get by on and left Chicago on a crowded bus bound for Tulsa. The journey down Route 66 took several days. There was engine trouble in Missouri and the bus stayed as hot as an oven. It was tiring and uncomfortable and a frightening experience for a young mother with a baby. "When we finally got to the bus station in downtown Tulsa, my father-in-law met us and took us out to the farm," says Pauline. "The roads weren't even oiled—they were still pure dirt. I had gotten all dressed up to meet my in-laws. I put on a pretty new dress with white shoes and a hat trimmed with ribbon. When we got out to the farm my mother-in-law, who didn't speak any

California, and in 1951 Warner Brothers had me play the part of my father in *The Story of Will Rogers.* Jane Wyman was my costar. She played the part of my mother. I recall one day we were sitting there when someone came up and told Jane it was time for her to shoot the scene where her first child is born. Jane smiled and looked at me and said, 'Pardon me, but I've got to go and bring you into the world.'

"In 1952 that movie was shown across the country when the Route 66 Association decided to stage a parade down the highway and rename the route after my father. They called it the Will Rogers Memorial Highway. The world premiere of the movie was held in Claremore, and there were bronze plaques about the new highway name placed at the borders of all the Route 66 states. After all, the highway did come right through Claremore and Oklahoma and it ended up out at Santa Monica not too far from where we once lived.

"I live down in Arizona now but I remember driving back and forth on the highway and seeing that plaque in the park by the Pacific in Santa Monica. But for me Oklahoma was always the heart and soul of Route 66 country."

English, welcomed me with a custom they brought with them from the old country. She sifted flour all over my new hat and poured a cup of water on my shoes. I was ready to turn right around and go back up the highway."

But she didn't leave. Pauline and her husband stuck it out, despite the fact that the Dust Bowl years had just arrived. "It was tough at first, but we made it. There were plenty of hard times, but nothing's easy. We learned how to raise every type of vegetable imaginable, and we worked that farm for more than fifty years. We're still going strong. But I still think about that day when we came down old Highway 66 and saw Tulsa for the very first time."

There have been tremendous changes through the years. At Admiral Place and Mingo Road, vehicles speed around a traffic circle where Cy Avery's popular gas station once stood. Avery probably twists a good deal in his grave, especially if he can see what's happened to his beloved highway in his own city. Route 66 through Tulsa had been pawed over and in long stretches is just plain seedy. Latter-day city fathers did not see the value of preserving the better architecture and

Left: "Oil Capital of the World," Tulsa, Okla., vintage postcard.

Below: Night skyline, Tulsa, Okla.

businesses along the city routes. Tulsa had been a major Route 66 booster. But like some other key points on the highway, including Oklahoma City and Amarillo, Tulsa for the most part turned its back on the old road and the businesses that made a living from highway traffic. Tulsa sold out for the fast lanes of the interstate.

Today, the Admiral Place section of Route 66 is lined with strip shopping centers, fast-food establishments, and auto body and welding shops. Among the franchise joints

Opposite page: A bygone 11th Street landmark, Tulsa, Okla.

remain a few Route 66–style eateries, including Hank's Hamburgers ("Since 1949"), Ike's Chili House, Family Diner ("Home Cooked Meals"), Wing's Hamburgers, and the East Side Cafe, open seven days a week for chicken and steak dinners.

Route 66 jogs back and forth on several downtown streets until it gets back to 11th, an avenue that still hints of the glory days when Tulsa was known as "The Oil Capital of the World." Many Route 66 motels and cafes fell victim to the interstate or the expressways that crisscross the city. When I-44 around Tulsa was completed, bigger and newer hotels, motels, and restaurants were built. Bigger and newer perhaps, but hardly any of them were any better than what had existed on the old highway.

Like the Admiral Place survivors, a few old motels and restaurants also remain on the 11th Street stretch of Route 66. But most are vacant or else a shadow of what they once were in the days before interstate madness swept the country. Several of the surviving motels, which used to cater to families, later had to resort to waterbeds and risqué movies in order to attract patrons. Some are used by transients, prostitutes, and drifters whose whole lives are spent in motels offering weekly rates.

Hardly anyone remembers the Pierce Pennant Terminal, the city's earliest motel and a Route 66 prize from the 1920s. The neon-lit sign of a cowboy mounted on a rearing stallion at the Will Rogers Motor Court, another 11th Street favorite, also disappeared along with the entire complex. Only a grassy lot and few pine trees remain. But next door, McCollum's Restaurant is still cooking. More than one Route 66 traveler has paused for a meal at McCollum's. Inside are booths and a lunch counter, glass cases stocked with several species of pie, a genuine malt and shake mixer, and a crew of highly capable waitresses who fill glasses from sweating pitchers of ice water before customers have a chance to open their menus.

Just up the highway, next door to the Oklahoma Academy of Hair Styling, another fine cafe named The Golden Drumstick was leveled and replaced with a plastic convenience store. But across the street, on a retaining wall that surrounds a school playground, the old restaurant appears in a mural. So does the distinctive U.S. 66 shield. Someone remembered and cared.

Unfortunately, not enough folks cared about the exquisite Will Rogers Theatre, just a few blocks away on 11th Street. A Streamline Art Deco gem with a marquee wrapped around a pencil-like tower and the words

"Nothing instant but the service," Route 66 Diner, Tulsa, Okla.

WILL ROGERS spelled out vertically in bold neon letters, this theater entertained thousands during its lifetime on the Mother Road. A mob of Tulsans and Oklahoma visitors crammed into the lobby when it opened, in 1941, with *Mr. and Mrs. Smith,* a Carole Lombard film. Prices were twenty cents and four mils for adults and a dime and two mils for kids. The theater closed in 1977, on the forty-second anniversary of Will Rogers's death, and a nearby church took over the property. First the church used the old theater marquee to advertise its services; then it tore down the Route 66 landmark and replaced it with a black asphalt parking lot.

Continuing on 11th Street, travelers pass a fine antique and collectible shop named The Browsery, the Oklahoma School of Poodle Grooming, and Skelly Stadium, located on the edge of the University of Tulsa campus. A blend of students, families, and Tulsa visitors stop for stick-to-the-ribs meals at the Metro Diner, a glitzy neon throwback to the old road days. The Metro was built long after the decertification of Route 66, but the interior walls are crowded with vintage signs and memorabilia. The young men and women slinging plate lunches and mammoth slices of cream pie on the tables recall the energetic waitresses from the good old days.

Route 66 hasn't been entirely forgotten in Tulsa. Another re-created old highway beanery is the Route 66 Diner, just down the street from the Metro and across the street from the Casa Loma Barber Shop. The diner lies on the other side of the large Bama Pie Ltd. bakery, where for many years commercial

Tulsa Monument Company built in 1936 on Route 66, Tulsa, Okla.

pies have been baked inside a big brick building decorated with plaques offering inspirational quotes from Woodrow Wilson, Abraham Lincoln, and Lawrence Welk. The 66 Diner, owned by Sherry and Debbie Higgs, uses the old highway shield for its sign and is in a building that dates back to 1935. Most of the people scarfing down burgers and fried spuds at the counter are locals, not travelers. None of the orders are written down, and the fry cook can flip four eggs at a time without breaking a yolk. A huge bean pot is always simmering on the stove alongside a pot of black-eyed peas. The mashed potatoes are real and even have lumps, and the French toast is

made with freshly baked whole wheat bread. The aroma of hotcakes, omelets, blueberry muffins, and rising hamburger buns fills the diner. Lunch specials include smoked brisket, meat loaf, and the popular Route 66 Diner's Philly Chicken. Nobody leaves *this* place hungry. The same is true at the Pancake Place, El Rancho Grande, and Mark & Mary's Good Food—all on 11th Street, all as Route 66 in style and substance as they can be.

On the road through Tulsa, 11th Street passes several important Art Deco buildings, including the Warehouse Market built in 1929 on the site of the old McNulty ballpark, where such sports greats as Babe Ruth, Red Grange,

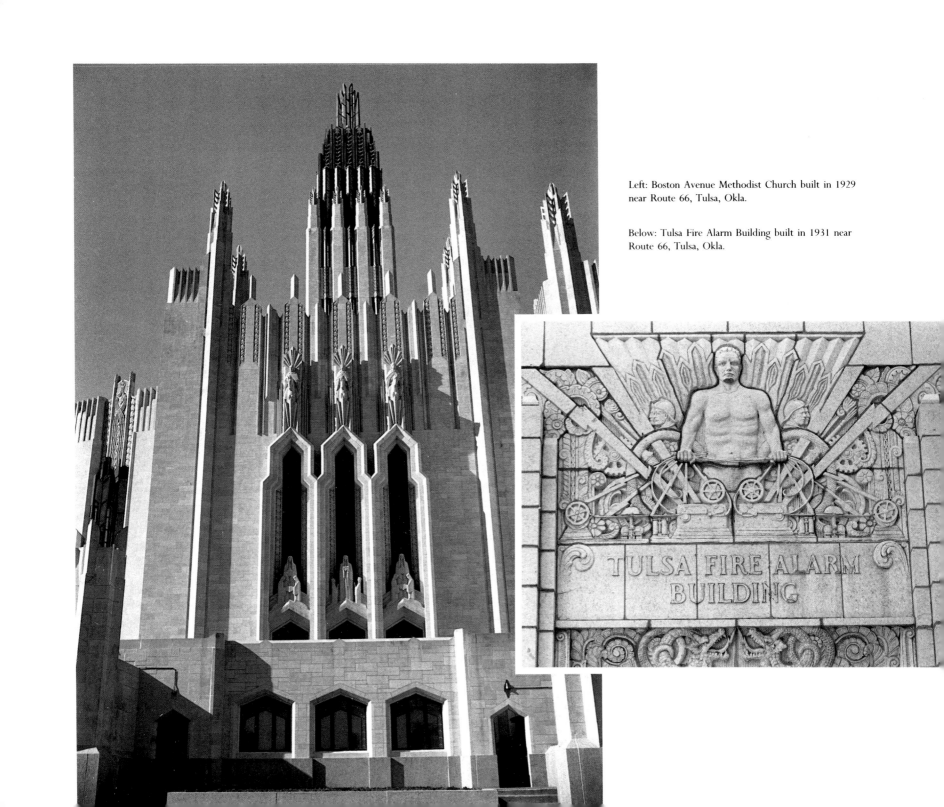

Left: Boston Avenue Methodist Church built in 1929 near Route 66, Tulsa, Okla.

Below: Tulsa Fire Alarm Building built in 1931 near Route 66, Tulsa, Okla.

TULSA FIRE ALARM BUILDING

and Jack Dempsey thrilled the crowds. The stadium also served as a shelter for black families during the city's shameful 1921 race riot. Eight years later, just as Route 66 was getting started, a developer transformed the park into a public market and erected the huge Deco building. A tower with brilliant polychrome terra cotta ornaments acted as a beacon to attract people to the market. The Depression closed the place, but a few years later it reopened as the Club Lido, where swingers danced to the music of Cab Calloway, Benny Goodman, Duke Ellington, and other touring performers. In 1938, it became the Warehouse Market and operated as a grocery store until 1978 when the building began its fall into limbo.

After passing the market building, the old city route flirts with the shadows of the famous Boston Avenue Methodist Church—an elegant Art Deco spire pointing like a finger toward heaven. Within minutes, travelers cross the Arkansas River on a concrete span built next to the 11th Street Bridge, originally erected in 1916, and now a blocked-off structure that serves as a shelter for the homeless who sleep beneath the old bridge.

On the other side, the route becomes Southwest Boulevard all the way through West Tulsa. This side of the Arkansas is a part of the city often overlooked, especially by some "proper" Tulsans who consider the west bank the wrong side of town. They say the west side is where you go looking for trouble. Some tales are true. For many years, the west side was as raw as Oklahoma crude. The area earned a reputation for being bare-knuckled

and always thirsty. In truth, the west side has cooled its hot temper and is home for generations of hard-working families who would not dream of living anywhere else.

"We keep the city honest," winks a gnarled old-timer over a mug of coffee in a Southwest Boulevard cafe. "Without the west bank of the Arkansas and what happened here, good ol' Tulsa would be just another podunk town that people pass through on their way to someplace else." The old man's reference is to the oil discoveries at Red Fork, a west bank community, and site of one of the biggest oil finds back in 1901. Red Fork really helped put Tulsa on the map. Then, a few years later, an even richer oil discovery was made at Glenn Pool.

That was all long ago. The oil dried up and so has much of the oil-related business on the west bank. The Park Plaza Court, a 66 relic on Southwest Boulevard for a half century, turned into a haven for low-income families and the disenfranchised. It was finally torn down in the late 1980s. Up the highway, only a short distance from where the Park Plaza stood, the ghostly 66 Motel has seen better times despite "reasonable rates."

But there's no need to despair. The best part of Route 66 in Oklahoma lies ahead. Travelers can switch on KVOO, the radio station that started down the road in Bristow with the call letters KRFU. During the Roaring Twenties, people started calling the station the "Voice of

Gladys Cutberth

Born: November 10, 1904
Occupation: Homemaker, former officer of the Main Street of America Highway Association, "Mrs. 66," widow of "Mr. 66"
Residence: Clinton, Oklahoma

"*I* was born and reared down around Kiel, Oklahoma, which became Loyal, Oklahoma, during World War I when there were a lot of anti-German feelings. All of my ancestry was German. My last name was Zobisch. When I was very small my parents moved to the town of Hinton where they operated a milling business. Then they moved to Butler, and that's where I met Jack Cutberth. We went to school together but I didn't

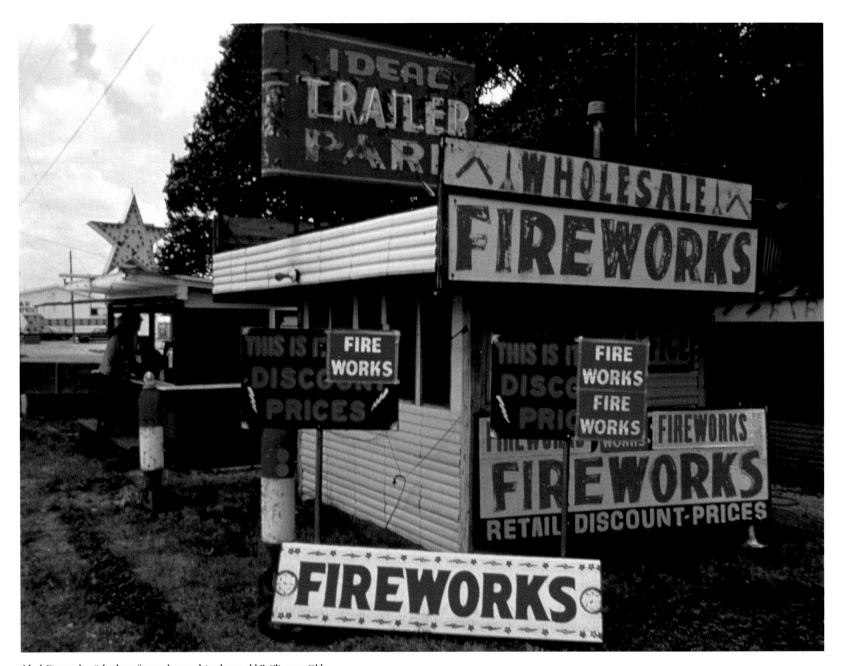

Ideal Fireworks, "the best fireworks stand in the world," Clinton, Okla.

Oklahoma" and the call letters were changed to match that impressive name. In 1927, KVOO moved to Tulsa, and ever since listeners have been treated to the music of Bob Wills and His Texas Playboys, Gene Autry, Hank Williams, and a legion of other country-western greats. Car radios can still get a good workout all the way to Oklahoma City as fingers twist the knobs back and forth picking up the strains of "Take Me Back to Tulsa" and "San Antonio Rose" or the Cardinals' doubleheader on another station.

Soon after leaving Tulsa, the old road works its way back into the country and heads for the little towns that will always be strong Route 66 havens. Along the old road between Tulsa and Oklahoma City stand ROUTE 66 MEMORIAL HIGHWAY signs. The two-lane is still well traveled and resurfaced through Sapulpa, Chandler, Luther, and the many other towns. In *A Guide Book to Highway 66,* Jack Rittenhouse describes this portion of the old highway.

This section of your trip takes you from Tulsa to Oklahoma City. The route is through rolling countryside—once the haunt of Indians, later the territory of cowmen and "badmen," but now devoted principally to oil and agriculture. Part of your route is through a section of the famous "Cherokee Strip." On weekends the traffic is somewhat heavier near Oklahoma City. The road is good, but the shoulders are soggy in wet weather. In the smaller towns, brick streets are often bumpy.

That description, written in 1946, remains accurate. Watch the soft shoulders and mind the bumps. Oklahoma City traffic is still a bear. For the traveler with some time to spare, a ride down Route 66 to Oklahoma City can be a side trip to a bygone era that can't be found anywhere else. No part of the long journey down the old highway provides the traveler with more kicks than this particular run. It is narrow and crooked and sometimes tedious, especially when a motorist gets trapped behind a time-warped farmer poking along in his pickup in one of the tiny towns. But for those who opt for the free road, it's worth every minute.

As the old highway winds through the countryside, the Frankoma Pottery Plant appears on the side of the road just before the town of Sapulpa. Founded on a shoestring in 1933 by John Frank, a young ceramics instructor at the University of Oklahoma, Frankoma Pottery moved to Sapulpa in 1938. Frank had received his formal training at Chicago's Art Institute, located at the exact spot where Route 66 begins its westward trek across the nation. That was in 1926, the year the highway was unveiled. The following year, Frank moved to Oklahoma and began his teaching career. In 1938, just after Frank and his wife, Grace Lee, moved to Sapulpa, a fire destroyed the plant. They started to rebuild, but when World War II arrived, the Franks could not get workers or materials for their pottery business. All production was halted as the family waited out the war. As soon as peace returned to the world, Frank fired up the kilns and started a training program for

pay any attention to him. I was friends with his sisters.

"Jack was born May 16, 1903, about twenty miles northwest of Clinton, Oklahoma, on the Washita River. He was one of nine children and his family were farmers. They mostly raised cotton. They had some Indian blood and that Cutberth family were the most soft-spoken people I've ever met. I never really gave Jack a second thought until I finished high school. In fact, I was engaged to marry another man. My hair was strawberry blond back then. I remember that Jack Cutberth was quite a dancer. We both went to Oklahoma City, where I went to business school and Jack attended barber college.

"We went together for about two months and then we got married on December 7, 1923, at the courthouse in Purcell, Oklahoma. We kept the wedding a secret because my family really didn't care for Jack. It was nothing you could put your finger on, they just didn't like him. We set up a barber shop in Stratford for a few years and our son Kenneth was born in 1925, but then the boll weevils came along and wiped out all the cotton crops and things went sour there. So in 1927, we moved to Clinton and Jack opened his barber shop here. This is where we stayed. The postmaster here in Clinton was Frank Smith, and he was involved

ex-GIs interested in learning the pottery trade. Tourists started traveling down Route 66 in greater numbers than ever before and Frankoma's business soared. Decades later, the pottery plant was charred by yet another terrible fire, but bounced right back.

Frank died in 1973. The plant remains a family operation and still turns out native clayware—dishes, vases, pitchers, tiles, ashtrays, flower bowls, and planters—sold throughout the Southwest. "People are interested in seeing pottery made, and they never get tired of seeing the new things that can be made from the earth," wrote Frank before his death. "It is for this reason that Frankoma Pottery is located on the main artery highway, so that passing tourists can stop by and see it made, and browse around enjoying the beautiful things we make from Oklahoma clays."

One of Frankoma's biggest fans is Norma Lee Hall, the woman who runs Norma's Cafe, a short distance away in Sapulpa, just past the big Liberty Glass Plant and across the street from the graveyard that also sits on Route 66. Norma wouldn't think of using anything but Frankoma dishes for her faithful customers. On the front window a sign proclaims, WOW! BREAKFAST 99¢. Inside, Norma bustles about setting tables with her pottery dishes and pouring coffee into diners' pottery cups. Hearty patrons go for her famous Tower of Power—scrambled eggs, bacon, cheese, and the works piled on Texas toast. But the breakfast special for under a dollar is hard to pass up. The price has not changed in years. Norma's Cafe has been serving good road food

since the '50s. Opal Glenn, the stoic woman cracking eggs and flipping pancakes in the steamy kitchen, has been a cook at Norma's most of her life and keeps getting better with age. At Norma's, almost everything is made from scratch. The chili, Irish stew, and smothered steak are worth dying for, and the ham and beans with corn bread can make a grown man weep with joy.

"The fast-food restaurants took away a lot of our business," says Norma during a rare pause between pumping quarters into the jukebox, dusting off the bowling trophies, and delivering a slice of chocolate pie to her granddaughter.

"We got all of 'em—McDonald's, Burger King, Arby's, Hardee's—anything you want except good food. The turnpike and the fast-food places really hurt us. Used to be we'd be open twenty-four hours a day. Anymore we stay open till about three in the afternoon. That just about catches everybody. But in those days before the turnpike was built, were we ever busy. Then one evening that ol' turnpike opened and the next morning we woke up and it was an entirely new world for us. Still we have our regulars who come through these parts every year on vacations. They still stop. They have a few more gray hairs and some wrinkles but we remember them."

Next door to the cafe is an old service station and truck stop, the domain of Norma's husband, Bob Hall. "We called it the Diamond

Truck Stop, and I ran it for thirty-six years and then retired," says Bob. "We had fifteen truck companies trading here and it took twenty-seven men working twenty-four hours a day to get the job done. I sold many a canvas water bag to hang on a bumper to some tourist headed out to California. Those were exciting times. Truckers knew they could always stop here for fuel and good food. Now the trucks have mostly left us for the turnpike."

Hall keeps old photographs he took of the truckers who were his regulars, standing by their rigs. Most of the photos are faded or have discolored with age. Hall wouldn't part with them for a sack of gold. "All of these men are dead. They were good fellas. They'd come back on vacations and bring their families to see us. One of them lived right up Route 66 in Tulsa and he died out on the highway. Had a heart attack. His family didn't have any pictures of him so they came out here and I got the negative and made them a photo."

Route 66 goes right through the heart of Sapulpa. Like so many Oklahoma towns, Sapulpa was named for an Indian who settled in these parts. At one time a hangout for such notorious gents as the James boys, the Dalton gang, and the Youngers, the town also became a rendezvous for cattlemen, railroaders, and roustabouts who worked in the nearby Glenn Pool field.

A few miles outside of town sit some forlorn motor court units—all made of the native rust-colored flat stones that look like patches on a giraffe. The old road goes below a concrete railroad overpass tattooed with fading lovers' initials and remembrances. "Kenny Loves Linda—Baby on the Way," and "Kenny, I'll Be Back in October—Don't Forget Me!!" The road rolls on through more little towns. There's Kellyville, remembered with some notoriety for Oklahoma's worst rail disaster—the 1917 head-on collision of two Frisco trains. Kellyville was also where the state's first, and mercifully only ski resort, complete with tons of artificial snow, was supposed to be built in the early 1970s. As one travel writer diplomatically put it, "The scheme was stillborn."

The highway crosses Little Polecat Creek and then Polecat Creek, scoots over the turnpike, and runs right into Bristow, a former Creek Nation trading post that developed into an oil patch town. As the highway bridges Catfish Creek and snakes toward Depew, another farm town laid out next to the Frisco tracks, the earth begins to change to the ochre color of western Oklahoma. Soon all the soil will be that famous iron red. In these parts, the locals drive slowly and wave at each other as they pass on the road. They take great pride in their roses and peonies, and raise irises the color of root beer and butterscotch.

The little towns and place names keep coming. There's Stroud, a burg that prospered by peddling illicit whiskey from its nine busy taverns until 1907, when statehood brought respectability. Later, the discovery of oil gave the town a more dependable income. The path through Stroud is brick covered, the Rock Cafe serves up big portions of stew, and "Old

66 Antiques" can't keep anything in stock that has "66" on it, especially the cherished highway shields. Next comes Davenport, home of Dan's Bar-B-Que, owned and operated by a retired Route 66 trucker, and then Chandler, "Pecan Capital of the World." In the city cemetery is the grave of Bill Tilghman, a famous frontier lawman from territorial days who died in what became known as the last "Old West–style" gun battle in Oklahoma. That took place in the oil town of Cromwell in 1924, only two years before Route 66 was officially opened.

The Lincoln Motel in Chandler, recommended in the Rittenhouse guidebook, is as neat and comfortable as it was when it opened in 1939. In front of each of the twenty cabins flutters a small American flag. After devouring a slab of pork ribs at PJ's Bar-B-Que, travelers can return to the Lincoln, ease into a canary-yellow metal lawn chair, and watch the evening traffic whiz past.

About 10 miles down the highway from Chandler is Wellston, the first permanent white settlement in Lincoln County and a former trading post on the Kickapoo Reservation. Wellston is where Harold Stephens hung his cap all his life. When he turned seventy, Stephens retired as the town blacksmith, a trade he religiously practiced every day since 1939 when he opened his shop less than a mile off Route 66.

"My dad came to Oklahoma in 1899 and brought his blacksmith tools with him," recalls Stephens. "I used those tools myself. His shop was over there, 'bout where that mimosa tree stands." Stephens, who spent his life

with the highway and the U.S. Highway 66 Association. He's the one who got Jack interested in Route 66. When they had a reorganization meeting for the association in Oklahoma City in 1947, he got Jack and me to go along, and then Jack became secretary of the Oklahoma chapter.

"The old Highway 66 National Association had been formed back in the 1920s, but over the years it sort of died down and then the war came along and, for all practical purposes, it ceased to exist. But after the war everyone started to travel and a bunch of folks out in Arizona started up a Highway 66 Association, and then New Mexico followed and Texas and Oklahoma, and pretty soon the whole association was back on its feet. Every one of the states had its own unit. About 1954, after Frank Smith died, Jack became the executive secretary of both the Oklahoma chapter and the national organization. There was a new president each year, but it was Jack who did most of the work.

"Jack devoted his life to Route 66. Altogether, he put in twenty-four years with the Highway 66 Association, and he worked up and down that highway. For years the national headquarters was right here in Clinton, in the basement of our house. We printed brochures about the highway and sent them out, and we

parently not twenty minutes old. This makes us doubly watchful tonight, as well as anxious, lest possibly we may lose a mule or two, to say nothing of the train." The following day, Beale noted, "We saw not a living thing but a prairie dog and antelope or two, and a crow, in crossing the extensive plain. Evidence enough exists that years ago buffalo have grazed on its fine grasses, but now there is not one to be seen, or the sign of one less than ten years old."

Although an officer in the U.S. Navy, Beale was no stranger to the West. While serving in the Mexican War—where he and the illustrious frontiersman Kit Carson carried dispatches for General Kearny through enemy lines—Beale came up with the ingenious idea of using camels for transportation across the great southwestern deserts. Soon after, Beale was given the task of continuing the survey of the routes west from Fort Defiance, about 180 miles southwest of Santa Fe, to the Colorado River and California. It was the perfect opportunity. Beale brought the camel proposal to his boss, Jefferson Davis, then secretary of war. Davis went along with the camel scheme. Soon the army bought seventy camels in Egypt and Arabia and brought them to the states along with some stubborn Greek and Turk camel drivers, prone to strong drink.

Beale became smitten with the plodding "ships of the desert," which could carry eight hundred pounds of supplies and surveying equipment anywhere from 35 to 75 miles a day. "It is a subject of constant surprise and remark to all of us, how their feet can possibly stand the character of the road we have been traveling over," wrote Beale in his journal. "It is certainly the hardest road on

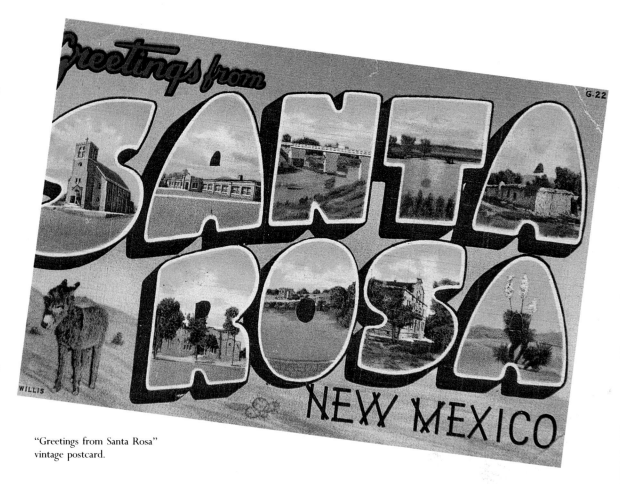

"Greetings from Santa Rosa"
vintage postcard.

the feet of bare-footed animals I have ever known. The harder the test they are put to, the more fully they seem to justify all that can be said of them. I look forward to the day when every mail route across the continent will be conducted with this economical and noble brute."

By the time the Civil War erupted, the camels' surveying work was completed and the

"brutes" were discharged from further military service. Some of the camels were sold to circuses or mining companies or else were turned loose to fend for themselves. For many years colorful stories circulated throughout the West about Beale's wandering camels. Some of the camel tales even became part of Indian legends. Beale also eventually left the navy and started a ranch near Stockton, California,

State and local officals at ceremonies in eastern New Mexico when Route 66 was dedicated as "Will Rogers Highway" in 1952.

where he kept a few of his prized camels. Before he ended his retirement to become minister to Austria-Hungary, Beale invariably created a hoopla when his carriage paraded into town pulled by a brace of the humped beasts.

Although he died in 1893—thirty-three years before Route 66 was opened—Beale would not have been surprised that the western path he surveyed developed into the nation's main transcontinental highway. As Beale had predicted in 1858, that path through the West would "inevitably become the great emigrant road to California."

Visions of the daring Lieutenant Beale and his camels abide in the stunning New Mexican landscape. Travelers still picture the alien pack animals ambling past prickly pear and cholla while sharp-eyed army scouts scan the brush for hostile Indians. Sleek cars and shiny new trucks flashing down the broad interstate highway cut through lands where prairie schooners brought homesteaders intent on settling the wild country and where, starting in 1926, a steady stream of traffic moved east and west on U.S. 66.

For many, the interstate highway that replaced Route 66 as the main thoroughfare across the state was heaven-sent. They remembered the old road between the Texas line and Tucumcari as dangerous. It was narrow, pocked with holes, and generally not well maintained. In some stretches there wasn't even a center stripe. Many people died on this section of the Mother Road. Some fell asleep at the wheel; others hit a deep pothole and lost control, or struck a cow

or deer that wandered onto the pavement. It was said that there was "only a few inches and a cigarette paper between you and death on Route 66." But even some of the old road's severest critics shed a few tears when the interstate nudged 66 aside.

If those who head westward on I-40 across New Mexico look hard, Route 66 still becomes apparent. It's in the nearby ranch-lands, or close by the railroad tracks, or hidden behind clumps of piñon, or, in many instances, still the main drag through several towns.

Less than 5 miles west of the eastern border crossing at Glenrio, memories of Endee, once a raucous cowboy hamlet, come rushing back. In this dot on the map, there were so many Sunday morning burials because of shoot-outs the night before that a trench was dug each Saturday on the edge of town. A few miles farther west at Bard, another trading point for ranchers, there was never much more than a few shacks and a gas station. Those buildings are gone, but a functioning post office is close enough for interstate wanderers to drop off postcards as they make tracks down the road.

Only 6 miles west of Bard is San Jon, a ranching and farming community on Route 66 that first boomed around 1904 with the coming of the railroad. Generation after generation of cowboys flocked to San Jon for Saturday night relaxation. Although the interstate dashes right by the small settlement, enough locals and passing travelers stop to keep the doors open at some of the old businesses that depend on highway trade. Sometimes out on a section of the old road on

Ribbon of old road west of San Fidel, N. Mex.

the eastern fringe of town, a big horned owl passes the day waiting for moonrise in a Chinese elm. Highway 66 is what they continue to call the main road through San Jon.

Down at the Rustler, a friendly cafe usually filled with old cowboys sipping coffee and gulping ice water, a big sign out front says EAT. In the summertime, the boxy "swamp cooler," attached like a metal leech to the side of the cafe, rumbles all day long. The primitive air conditioner keeps the temperature inside tolerable so folks can enjoy fish or chicken dinners and candy bars or dishes of ice cream.

During the winter months, plenty of would-be skiers—mostly from Oklahoma and Texas—pull off I-40 for gas at a nearby Exxon station. A herd of Texans in two matching red jeeps, with ski racks on top and Christmas wreaths tied to the front grilles, screech to a stop beside the pumps. All of them pile out to use the restrooms and stretch. Within two minutes the Rustler's business damn near doubles when one of the Texans notices the EAT sign and convinces his companions that it's time for some real food and not another round of slop from some tasteless fast-food restaurant on the interstate.

Just a short distance away from the crowded cafe back on the old road, a three-legged bulldog, spotted black and white like an Indian pony, stands vigil outside the Someplace Else Lounge. The bulldog sniffs the air and scowls at a monstrous recreational vehicle called "The Prairie Schooner," parked on the old highway in front of a block-long building covered with a mural of scenes from the Old West. Grass sprouting up through the

sidewalk makes the concrete look like it's part of the mural. The scene painted on the wall shows wranglers moving longhorn cattle and there are yucca plants, running buffalo, and a nest of rattlesnakes. The artist was Leona Mills Head, and she painted the scene in 1976 to honor the nation's Bicentennial.

"I call it the 'Route 66 Mural' because that's what this street is named," says Dan Parnell, the old man who lives in an apartment behind the faded scene of the cattle drive. "This town used to really be something. Everybody came right down this street and most of them stopped. There were six or seven cafes going night and day. Then that interstate came along and changed everything." Parnell sips a small bottle of Coca-Cola to help soothe a throat that's raw from cheering for favorite football teams on the television all afternoon. Then he says,

"I was born in 1905 in Selma, Alabama, and then in 1926 I went out to California to see a Rose Bowl game. That was just when ol' Highway 66 was getting started. I got out there and saw the game and then I stayed for sixteen years. I left to serve in the air force during the Second World War. Demolition was my job. If a bomb didn't go off then I had to take care of it. I came over to this part of the country because of my allergies. I lived in Houston and then I went to Amarillo for a few years and then I came here and liked this town better. It's a nice place and I know everybody and when you're all alone like I am that sure does make a big difference."

After finishing his drink, Parnell walks behind the mural, puts the empty bottle in a wooden rack, and heads for the back door to resume watching football. Behind the building are rolls of wooden storm fencing used to catch drifting snow along the old highway. There are also several rusted car bodies, including a convertible filled with empty beer cans. The "rag top" is an old-model Cadillac, with huge rear speakers and pointed chrome tail fins. The big gas-guzzling Caddy—as obsolete as a dinosaur—is destined to act as a poor man's Cadillac Ranch sitting in a plot of weeds behind the painted walls.

Twenty-five miles west of San Jon is Tucumcari, a classic Route 66 town in every sense of the word. The interstate may have slapped Tucumcari hard in the face, but this highway town survives. Travelers continue to stop in Tucumcari and drive the old road where more than fifty motels once did a booming trade serving people attracted by the famous signs that promised TUCUMCARI TONITE! 2000 MOTEL ROOMS.

An eastern New Mexican oasis, Tucumcari has used other aliases through the years. Back in the 1880s when life was truly fierce, raw, and wide open, the settlement was known as Liberty. After the coming of the twentieth century, when the railroad was built, citizens called the construction camp Six-Shooter Siding. But by 1902 the town was renamed Tucumcari, after the nearby mountain.

Some credit the name to a folktale tied to Geronimo about a pair of star-crossed Apache lovers named Tocom and Kari. It seems an Apache maiden named Kari, daughter of Chief Wauntonomah, was smitten by Tocom, a handsome young brave. When Tocom was killed by a rival, Kari is said to have stabbed to death her sweetheart's murderer and then taken her own life with the bloody knife. Wauntonomah was so distraught when he found out his daughter and future son-in-law were both dead, the chief seized Kari's knife and plunged it into his heart as he wailed his dying words, "Tocom! Kari!" In truth, the Tucumcari area was more Comanche territory than Apache country. Old Comanche warriors used the peak for smoke signals across the valley to the plains. The mountain was an ideal lookout for war parties. Linguistic experts explain that the name in Comanche is *Tukamukaru,* which means "to lie in wait for someone or something to approach."

This latter version of how the town got its name makes more sense. Folks in Tucumcari have been lying in wait for a long time, ready to serve up a hamburger or bowl of posole, peddle some postcards, pump a tank of gas, or rent a motel room.

Lillian Redman, the woman who values sunsets, knows about waiting. Every day for decades she has staged a daily vigil, waiting for guests from points east and west to arrive at the old Route 66 relic she calls the Blue Swallow. "I end up traveling the highway in my heart with whoever stops here for the night," says Lillian.

The venerable *Smithsonian* magazine declared that "the Blue Swallow may be the last, best and friendliest of the old-time

motels." Few would argue otherwise.

Born in Texas in 1909, Lillian came to New Mexico in 1915 in a covered wagon when her father homesteaded near Santa Rosa. After she completed school, Lillian put in yeoman's service for years as a waitress and cook at Fred Harvey Houses throughout the Southwest. She finally settled in Tucumcari, where she met and married Floyd Redman, a man who ran a trailer park and pawn shop on Route 66 for many years. In 1958, Floyd presented Lillian with an engagement present —the Blue Swallow. Built in the 1940s, it was the best present she ever received. From the first night they took in guests, Floyd and Lillian made it a point to put their customers first. When folks didn't have the money to rent a room, the Redmans took personal belongings, including old television sets and bowling balls. If the people were really in a jam, they got the room for free.

Floyd died and so did her parents, and Lillian eventually had to go to Amarillo and get a new right eye, but through it all, she managed to hang on to the Blue Swallow Motel. Rooms rent for 1960s prices, and there is a well-worn Bible on the check-in counter. Over each garage flickers a blue neon bird.

"We've had all kinds of people stay here," says Lillian, her blue eyes as warm as they were when she was a Harvey Girl.

"Once we had a 'streaker' and he stayed a week. At sundown he liked to take off his clothes and run around the block. Boy, did he cause a commotion. About his fourth night, the police were waiting for him. A lot

A Route 66 Portrait

Ron Chavez

Born: June 18, 1936
Occupation: Owner of the Club Cafe, writer
Residence: Santa Rosa, New Mexico

"*I* was born just eleven miles southeast of Santa Rosa in the village of Puerto de Luna. The name means 'gateway to the moon,' because there's a narrow gap in the tall mountains near the village where at certain times during the month the moon shines through into the river valley. It's a very old village. Billy the

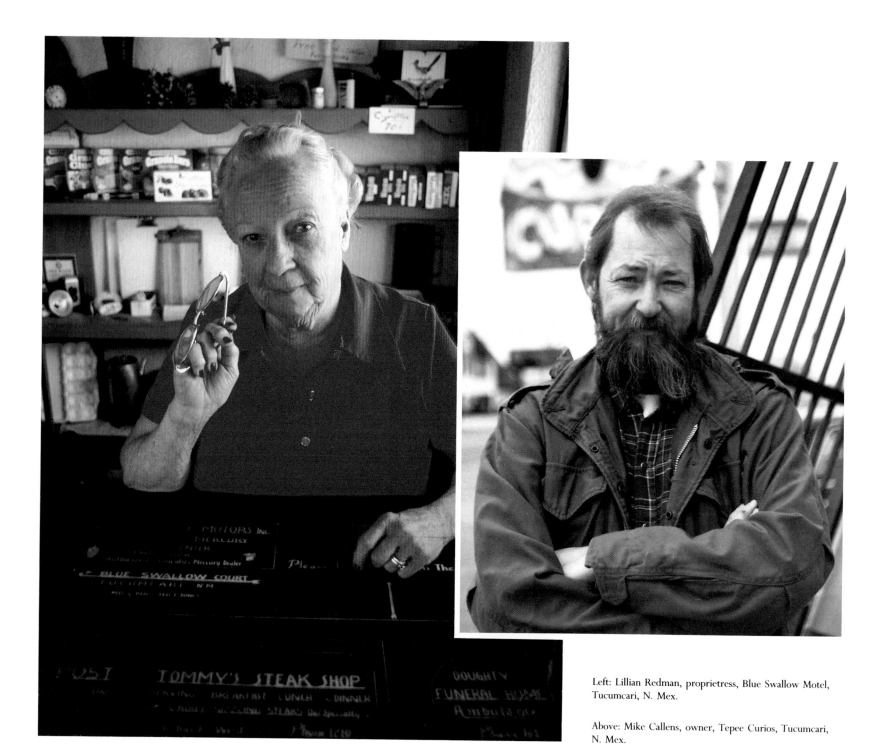

Left: Lillian Redman, proprietress, Blue Swallow Motel, Tucumcari, N. Mex.

Above: Mike Callens, owner, Tepee Curios, Tucumcari, N. Mex.

of repeat customers stop, too. One couple honeymooned here in 1965 and every year on their anniversary they come back and get the very same room. We see more vagabonds than in the past. We always have our people of the road. They're not coming from anywhere in particular and not headed anywhere special. And when they get someplace, it's not where they want to be."

No matter who checks in, Lillian treats them all alike and hands every guest a card with a simple but eloquent message.

Greetings Traveler:

In ancient times, there was a prayer for "The Stranger Within Our Gates." Because this motel is a human institution to serve people, and not solely a money-making organization, we hope that God will grant you peace and rest while you are under our roof.

May this room and motel be your "second" home. May those you love be near you in thoughts and dreams. Even though we may not get to know you, we hope that you will be as comfortable and happy as if you were in your own home.

May the business that brought you our way prosper. May every call you make and every message you receive add to your joy. When you leave, may your journey be safe.

We are all travelers. From "birth till death" we travel between the eternities. May these days be pleasant for you, profitable for society, helpful for those you meet, and a joy to those who know and love you best.

Sincerely Yours,
Lillian Redman
Blue Swallow Motel
Tucumcari, New Mexico

And when the sun rises and it's time to get back on the road, there are no wake-up calls at the Blue Swallow since none of the rooms have telephones. Instead, Lillian gently knocks on every door and says, "Good morning." With folks like Lillian Redman living on the old road, named Tucumcari Boulevard through the length of town, it is little wonder that Tucumcari prospers despite the presence of the interstate. "Route 66 has a definite feel to it," says Lillian. "It makes you feel warm all over. When it was closed to the majority of traffic and the other highway came in, I felt just like I had lost an old friend. But some of us stuck it out and are still here on Route 66."

Across the highway from the Blue Swallow is Tepee Curios, another veteran road business. Mike Callens and his wife, Betty, run the souvenir and gift shop, which has been carefully passed down through several owners, including Jene Klaverweiden, Callens's uncle and a former mayor of Tucumcari. "I was born here in 1947, but my family moved to California in the mid-1950s," says Callens. "I have so many relatives in this town. Both my grandfathers were in business in Tucumcari. One of them ran a pool hall called the

Kid danced there and my family lived there for many generations.

"We were very isolated. There was only a ribbon of 66 going through these parts. That was our touch with the world. We were also poor, but we never lacked for anything. My father had gone to Colorado and California when he was young and worked in the fields. He picked sugar beets and was a dirt farmer. Times were hard during the Depression. Those were terrible years. I paid my dues too. When I was a kid, I shined shoes right out front of this cafe. I worked as a busboy here and then became a cook. Phil Craig and Floyd Shaw owned the place back then. There were eight waitresses in the morning and ten more in the evening.

"The Club Cafe was a jumping son of a gun. It was always busy. I remember seeing my first Bermuda shorts here. A man walked in with shorts on and I fell over. I had never seen anything like that. After working as a busboy, I became a dishwasher, which paid a little better, and little by little I started cooking. Phil Craig took me aside and taught me how to bake sourdough biscuits and pies and cinnamon rolls. Phil was one of those Depression guys who came out of Texas on a freight train. He was poor as dirt and he married a local girl named Ruby, and her father had the cafe and Phil started

Rattler's Den. I'd come back on the train every summer and visit and then after I got out of the army and worked for several years in the aircraft industry, we decided to move back with our two sons. It was the smartest move I've ever made. Being here on Route 66 in Tucumcari is as good as it gets."

Callens took over Tepee Curios in 1985, four years after the interstate bypassed Tucumcari. The front entrance to the building is shaped like an Indian teepee, and a friendly mixed-breed dog, a Doberman-husky with the ominous name of Trouble, greets customers and patrols the premises at night. The Callenses handle a brisk trade in quality Indian jewelry and crafts, as well as hawk an array of inexpensive trinkets that most self-respecting tourists cannot seem to live without. "We get the classic *turista*-types here," says Callens. "Mom, dad, and the kids. They pull up in the station wagon, and the whole family hops out and poses in front of the teepee, and dad snaps a picture. Sometimes they come in and browse and pick up a few gifts for the folks back home. The whole process takes two and a half minutes."

Top: Flying M Ranch, Tucumcari, N. Mex.

Below left: Route 66 Plaza, Central Avenue, Albuquerque, N. Mex.

Near left: Tepee Curios, Tucumcari, N. Mex.

Opposite page: Buckaroo Motel, Tucumcari, N. Mex.

The outside plaster walls of the building are adorned with colorful paintings of Indian dancers. There is a stunning Route 66 shield, painted one windy afternoon by Robert Waldmire. An itinerant artist from Illinois, Waldmire has championed many causes, including vegetarianism, nuclear alternatives, and the salvation of rain forests, whales, and fur-bearing creatures. But nothing arouses the artist's passion more than the Mother Road.

"I still get my kicks and I still take my trips," Waldmire says about a life spent mostly traveling from state to state along the old highway. Waldmire's catalog of artwork includes bird's-eye-view posters of Illinois, Missouri, New Mexico, Arizona, and California. There are also drawings of scenes along Route 66—the starting point of the highway in downtown Chicago; an antiques store in Halltown, Missouri; diner car ruins north of Quapaw, Oklahoma; the round barn at Arcadia, Oklahoma; Tijeras Canyon east of

working here. He took me under his wing. I learned the food business and how to deal with the public. I developed an affinity for this place and for the people who come down that highway out there. That's why I continue to work hard to keep the cafe going and keep the highway alive.

"I have six children and one of my sons and a daughter are involved in the business. I started my son out as a dishwasher, and at first he didn't understand why he had to do that. He wanted to be out front wearing a white shirt and a tie and smiling at everybody who came in here to eat. I told him if we're going to make this cafe into a dynasty all the white shirts and smiles in the world won't help. You have got to learn the business. You have got to know how to make the best salad, prepare the finest chili, cook a steak, bake sourdough biscuits, make real gravy, and you have to know how to wash dishes. I told him we have to build a reputation for this place that will never be anything but excellent. Without that, we might as well step aside and let the tumbleweeds come into town and run down the road.

"I spent eighteen years working out in California. When we came back here in 1973, this cafe had almost died. The town was bypassed and people were deserting the highway left and right. I

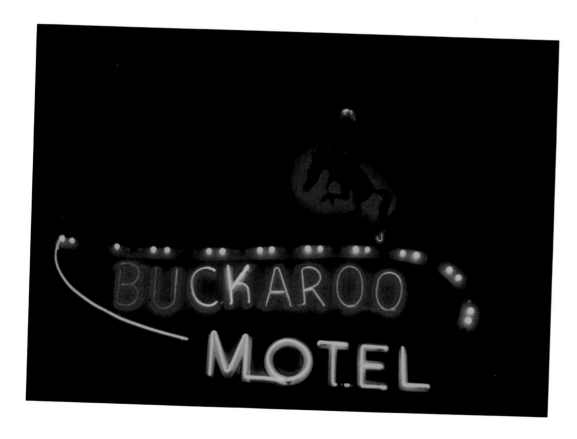

Albuquerque; and the end of Route 66 at Santa Monica Boulevard and Ocean Avenue at the Pacific Palisades Park. Wearing a beard, a smile, and an "Earth First" T-shirt, Waldmire started traveling the highways of America in 1963 in his dad's 1955 Pontiac. He soon became a familiar sight on Route 66, driving slowly in his van with a 66 shield and the words "Unofficial Old Route 66 Mobile Information Center" on the door. "I've fallen in love with old Route 66," says Waldmire. "I want to show the beauty of the land of this

continent. You can't appreciate it from the interstate."

Other Route 66 stalwarts call Tucumcari home. They can be found at the motels named Paradise, Royal Palacio, Safari, Cactus, Buckaroo, Sahara Sands, Aruba, Pony Soldier, Lasso, Apache, and the Palomino with its colorful "Whoa Palomino" electric rendering of a rearing horse. There are unwavering

Route 66 partisans at Tucumcari restaurants named Del's, Dean's, Blake's, and La Cita, with its big pointed sombrero out front, and inside—surrounded by garish paintings and potted plants—the many tables covered with oilcloth the color of mustard.

Other Route 66 sentinels are scattered down the highway to the west of Tucumcari. Travelers pass traces of the small towns of

remember this highway after World War II. It was really something. Cars were being manufactured again, and people started making money and taking vacations cross-country. Many of them had never been out in the Southwest. The big fat-man signs attracted them. The signs were Phil Craig's idea, and they were painted by a billboard artist named Jim Hall.

"People can still see the signs and they can also see other fantastic things —wide-open spaces and panoramas, cars boiling over by the side of the highway, rattlesnake pits, and Indians. They can sleep in motels that look like teepees and eat food that they'd never had before. There were changes when all that interstate highway talk started. It was Eisenhower who got the interstate going. He'd seen those highways in Germany. But even though the interstates came along and tried to knock 66 out of the picture, the old highway has never died. I don't think it ever will."

Far left: Club Cafe billboard west of Santa Rosa, N. Mex.

Center left: Club Cafe, "An Original Route 66 Restaurant Since 1935," Santa Rosa, N. Mex.

Near left: Highway sign, west of Tucumcari, N. Mex.

Above: Katherine Wilkerson and a road veteran at rest, Newkirk, N. Mex.

Montoya, Newkirk, and Cuervo. They follow the pavement into lands where the old highway climbs the bluffs of the Llano Estacado and enters the Pecos River country.

In Santa Rosa, the old town on the banks of the Pecos, lives one of the strongest custodians of the old highway. Ron Chavez is his name. He owns the Club Cafe, a significant Route 66 establishment since 1935, located on the old highway in the center of town. Even though I-40 bypasses the city, several of the famous Club Cafe billboards, depicting a grinning fat man, remain on the interstate. The big signs beckon all comers to get off at Santa Rosa and try some of the cafe's "honest-to-goodness, authentic sourdough biscuits, hamburgers made with 100% ground beef, homemade chile and chicken-fried steaks made with tender, fresh meat and served with old-fashioned, iron-skillet gravy."

Chavez was born in a tiny village on the Pecos, a few miles south of Santa Rosa, only a year after the Club Cafe was founded by Newt Epps. In 1939, Phillip and Ruby Craig bought the restaurant and served hot meals to weary tourists and truckers until 1973 when Chavez, who as a boy shined shoes in front of the Club, bought the place. For Chavez, owning and operating the Club Cafe is literally a dream come true. The fresh green chile used in the Club's dinners come from Puerto de Luna, the village where Chavez was born. Breakfast customers are at the door by six A.M., and the New Mexican–style lunches and dinners are washed down with cold beer. Some of the paintings decorating the cafe are by Santiago Chavez, Ron's brother. There are also mounted collections of arrowheads and old Indian jewelry, and next to the cashier is a room filled with highway souvenirs and curios. Ron's children work alongside him, learning every aspect of the business, and sometimes Chavez finds time to sit in one of the red vinyl booths and write a short story about life in New Mexico. He points with pride to the sign out front, which says "Original Route 66 Restaurant Since 1935," and the Route 66 shield and mural painted on the dining room wall. But the Club's familiar fat man signs out on the highway have a special place in Chavez's heart.

"Everybody who's ever traveled in this part of the country has seen the fat man

Club Cafe night shift, 1954, Santa Rosa, N. Mex.

Richardson's Store, Montoya, N. Mex.

signs," says Chavez. "Phil Craig wanted to create an image of someone who appreciated good food and had a satisfied look on his face. People still come in here and actually ask to see the fat man."

Nobody, however, expects to find fancy dishes on the Club's ample menu. Chavez serves only what he calls "real food"—piping hot and right off the griddle, just as in the boom years of Route 66. "They've ruined food," says Chavez. "Fast-food places have done it. I call it the 'blanding of America.' The food comes out of machines and is made of plastic and has chemicals in it. But not here. No way. We have stood the test of taste and time. In the Route 66 days there was nothing frozen, flash-fried, or microwaved. I have customers who stopped here to eat when they were kids. They want that same kind of food and that's what we serve. They're amazed to see that nothing's changed. Sometimes they even get emotional."

Leaving the surviving cafes, trading posts, and motels of Santa Rosa behind, those traveling west need to know that Route 66 used to head northwest through the village of Dilia to Romeroville, where it turned southwest. In those early years just after the creation of Route 66, some motorists left the Mother Road and visited Las Vegas (New Mexico), the seat of San Miguel County and a railroad and trade center in its own right. In the pre–World War II years of Route 66, travelers

found lodging at the Plaza Hotel on the historic Las Vegas plaza, just as they do today. Those driving west from Romeroville continued through the small towns of Bernal, Rowe, Pecos, the site of an ancient Indian ruin, and Glorieta, the scene of a decisive Civil War battle that spelled defeat for Confederate forces in New Mexico.

Beyond waited the many adobe hotels or motor courts in the ancient state capital of Santa Fe—the city of "Holy Faith" and the oldest European-settled community west of the Mississippi.

Santa Fe was also the terminus of the famed Santa Fe Trail. This indirect routing of the Mother Road, which brought motorists to the magical mountain city, came about because it followed the old trail blazed by Marcy and Simpson in 1849 for gold seekers headed from Fort Smith to California. During the years

Early general store and merchants during the "good ol' days," Santa Rosa, N. Mex.

Santa Fe was on Route 66, both Cerrillos Road and Old Pecos Trail served as the old highway's route around the city. After Santa Fe, the highway then headed south through Indian lands to Albuquerque.

By 1937 a straight paved section of Route 66 was completed which allowed travelers to bypass Santa Fe and the other northern towns and villages. Tourists and truckers could now drive directly east or west between Albuquerque and Santa Rosa. By dropping the northern loop from Route 66, travelers were able to save as much as four hours when crossing New Mexico.

The newer path of Route 66 past Santa Rosa eventually became Interstate 40. People driving to Albuquerque and points west still have a view of the sweeping New Mexican landscape, a scene replete with juniper and piñon. Just west of Santa Rosa, Cerro Pedernal ("rocky peak") can be seen jutting above the land. Then Clines Corners, an old tourist stopover at the junction of Route 66 and State Highway 285 leading to Santa Fe, comes into sight. Named for Ray Cline, the fellow who established a gas station at this point in 1934, Clines Corners became an interstate highway tourist trap, selling truckloads of beaded belts, key chains, steer skulls, buffalo horns, laminated pictures of Jesus Christ, cactus

honey, prickly pear syrup, green chili jelly, serapes, rubber snakes, bullwhips, placemats, jawbreakers, and ceramic butterflies.

Only 56 miles to the west of Clines Corners lies Albuquerque, the largest city in the state. But first one must go through the towns of Moriarty, Edgewood, Barton, and Tijeras. The interstate has passed all of them by, but the fragments of Route 66 offer travelers opportunities to stop in every last one. In this area—almost paralleling the old highway—was the trade route established by

Above: Bob Audette, guardian of The Mother Road, Barton, N. Mex.

Right: The Longhorn Ranch vintage postcard, "Welcome, Light and Set a Bit," near Moriarty, N. Mex.

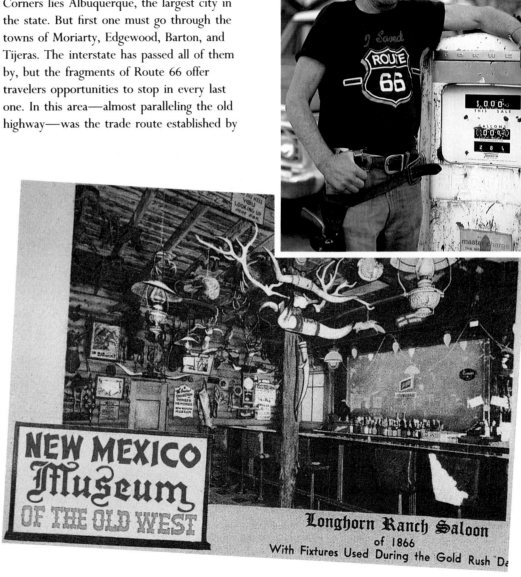

NEW MEXICO Museum OF THE OLD WEST

Longhorn Ranch Saloon
of 1866
With Fixtures Used During the Gold Rush Da

Josiah Gregg, a frontier figure from the mid-1800s, who blazed the return trail from Santa Fe back to Fort Smith, which became popular with gold seekers in 1849.

Forty-five miles east of Albuquerque is Moriarty, a town named for a rancher who came to New Mexico from Indianapolis seeking a cure for rheumatism. Here are the remains of the Long Horn Ranch. Started on Route 66 by a cop from back East, the Long Horn grew from a tiny cafe with a few stools to a full-service hotel with a restaurant, coffee shop, cocktail lounge, and, of course, curio shop. The slogan at the Long Horn was "Where the West Stops to Rest." At the Long Horn, travelers on the old highway were often startled to see a red and gold stagecoach, pulled by a team of four paint horses, bouncing along the side of the road. After that it was difficult not to stop and listen to Wild West yarns from one of the many ranch hands, such as Hondo Marchand, a tall, handsome wrangler typically decked out in western attire that included a silk neckerchief, tooled cowboy boots, silver and turquoise jewelry, and a big Stetson hat. Like the Cherry Hill Cider Stand, another popular tourist stop located just down the highway near Edgewood, the Long Horn went into a tailspin when the old highway was decommissioned and I-40 appeared.

The Long Horn and Cherry Hill may be gone, but they are not forgotten. Down the road near the small mountain town of Barton is a man who remembers. Bob Audette, a retired steeplejack and iron worker, gets as emotional about Route 66 as Ron Chavez and

the other guardians of the old highway. Born in a family of high climbers from Canada, Audette broke almost every bone in his lean body at one time or another during a long career spent climbing towering steel girders. The motto printed on his letterhead reads "Danger Is My Business, High Risk Specialist." During World War II, Audette was an underwater demolition expert in the navy. He came back to continue climbing and putting his life on the line high above the earth.

Cloistered in a ramshackle house that was once a gas station on the old highway, Audette lives with a watchdog named Buck, a brace of guns, and a lifetime of remembrances. He tends a small patch of tomatoes not far from an abandoned gas pump last used when the price was a mere nineteen cents a gallon. On bitterly cold winter nights he stokes piñon logs in the stove, plays his sweet dulcimer, and thinks about the Mother Road. Like others, Audette regrets that some stretches of the highway were neglected. At one time he helped lead a battle to purchase Historic Route 66 signs to post along the road. He sent out letters, sold T-shirts, circulated petitions, and tacked up posters about benefit dances to raise funds for the highway signs. He says,

"This is history we're talking about. Route 66 is a ribbon of history across the country and there are lots of memories. I remember Okies going out to California in their old cars and trucks with everything they owned tied down—rocking chairs, chicken coops, and bedsprings. If you were driving through

The Interstate, Las Palomas, N. Mex.

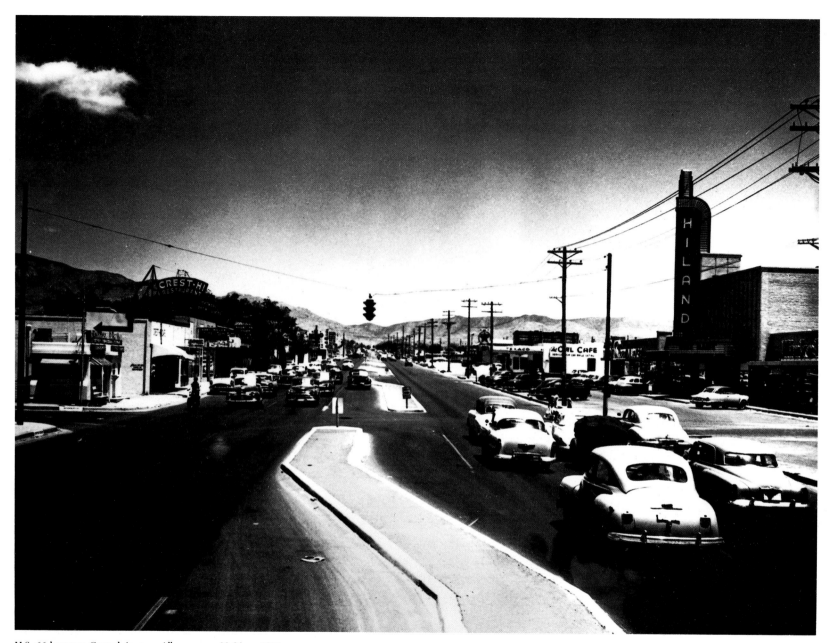

U.S. 66 becomes Central Avenue, Albuquerque, N. Mex., 1954.

Tijeras Canyon in the old days, you had to honk your horn before going into a turn because there wasn't enough room for two cars. I remember that narrow road. You had to be careful to not sidewipe someone. I remember the war convoys. I remember everything about Route 66. There was danger but still the world was better then and maybe that's why we should always remember the old road."

Audette was raised in Albuquerque, not too far from the University of New Mexico campus, and he went to the old high school on Central Avenue, one of the busiest sections of Route 66 in the country.

As the old road twists and dips through Tijeras Canyon and enters Albuquerque as Central Avenue, the city spreads out beneath the Sandia Mountains over the broad Rio Grande valley. Because Central Avenue, an unimproved dirt road until the early 1930s, remained a busy thoroughfare in the city, Route 66 is a strong artery in Albuquerque.

For years the first Albuquerque sight spotted by most motorists when they entered the city from the east was Manny Goodman's Covered Wagon Trading Post. A landmark store and tourist attraction, Goodman built the large rectangular building behind a massive concrete and wooden covered wagon. All around the building were six-foot tall jack rabbits, palomino horses, and other critters

fashioned of papier mâché or fiberglass. "I planned the store so that travelers coming around the bend into town first saw a huge covered wagon pulled by a pair of papier mâché oxen," says Goodman. "As they got closer to the wagon, they could see my store stretched out beyond it." Years later Goodman dubbed his souvenir haven "a poor man's Disneyland." The busy Route 66 institution was demolished to clear a path for Interstate 40. But instead of retiring, Goodman just moved a little farther down Route 66. He set up a new Covered Wagon store in Albuquerque's Old Town district, a block off Central Avenue, so he could continue to sell Indian jewelry and curios as well as dispense cigars to old pals, boxes of Cracker Jack to kids, and colorful yarns to wide-eyed tourists.

Although there have been changes through the years, much of the neon and glitz from the days before the interstate came is still evident in Albuquerque. For miles, both sides of Central Avenue are crowded with commerce—car lots, chicken and burger joints, gas stations, and countless motor courts and motels with names like Loma Verde, La Mesa, Rose Villa, La Puerta, Tewa Lodge, Lazy H, El Cid, Trade Winds, Zia, De Anza, Royal, El Vado, and Aztec. Travelers can still get big homemade cinnamon rolls dripping with butter or steaming plates of enchiladas and burritos smothered in fresh green chile. At the Monte Vista Fire Station, the firefighters and their spotted Dalmatians are long gone, but the distinctive adobe building—built in 1936 and one of the finest examples of pure Pueblo Revival architecture—remains as a handsome

A Route 66 Portrait

Michael Martin Murphey

Born: March 14, 1945
Occupation: Singer, songwriter,
wandering troubador
Residence: Taos, New Mexico

"I was born and reared in Texas. Early on I had an interest in music. At the same time, while traveling with my parents and my kid brother, Mark, I developed an abiding love for the

Right: Sky Court vintage postcard, "The Best for the Money," Albuquerque, N. Mex.

Below: Foyer, KiMo Theatre, "the cultural cornerstone of downtown Albuquerque," built in 1927.

restaurant and bar. On the corner of 5th and Central, in the heart of Old Town, is Lindy's, where cooks since 1929 have been ladling out the "best chili in town." Central Avenue is as busy as it was before the historical 66 signs were erected when the street still proudly bore the genuine Route 66 shields.

Like Santa Fe and Taos, the history of Albuquerque is as rich as a hunk of truck-stop cake. Founded in 1706, the city was located on the Chihuahua Trail, an extension of the Santa Fe Trail into old Mexico. For a long time growth was slow in Albuquerque. From the year of its founding until 1940, the city grew only to a population of 35,449. Then nuclear research gave Albuquerque a boost,

and the city boomed. Ten times as many people came over the next four decades as did in its first 234 years. Albuquerque evolved into the industrial and population hub of New Mexico and sprawled out alongside the Rio Grande, between the Sandia Mountains, Indian reservations, and Kirtland Air Force Base. Many landmarks—including the Alvarado Hotel, one of the last Mission Revival–style Harvey Houses—have vanished. But there are reminders of the old days and even some newer attractions that memorialize the Mother Road.

One Central Avenue gem that harks back to the good old days is the 66 Diner. It was opened in the late 1980s—years after the highway lost its federal status—only a few blocks from the University of New Mexico campus in an old stucco Phillips 66 gas station that dates back to the 1940s. The walls are covered with Route 66 photographs and the jukebox plays vintage tunes. At lunchtime every booth, counter seat, and table is jammed with downtown office workers, university students, and, of course, tourists eager to gobble meat loaf, grilled liver and onions, or chicken-fried steak. For chasers there are milkshakes, malts, cherry Cokes, or icy beers. "We get a lot of out-of-town people who come by and tell us they remember driving through Albuquerque on old 66 when they were kids," says a busy diner waitress. "The concept is a winner. Where else can a customer be seated by someone wearing a bowling shirt, enjoy a green chili cheeseburger, and boogie with a waitress wearing a poodle skirt?"

One of the regulars at 66 Diner is Marianne Dickinson, a New Yorker who fled to New Mexico to continue her successful journalism career. Dickinson edits *Route 66* magazine, an arts and entertainment publication that discusses the issues, trends, and lifestyles of the time when Route 66 was as strong across the country as it remains in Albuquerque. "It's actually a metaphorical name," says Dickinson of the magazine's title. "We're interested in the arts and architecture of the area that was part of 66, and we're part of the movement to revitalize the area. Route 66 gave people romance. It was a highway they came west on to build new lives and find new opportunities. It meant adventure, and I

think much of that is still alive. People are still coming here looking for the golden West—the wild and free West. Remember, the romance of the automobile still holds sway here."

Another local editor and writer, Jack Rittenhouse, previously mentioned as the author of the famed Route 66 guidebook first published in 1946, ended up living in Albuquerque, just a short distance off Central Avenue. Retired from the University of New Mexico Press, Rittenhouse and his wife quietly run a rare-book catalog business from their home.

One of Albuquerque's older motor courts, which provided refuge for many of Rittenhouse's readers, is El Vado on west Central Avenue, near Old Town Plaza and a short distance from the bridge spanning the Rio Grande. El Vado, with its white adobe walls and electric Indian sign, is much the same as it was in 1937 when it was built by Dan Murphy, an Irishman who had previously worked at the Waldorf-Astoria and managed Albuquerque's Franciscan Hotel. Some say El Vado is the purest Route 66 motel surviving in Albuquerque.

One of the main reasons for El Vado's survival is Ali Hakam, an affable man who was born in India, lived in Pakistan and Sweden, studied urban planning, and mastered five languages. Hakam, his wife, Salma, and their three children took over the management of El Vado in 1985. "People enjoy staying here because it's like stepping back in time," says Hakam. "It's a very special place. Most of the customers are regulars. I know many of their

American West. Route 66 was one of my earliest memories, and it was during those long trips down the old highway with my family that I got locked into nature. That old road connected me to the land and the people who lived there. We were able to travel through New Mexico and Arizona and see truly wild places—mountains, deserts, canyons.

"I recall one trip in 1952 in my dad's 1947 Chevrolet on Route 66 driving through New Mexico headed out to the Grand Canyon. In far West Texas, we stopped and picked up two turtles off the road. They kept us busy in the backseat, but after a while my brother and I got bored and put the turtles down on the floor. Several hours later one of those turtles crawled over my mother's foot. She was wearing sandals and when she felt those claws she let out a scream. There was a screech of brakes and a sudden stop on the highway. Two well-traveled turtles found new homes in New Mexico somewhere near the Arizona border. I have other strong memories of the old highway—memories of canvas water bags and radiators boiling over. I also clearly remember falling in love with New Mexico on those trips. I remember the plaza at Santa Fe and when I was about twelve I bought my very first Kachina doll. I vowed that someday I'd live in New Mexico.

names. They say staying here is just like coming home."

All up and down the old stretches of Route 66 and the interstate highways in the West are motels that are managed by natives of India or Pakistan, many of whom are part of a syndicate backed by Indian money. The odor of curry wafting from the manager's kitchen is not uncommon in motels in Oklahoma, Texas, New Mexico, and across Arizona. To distinguish themselves from these Indian-managed businesses, many motel operators hang American flags or signs that boldly state AMERICAN OWNED in the windows. But Ali Hakam was one of those who cared about the old motor court he managed and had a love for Route 66. "No prostitutes or drug addicts can check into this motel," says Hakam. "That wouldn't be right. This is a remarkable place and it's filled with the spirits of people who have been coming here for a long, long time."

Across Central Avenue from El Vado is Casa Grande Restaurant, once part of a Route

66 complex that included a hotel, bar, and gas station. Breakfast is served anytime at Casa Grande and for regulars that means huevos rancheros, chili omelets, eggs with Polish sausage, or golden waffles. For lunch and dinner the list is endless, but discerning road-food gourmets usually settle for one of the popular Mexican dishes or order a gringo entree— club steak, pork chops, breaded veal cutlet, fried chicken, baked meat loaf, roast turkey, or rainbow trout. The gravy for the mashed potatoes is as smooth as chocolate sauce. A note in the menu says "Thank You for Your Patronage," and there's a big old-fashioned scale that costs only a nickel. Portraits of conquistadors, a picture of the Statue of Liberty, and a reproduction of *The Last Supper* hang on the walls.

After leaving Casa Grande, travelers heading west cross the Rio Grande and pass through an area clogged with shopping centers, burger drive-ins, drugstores, and palm readers. At the edge of the city, the highway begins to climb the steep grade out of the Rio Grande valley and onto the plateaus. This is old Route 66 and the long hill rising to the horizon is Nine Mile Hill, a local landmark that got its name because the crest of the hill is exactly 9 miles from the geographic center of Albuquerque at the intersection of 4th Street and Central Avenue. On the way up the hill, an old roadside sign for a reptile farm says "See 'Em Alive—Free Snake Garden." There's only a concrete foundation left and pieces of broken porcelain from the toilet. Scraps of paper and shingles are piled up with huge tumbleweeds. All the caged snakes are gone; only wild snakes are left. On summer mornings they bake on the patches of cement and then slither off to their desert holes when the sun starts to dip. Farther up the road, from the peak of Nine Mile Hill, all of Albuquerque and even Sandia Peak sits under a layer of haze and clouds.

To the west the old highway becomes a frontage road and disappears into the mesas and desert—a vast and varied land colored blood red, jet black, purple, and brown. A land of ancient cultures and fiery lava gone stone cold. A land of cactus and scrub brush. Near the old road a concrete tunnel runs below the interstate. Cattle cross here, slow and plodding under the fast pavement, and tumbleweeds blow through and bounce out into the arid ranchlands. Prancing coyotes— called God's dogs by the Indians—leave their tracks in the soft dust covering the floor of the tunnel. Lewd words and people's names are spray-painted on the concrete. One message is angry. "I Am Rage, I Am Terror, I Am Obscene." Another reads "The Thrill Can Kill." It is signed *The Vampire*.

Ahead is the Rio Puerco, a stream that rises at the southeastern corner of the Jicarilla Apache lands and looks like an ordinary gully as it edges the Laguna Indian Reservation and flows south to empty into the Rio Grande. At the Rio Puerco crossing, travelers may stop for gasoline or food or to buy a pair of moccasins. This place used to be famous for the stuffed polar bear inside a glass case at the old trading post. On occasion, the bear would be brought outside near the gas pumps. Tourists always looked for the big polar bear

"As far as my music, the singers from the old highway also were a major influence on me—Hank Williams, Bob Wills, Woody Guthrie. In 1965, I took off to go to UCLA with a couple of my friends, and we packed up our stuff in a Volkswagen and headed west. Driving out to California with a guitar and harmonica, I came up with a song called 'Once a Drifter.' Here are the words:

Sittin' in the back where the chairs are
stacked
I'm warmin' up the stove.
Thinkin' about my old Ford stomped to the
floorboard
Chuggin' out of Pleasant Grove.
Blazin' off to California
Like a dust devil dancin' on a dime.
Guess I was a red-eyed backslider
Now I'm tired of the ride.
But once a drifter, always a drifter.
Once a drifter, always a drifter.
Mama standing in the driveway.
Too choked to say goodbye.
I turned my collar and turned my back
Went a mile and started to cry.
Johnny, Donny Brooks and me
Singing songs to pass the time.
Long before the war came.
Long before the star game.
Long before I came to find . . .
So here I am, uncertain again
Headed for no place to go.
Settin' down, leavin' town,

El Vado, built in 1937, Albuquerque, N. Mex.

at Rio Puerco but then one night someone stole the bear and it was later found all torn apart in the upper reaches of the Sandias. Hopefully, the culprit later ran into *The Vampire,* who provided some thrills.

On the other side of the steel bridge over the Rio Puerco the old road continues through the Laguna Reservation, offering side trips to Indian ruins and uranium mines. At one point about 30 miles west of Albuquerque, an exit off the interstate leads to a stretch of the old highway at a forgotten point called Correo, the Spanish word for "mail." Correo used to support not only a post office but a gas station, general store, a small cafe, and a few cabins. For many years a story made the rounds of Route 66 in both directions about a dwarf who lived near Correo in a hidden desert dugout. It was said that travelers would sometimes see the strange little man with shaggy hair and beard at the tourist court and someone would usually wind up in a card game with him. The tourists never won a pot because the dwarf cheated and carted off the winnings from the game to his secret hideaway.

There are no more card games or tourists at Correo and no sign of the mischievous dwarf. A sign talks about the Wild Horse Mesa Bar and there are concrete slabs and piles of debris stuffed in the arroyos near the old road. In the piles are empty wine bottles—killer Tokay that cooks brains and has taken its toll on generations of Indians. There are also discarded beer cans and somebody's old quilt and disposable diapers and soggy magazines and seed catalogs and a hot water heater plugged full of bullet holes.

Route 66 is a real ghost road at this point. It runs off past a wire ranch fence toward Albuquerque in one direction and to the west the road crosses the Atchison, Topeka, and Santa Fe railroad tracks and arches seemingly toward the sun. The crossing over the tracks is battered and worn and at twilight, when the mountains and desert turn rosy, travelers on the old road can stand on the bridge and see the trucks on the distant interstate moving like big white slugs under peach-colored clouds. Pairs of shiny black crows dance on the telegraph wires next to the tracks and off in the distance a train moans and then draws closer and closer until the big yellow and blue AT&SF engine hauling

Abandoned watering hole, west of Albuquerque, N. Mex.

Opposite, above: Tourist stop and Rio Puerco bridge, west of Albuquerque, N. Mex.

Opposite, below: Railroad tracks from old highway bridge, near Correo, N. Mex.

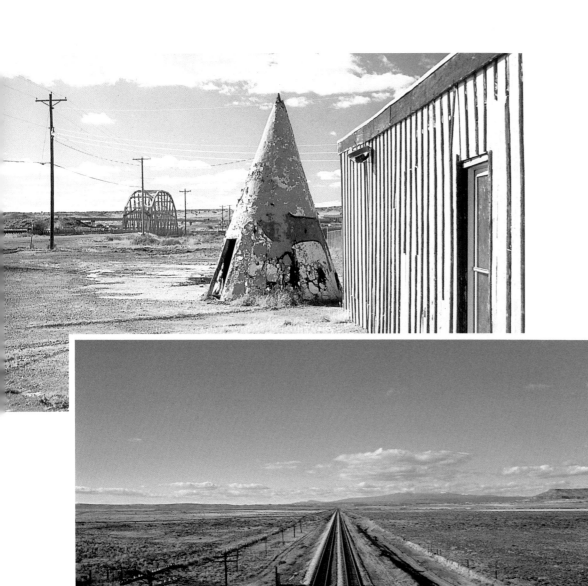

Family man, ramblin' man,
I just pretend it's part of the show
One too many childhood movies
With strangers riding off in the sun
Taught me you can't talk it out
When you feel like walkin' out.
The sequel's already begun.

I thought about all the people who traveled back and forth on Route 66. I thought about the people from Oklahoma in the thirties who headed west to find relief. Driving through the Hopi and Navajo country on that trip was very important to me. I became involved with Indian rights activists and wrote a song called 'Geronimo's Cadillac,' which became an anthem for the Indian Rights movement. In the early seventies I lived in Austin and then I moved to Colorado. There I wrote more music—'Wildfire' and 'Carolina in the Pines' and 'Cherokee Fiddle.

"My wife, Mary, is from Montreal and she was a Wilhemina fashion model. We met in New York and she had never been out West except for trips to L.A. I took her to the heartland—to the old Route 66 places. We lived in Los Angeles for a brief time.

"In 1978, we moved to Taos, New Mexico, and my boyhood dream came true. I love every corner of this state and I enjoy playing everywhere from Farmington to Artesia. I think coming

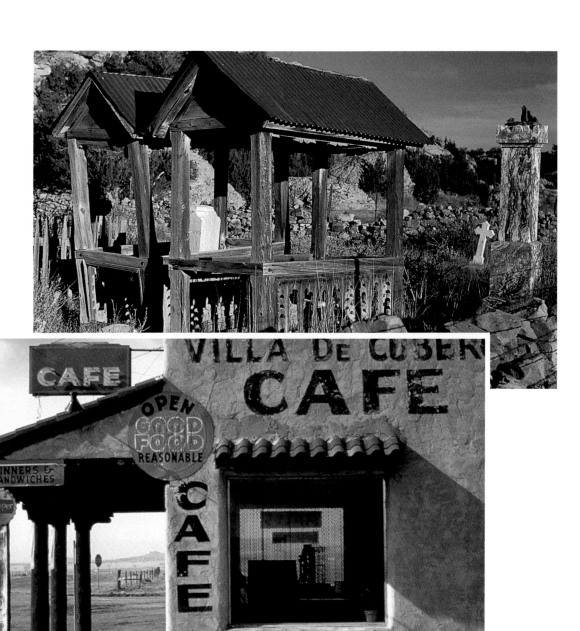

a long line of freight passes below the bridge. Hot air rushes over the old road and the train moves west down twin rails shining like silver ribbons in the sun. At that precise moment, when the train engineer, a pipe clenched in his teeth and the sun's rays glinting off his eyeglasses, blows the diesel horn and the warmth of the train washes across the worn and cracked pavement, the Mother Road comes to life.

The old road—Route 66—can still be followed past crumbling tourist courts and open range where falcons hover above the weeds and ride the wind looking for their next meal. These are Laguna Indian grazing lands. Beyond Mesita village, the old road curves around pueblo ruins on the mesas instead of plowing right through the rock and earth as the nearby interstate highway does. Route 66 honored the land and adjusted to the terrain and did not chisel into buttes and mountains or interrupt entire cultures. The frontage road is the old highway and it winds toward Old Laguna and dips into the San José river bottom. Across the site of the bridge that burned in 1952 and took a trucker's life, holding up Route 66 traffic for twelve hours, is the Old Laguna church and a trading post where gasoline, Pendleton blankets, and groceries are sold, and video tapes are rented.

From Laguna west to Grants the road

takes the name New Mexico 124, and the pavement courses by New Laguna, bounded by meadows of blond-colored grass and Indian schools. Travelers pass the village of Paraje and roads that offer side trips to Encinal and the famous "Sky City" of Acoma—the oldest Indian pueblo in America on top of a high mesa only a dozen miles south of Route 66. Acoma was a well-established settlement a thousand years before Coronado reached New Mexico in 1540.

Continuing westward on New Mexico 124, the Mother Road takes travelers to Budville, consisting of a few buildings on the highway just 23 miles east of Grants. Budville was named for H. N. "Bud" Rice, the fellow who started an automobile service and tour business at this place in 1928 when Route 66 was young and vibrant. During the hectic years of the old road, any cars that broke down or ran into problems between Albuquerque and Grants were towed to Budville by one of Rice's wreckers. A loop road off the old highway takes travelers to the village of Cubero with its old graveyard, a stream that cuts through solid stone, and stands of stout cottonwood trees. The loop comes back to old 66 near a once popular spot called Villa de Cubero, where at one time there was an active trading post and motor court and where the Gunn family ran a slick cafe that served plates of succulent lamb. Just west of Villa de Cubero is San Fidel and off in the distance stands snow-capped Mount Taylor, the highest of the San Mateo mountains, named for Zachary Taylor and a landmark on the southern border of the Navajo's world.

Those who stay on the old road soon come across Santa María de Acoma, also known as McCarty's, a trading community on the Acoma reservation on old U.S. 66, 13 miles southeast of Grants. Just above the settlement, clinging to the side of a rocky mesa, is a mission church built by the Indians in 1933. Inside the church are wooden pews and hand-carved beams, saints, and religious figures, and rows of burning vigil candles. Indian parishioners often leave a sacred feather or a turquoise bead instead of lighting a candle. Baskets of squaw bread are sometimes placed on the altar. On some winter mornings on the steep slope behind the building, the fresh tracks of a mountain lion can be found in the new snow.

Between McCarty's and Grants, the old highway passes through ancient black lava flows hardened into sharp-edged formations on both sides of the road. This area is the New Mexican badlands or *malpais,* Spanish for "bad country." Navajo folklore claims that the strange dark masses with razor edges are actually the dried blood of a horrible monster killed by the Twin Gods of War when they were traveling through this country. Scientists believe the malpais is the result of volcanic activity that occurred a million years ago when cinders were blasted through the heavens and hot lava flowed on the ground. To the road crews charged with building Route 66, it mattered little which version of the story was true. All they knew was that the malpais was an obstacle that presented serious problems. They routed the Mother Road around the lava flows and built their bridges on the edges

from New Mexico and Texas is exactly what I'm most proud of. It's nothing I ever want to cover up. It's done nothing but help me. I get out with my group in our tour bus, and we travel the highways. We ride Interstate 40 all the way back to Nashville and we ride out to the West Coast on the other interstates and we still get off at the old Route 66 places along the way. The old road is still there in Albuquerque and Gallup and the other towns. That's why I decided to do my own version of Bobby Troup's great song, 'Get Your Kicks on Route Sixty-Six.' It was a perfect fit for my *Land of Enchantment* album. The old highway keeps alive that part of me I absorbed as a kid driving across the Southwest in my dad's car."

Route 66 (foreground), Interstate 40 (in the distance), McCarty's, N. Mex.

of the badlands. Decades later when the interstate highway engineers came upon the scene, they had more bucks and a lot more technology so they simply cut right through the jagged lava beds. It gave travelers a safer but less interesting route.

Ahead is the railroad town of Grants, where miners once thrived thanks to the nearby uranium deposits, counted among the largest in the world. The Grants uranium boom began in 1950, when Paddy Martinez, a Navajo Indian, discovered the first vein of ore at Haystack Mountain. Before the uranium craze, Grants was a sleepy highway town and railroad base camp that had once been called Nahto-Si-Ka'i, or "place of the friendly smoke," by local Indians because a peace treaty was signed there between Kit Carson and Chief Manuelito. Through the city, old

Route 66 is still called Santa Fe Avenue, and in those glory days when everyone had plenty of cash to spend thanks to uranium, the shops, cafes, and bars were jumping with miners, railroaders, construction crews, and a sprinkling of tourists. Maria's Diner, the Silver Moon Bar, Pat's Lounge, the Zia Motel, and Speak Easy Grill are reminders of those days and nights when cold cash, not credit cards, served as the coin of the realm.

In *Route Sixty-Six Revisited: A Wanderer's Guide to New Mexico,* a magical self-published guidebook filled with memories from the Mother Road, photographer D. Nakii and writer K. Hilleson tell the story of how Grants prospered before the mining boom. Hilleson weaves the tale through the words of an unnamed peddler who spent his life traveling Route 66.

I'll never forget the first time I saw the carrot fields of Grants. It was in 1945. They tell me that some sights can change your life, or at least, change your point of view. I think the carrot fields did that. They filled me with awe. They made me realize what water could do. They made me think of New Mexico as a sleeping field, just waiting for enough water to wake it up and turn it into a great green empire. Of course that might never happen. There probably isn't enough water to do that for all the desert land, but there was enough for those carrot fields. Those fields were so green. They were soft and alive, compared to the desert surrounding them, compared to the desert I had just driven through. Dotted among all of

the greenery were bright little specks of color: orange, red, and purple. Even the grey was sort of luminescent. All of those colors were the velvet shirts of the Navajos picking those carrots by hand.

Those carrot fields covered thousands of acres between Grants and Bluewater. Those carrots were the base of a financial empire and most of the work was done by hand and done by the Navajos. Those carrots were planted, cultivated, and pulled by mostly manual labor.

Those carrots were shipped out by railroad. There weren't any refrigerated cars then, everything perishable had to be packed in ice. Eventually the carrot business got so big that a modern ice plant was built in Grants near the railroad tracks. It was built right where the Diamond G Home Center is now. It was a big facility that could make ice, chip ice and then blow it into the railroad cars filled with carrots. Those cars, everyone called 'em reefers, would speed along the tracks to St. Louis and Chicago and you could see the water dripping out of them as that ice melted. Then they built a big box factory next to the ice plant. Everyone had jobs there. The Indians would pull the carrots and load them on to a horse-drawn wagon and take them to the washing sheds near the fields. Then the clean carrots would be taken over to the railroad siding and packed into boxes or just packed into the reefers. They'd blow in the chipped ice and then all the carrots would be gone, east and west. You know, it takes two years to grow a carrot. The whole enterprise was

Left: Budville, N. Mex.

Below: Deteriorating road, 1965,
southeast edge of Cubero, N. Mex.

Above: Sunning hubcaps and license plates, Bluewater, N. Mex.

Below: Wall mural, Thoreau, N. Mex.

the mining companies, the carrot empire folded. No one needed to grow carrots if they had all of that money in the bank. No one needed to work in the carrot fields if there was work in the mines.

I regretted the end of the carrot fields. I used to look forward to driving through Grants at dusk. There was a collection of small hoghááns for the Navajo field workers you could see from Route 66. It was sort of a company town, I guess. I imagine that the living conditions might not have been the best. But it was so peaceful to look away from the highway to that scattering of little, round houses. Each one had a piñon fire in front and you could see the Indian ladies in their long graceful skirts cooking dinner over bright little fires. Those people had work and food and shelter. Their little piñon fires shone so brightly in the dim light. It couldn't have been all bad.

a wonderful success story, a remarkable business and it lasted many years.

In the late forties, those little plastic bags appeared. You could put carrots in them and they would stay fresh without ice. It was just like now. You didn't need to pack carrots into special boxes from the box factory. You didn't need to cover them with chipped ice from the ice plant. Just load them up on a wagon in the field and take them to the washing shed. Wash them, bag them and there you were. No boxes, no ice. I guess after they sold the water rights to

Besides the railroad, carrots, and uranium, Grants was also known as the jumping-off place for side trips. There was El Morro National Monument, a towering mass of rock covered with Indian petroglyphs and inscriptions of early Spanish and gringo explorers, and the Perpetual Ice Caves, 7,300 feet above sea level and formed from the lava flow of a volcanic cone called Cerro de la Bandera. West of Grants the old road passes Bluewater, Prewitt, and then, 31 miles east of Gallup, reaches Thoreau (pronounced either "thru" or "thuh-roo" in this region) named for the author Henry David Thoreau.

About 6 miles west of Thoreau the old

road crosses the Continental Divide, the line geographers have labeled the "backbone" of the nation. At 7,275 feet, the Divide is the highest point on the entire length of U.S. Route 66. It consists of a ridge of high ground that runs north and south through the Rocky Mountains. The Divide separates eastward-flowing streams from those flowing to the west. Water falling east of this line flows to the Atlantic by way of the Gulf of Mexico, and water falling west of the line drains into the Pacific.

A huge complex called the Giant Travel Center is located at the base of the western slope of the Continental Divide. Before the advent of the interstate there were several successful establishments at the peak of the Divide, such as the Great Divide Trading Company, the Continental Trading Post, and the Top o' the World Hotel & Cafe. After World War II, soldiers stationed at a nearby military base frequented a juke joint on the Divide. They drank and danced to their hearts' content with the taxi dancers who kept the wolf from the door by hustling their living on the floor. It is quieter on the Divide, but there is a Stuckey's and a trading post, and tourists still stop to get gas or buy ten-cent coffee or Kodak film and fill their chests with bags or blocks of ice.

The Mother Road and Interstate 40 soon leave New Mexico and enter Arizona. But first the highway passes Fort Wingate, a military reservation since 1868; another road leading to Kit Carson Cave, where the Indian fighter was besieged for many days during the campaign against the Navajos in 1864; and magnificent red sandstone cliffs, especially at sunset, that precede the entrance to Gallup, one of the great Indian trading centers of the entire Southwest.

Travelers driving through Gallup after twilight on the Mother Road pass in review by motel after motel festooned with bright neon. During the terrible 1930s when the Okies came this way, their path was made brighter by the lights of Gallup. Breathtaking sunsets and glowing ribbons of neon still light the way for motorists making the same trip.

Gallup was founded in 1881. Old-timers recalled that the early railroaders would announce that they were "going to Gallup's," which meant it was payday and time to collect wages from David L. Gallup, the railroad paymaster. Besides the railroad and coal mining, trading with the Zuni, Hopi, and Navajo Indians—all renowned for their fine arts and crafts—also became important to Gallup. Trading posts sprang up across the large Navajo reservation and Gallup became the leading trade center. Tobe Turpen's Indian Trading Co., Thunderbird Jewelry Supply House, Richardson Trading Company, and other businesses built around the Native American arts and crafts were established.

With the development of Route 66 through the very heart of the town, Gallup was opened up to highway travelers from across the nation and became a popular resting place for travelers. Big signs aimed at the tourists are posted from Albuquerque to the east all the way to Flagstaff, boasting that Gallup is "The Indian Capital of the United States," chiefly because the town is surrounded by the huge Navajo Reservation, the largest in America.

For many years home for the famed Inter-Tribal Indian Ceremonial, Gallup developed a tarnished image because of the many Native American alcoholics who haunted the liquor stores and became familiar figures

Bluewater Trading Post, northwest of Grants, N. Mex.

shuffling up and down 66 when the bars opened up early each morning. The "dreary march," as it is described, continues until two A.M. the next morning, when the bars go dark for a few hours. Mother Teresa, the venerated nun who champions the oppressed around the world, placed Gallup on her list of forsaken places along with Calcutta. Truckers gave Gallup the code-name "Drunk City." Finally, in the late 1980s, the city launched serious efforts to change its image by enforcing massive crackdowns on the town's drunks and liquor stores not abiding by the law.

"It's my plan to polish Gallup's image and restore people's faith in Route 66," says Judi Snow, one of the chief boosters of Route 66 in New Mexico and a native of New Brunswick, Canada. She came to Gallup after living in California and Albuquerque. "In some respects Gallup has gotten a reputation it doesn't deserve. It's a colorful town and there's so much history. It's living history. People can drive into town on the old road and see history for themselves. Route 66 was a big part of all that and it's still here. The interstate didn't kill off Gallup. There are almost eighteen hundred guest rooms, and although we may not have French cuisine, we serve up the best Navajo tacos in the entire world."

Image aside, a visit to Gallup is usually never dull. Characters abound. Some are imports; others are locals who look like they just stepped out of one of Tony Hillerman's

Above: El Rancho 1980s postcard, "In the Heart of Navajo Land," Gallup, N. Mex.

Left: "Feliz Navidad," El Rancho lobby, Gallup, N. Mex.

Navajo-centered novels set in the Gallup region. Then there's Octavia Fellin, the spirited director of the Gallup Public Library since 1947 and Gallup's own national treasure.

One of the town's principal tourist palaces is El Rancho, a former Route 66 phantom that has now been completely resurrected. The original luster of the hotel was restored by Armand Ortega, a well-known Indian trader who bought the property, rolled up his sleeves, broke out his checkbook, and put the grand old place back on its feet. After a traveler spends a day driving through the natural beauty of western New Mexico, this classic hotel remains a worthwhile stop, if only to look at all the photographs of celebrity guests covering the lobby walls.

First opened as the Depression was nearly at its end in 1937, El Rancho was from the beginning a gathering place for the stars. Attracted by the many films made in the region, El Rancho's guest register logged such greats as Spencer Tracy, Katharine Hepburn, Kirk Douglas, Alan Ladd, Humphrey Bogart, and Jack Benny. A thirsty Errol Flynn rode his horse into the bar, and Ronald Reagan slept beneath cool sheets at El Rancho long before he became a political figure. The hotel housed one of the largest gambling operations in the state, complete with dice tables, a roulette wheel, slot machines, and a continuous poker marathon.

"She's a glitzy lady," Ortega says of his hotel. "This was the home of movie stars and cross-country travelers. It brings back a taste of another time."

What Ortega calls a taste of another time is the same story all across New Mexico. From east to west, whether in Cuervo or Tijeras, Laguna, Thoreau, or Grants, there are those who can recall with pride when Route 66 was the main transcontinental highway, which left Gallup as a big broad boulevard and headed to Arizona only 26 miles to the west. As elsewhere in New Mexico, definite traces of the Mother Road exist between Gallup and the state line—out in the open spaces, near trading posts and curio shops, and in the village of Manuelito, named for a famous Navajo leader. People in these places all along the old highway know Route 66 is still the open road. If they're in the right mood, most of them will say they have sweet memories of those days when there seemed to be more time. Those days when time was a precious treasure. When there was time to stop for a

Route 66, east of Gallup, N. Mex.

home-cooked meal in Santa Rosa, time to play a round or two of miniature golf in Albuquerque, time to stretch out in a room cooled with refrigerated air in Grants, time to scribble postcards in Gallup. And time to pause—if just for a minute—to watch the sunset.

That's what Route 66 was all about. It still is.

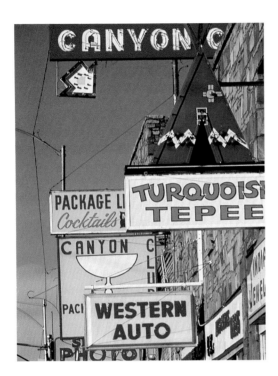

CHAPTER EIGHT

Arizona

"It is because in Arizona the arresting framework, the very skeleton of the earth, is exposed that the scenery is so compelling and meaningful. Its bone structure is superb."
—Josef Muench
Southwestern photographer

Arizona is one of the Route 66 states where tourists can gorge themselves with attractions. The Grand Canyon, Painted Desert, Petrified Forest, and Meteor Crater alone can keep an army of camera-toting travelers occupied for weeks. There are also subtle enticements to be discovered in the Arizona canyon lands, mountains, and high desert. Many of these are tied to the Mother Road. With a bit of luck, they can still be found.

Folks passing through Arizona who are lucky enough to find Nyal Rockwell and his two hundred acres covered with wrecked cars, old horse barns, stone ruins, and chunks of petrified wood, often believe they have arrived at some sort of time warp. They haven't. Nyal Rockwell is not an aberration. He's as genuine as the vestiges of the Mother Road, which remain only a few paces from his house trailer.

Rockwell lives on a slice of the old highway 24 miles east of Holbrook and only a few miles from Adamana, at one time a Santa Fe railroad station on the north bank of the Rio Puerco near the southern boundary of the vast Petrified Forest.

Left: Storm clouds gather over horses grazing next to the highway near Arizona's Aubrey Cliffs.

Above: Main drag, Williams, Ariz.

In the late afternoon when his chores are mostly done, Rockwell, dressed in an open-collar white shirt, jeans, and cap, slowly walks over the high desert landscape accompanied by Zeus and Smoky, his faithful dogs. "This is historic land we're walking on," says Rockwell, waving his arm before him like an Old Testament prophet.

"A stagecoach station stood right here, and when we came out to this land we called it the 'store building.' The old stage station that was torn down was made from these rocks and it was built in 1886. These are all native stones that were used for that building. Each stone has a story. We stacked the rocks right here.

Nyal Rockwell, near Adamana, Ariz.

"My horse barn is up there against the National Monument fence and there's a trail that comes down from over the hill. That was the road that went all the way from Fort Defiance to Fort Apache. It was a military road and the old stage station was built here because the soldiers were always passing back and forth. I have a big pile of wooden stakes I picked up from out there. Calvary troopers tied their horses to the stakes and when the Indians came and tried to steal the horses, the dragoons stood inside the stage station, at windows shoulder high, and they shot at the Indians."

Rockwell pauses to let his story sink in and he wipes his tinted eyeglasses clean with a handkerchief. "For many years people have been passing through this place. Indians were coming this way long, long ago and then the Spanish explorers and the white soldiers and settlers and finally the tourists."

At the corner of the property, Rockwell turns his back to the wind and pulls a bur from the paw of a grateful Zeus. "See, these signs here are from the National Old Trails Road, which was the highway through this land before Route 66. It was only a dirt road and those early automobiles came right through here on it. See the old sign? It says 'National Old Trails Road Association. Ocean to Ocean Highway. Holbrook 24 miles, Winslow 57 miles, Navajo 19 miles, Gallup 78 miles. Auto Club of Southern California.' That outfit helped sponsor it. See the sign? Some fool came by and put those bullet holes in it, but I've kept the old sign posted right

here to mark that early highway."

Born in 1913 in the Route 66 town of Weatherford, Oklahoma, Rockwell was three years old when his family moved to a Colorado farm. Within a few years they moved to Arizona. The family lived on ranchland near Holbrook, and they lived in Globe and Stafford and Winslow, where Rockwell finished high school. Then they went on to Phoenix where he went to junior college. During World War II, Rockwell took a job in an aircraft plant and afterward he worked as an engineer and owned his own business. In 1954, he sold out of Phoenix and he and his wife and son moved to the land where the old stage station stood and where the National Trails Road once ran—out on busy Route 66.

"My wife's name is Helen, and we got married in 1935. I was working at Babbit's in the meat market at Grand Canyon, and she came out on the train from Chicago to visit her grandmother and I wouldn't let her go home. My son spent his summers out here. He went to college in Flagstaff and became an educator. He teaches at the high school in Winslow."

Rockwell and his dogs turn to look back at the cluster of buildings and the trailer. Four lanes of Interstate 40 run nearby and divide Rockwell's acreage into two separate parcels. Highway fences keep people from leaving the interstate to visit the old man. Without saying a word, Rockwell curses the superhighway that came along and changed his life.

"Those old cabins over there were once filled with people," says Rockwell.

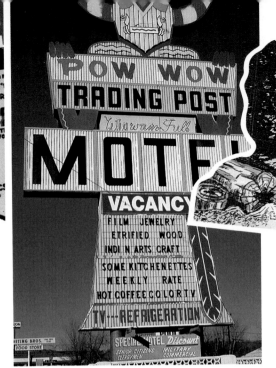

Above: Arizona state decal.

Near right: Kachina sign, Holbrook, Ariz.

Far right: Petrified Forest vintage shipping tag.

Below right: Piñon vintage shipping tag, "With best wishes from the Land of the Navajo."

"We hired a man and his wife to help us, and they lived in one of the cabins. We had wrecker drivers out here too. We had a busy garage and gas station and a wrecker service. My main business was the tourists and anything they wanted, we tried to have. I called this place 'Rocky's Old Stage Station.' When we first came, there was only one service bay but we added two more on the back of the station and the three gasoline pumps out front were always going. I had six regular workers and in the summertime when things got real busy, I had some school boys working for me.

"We didn't have a motel but we let people camp here. Lot of folks carried tents

and bedrolls back then and they'd just sleep out on my land. We were selling more gasoline than Fred Harvey was selling up at Petrified Forest National Monument. People liked coming here. Our beer was cold and my wife made some of the best chili you ever tasted. Sheriff's deputies would chase a few cars up and down the highway and they'd stop here to eat. Truckers would stop too and get a bowl of chili or eat a sandwich and sometimes we'd have ten or twelve trucks crowded around here."

In 1965, the interstate highway was completed in this section of Arizona, and Rockwell's life was never the same. "When they put in I-40

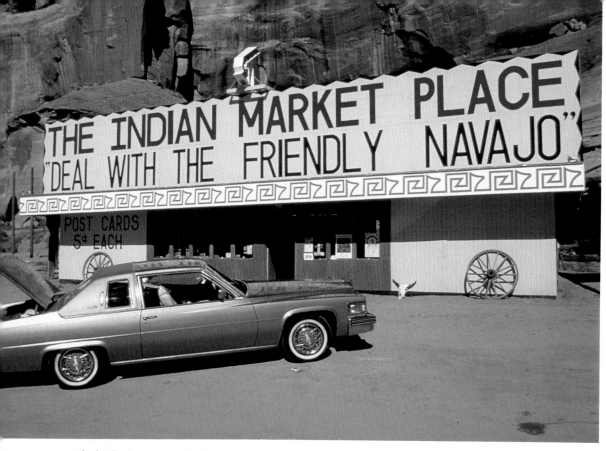

Chief Yellowhorse Indian Trading Post, Lupton, Ariz.

Route 66. Like the stones from the old stage station, each vehicle has a story. Rockwell knows them all by heart.

"That 'fifty-six Lincoln came in off Route 66. And that Dodge pickup over there was pulled in shortly after we came here in 'fifty-four. I got that 1948 Ford truck over there at a government sale. That trailer has a sad story. A couple lived in that trailer and one evening when she was cooking supper something boiled over and it caught fire and the woman died inside before they could get her out. The Barracuda over there had a bad transmission but the fellas driving it couldn't afford to get it fixed so it was junked. I sold parts off a lot of these cars and trucks— engines, windshields, tires, radiators. We had many of the cars crushed too. A big portable crusher would come in and crush ten cars in one hour."

By the time the sun sets, Rockwell and the dogs have ended their patrol. He stops at a storage shed, filled with supplies and tools, to feed the dozen cats who reside there, and then he plods toward the house trailer where Helen waits and the best pot of chili in the world simmers on the stove.

Travelers who revere a land where time does indeed stand still find plenty of hidden pockets filled with human and natural treasures, such as Nyal Rockwell, along the route of the

the government claimed I had been taking petrified wood from their park and so they cut me off with a fence and then the new highway sliced through here, and they didn't leave me a gate or an access ramp, so I was marooned. They tore up Route 66. You see that black stuff and that gravel there? That's part of the old 66 roadbed. Route 66 ran right in front of my building but the government took it all away. There are just little stretches of the old road left."

Despite what the interstate highway did to his family and livelihood, Nyal Rockwell held on to his land. No one could stop for a bowl of Helen's chili or buy a tank of gasoline, but Rockwell continued the wrecker service until 1987. Each evening he and the dogs stalk the rows of wrecked cars, trucks, and campers lined up near the interstate like a last forma-tion of automotive relics gathered in tribute to the Mother Road. Many were pulled in from the interstate, some are from the days of

Mother Road across Arizona. Thanks to air-conditioning and the internal combustion engine, it's a more hospitable place than it was when early adventurers such as Coronado, Kearny, and Beale made their way through the territory. Even John Steinbeck's Joad family in *The Grapes of Wrath* feared the brutal heat of the Arizona desert—undoubtedly, along with the Mojave Desert, the most inhospitable segment of their long trek to California. Steinbeck hinted at bad times to come when the Joads reached the Arizona state line and a border guard confronted the family.

They climbed into the high country of Arizona and through a gap they looked down on the Painted Desert. A border guard stopped them.

"Where you going?"

"To California," said Tom.

"How long you plan to be in Arizona?"

"No longer'n we can get acrost her."

"Got any plants?"

"No plants."

"I ought to look your stuff over."

"I tell you we ain't got no plants."

The guard put a little sticker on the windshield.

"O.K. Go ahead, but you better keep movin'."

"Sure. We aim to."

The 376 miles of the Mother Road from Lupton in the east to Topock in the west may have been tough going for the Joads and the other migrant families traveling the highway during the 1930s, but the fact remains that the old road in Arizona is lined with history —both natural and man-made.

Coronado's two-year journey in quest of riches took him to the lofty San Francisco peaks not far from present-day Flagstaff and also to the vicinity of the majestic Grand Canyon, one of the most popular targets for latter-day Route 66 pilgrims. The old highway also follows Lieutenant Edward Beale's 1857 survey trail along the 35th parallel. Beale and his camel caravan traversed Arizona while plotting the wagon road from Fort Defiance in New Mexico Territory to the Colorado River. In a report about Arizona sent back to Congress in 1858, the surveyor wrote, "The region is altogether valueless. After entering it, there is nothing to do but leave." Nonetheless, Beale and his camels left their tracks. For many years, north of Kingman in the western part of the state, locals could point to wagon ruts made by Beale's party.

In the twentieth century, the course of what became Route 66 across Arizona was used by early travelers, ranchers, and Indians headed to any of the larger towns that grew along the way. By 1927, the road was officially named U.S. 66, although some folks still occasionally used the old route names such as National Trails Highway or Evergreen National Highway. The road conditions varied for many years when there was no hard surface and most of the highway was simply oiled gravel or just graded earth. By the late 1930s, the highway was paved. After World War II, armies of tourists swarmed across Arizona

anxious to see the state's Indian country, Painted Desert, Petrified Forest, or Grand Canyon. The interstate carries the brunt of the traffic passing through Arizona, but reliable threads of the old highway remain, including a particularly noteworthy segment between Seligman and Kingman, one of the best-preserved stretches of the Mother Road between Chicago and Santa Monica.

The first spot of any consequence a motorist driving west on Route 66 encounters after leaving New Mexico is Lupton, named for G. W. Lupton, an early trainmaster at Winslow and later the Santa Fe railroad superintendent at San Francisco. In this portion of the state, several of the "tourist traps" have shifted from the old road to the banks of Interstate 40. There are plenty of signs advising travelers of the availability of tax-free cigarettes, "museum quality" pottery, ice-cream cones, Indian moccasins, Navajo rugs, steer horns, velvet paintings, and clean rest rooms. Between the state line and the first large town of Holbrook are several trading post–railroad station settlements that are similar to Lupton. They include Allantown, Houck, Querino, Sanders (sometimes called Cheto), Navapache, Chambers, Navajo, and Adamana—most of them named for early settlers, Indian traders, or railroad officials.

The highway cuts by the Petrified Forest National Park, with its thousands of acres of petrified trees and huge chunks of agate, carnelian, onyx, and jasper. Adjacent to the ancient desert forest is the famous Painted Desert, where the soil and rocks are tinted blue, chocolate, purple, rose, and vermilion.

Continuing west, the highway streaks past the Old Stage Station and descends into Holbrook, founded in 1882 and seat of Navajo County. Holbrook always had a regular flow of travelers. The region was opened to settlers and early traders stopped for rest and refreshment after the railway across northern Arizona was completed in the year the town was founded. Cattle spreads were established in the area such as the Hashknife Outfit, one of the largest in the country, and cowhands rode into Holbrook to drink their fill at the Bucket of Blood Saloon.

The romance of the West and its untapped resources attracted many easterners. As a result, tourism became the mainstay of the local economy. One of Fred Harvey's first restaurants was in Holbrook, housed in several old boxcars on a rail siding. Early tourists hired wagons to take them to see the nearby Indian reservations and the Petrified Forest, which became a national monument in 1906. The White Motor Court, purported to be the

nation's first tourist camp, was built in Holbrook. An array of other tourist facilities followed after Route 66 became the official transcontinental highway. The old Brunswick Hotel, once the headquarters for the Hashknife Outfit, was converted into the Arizona Rancho Motor Lodge. The Green Lantern Cafe had a reputation for good food, and Campbell's Coffee House served as a meal stop for tour buses and motorists hungry for "Son of a Gun Stew."

After the gas shortages of World War II ended, tourists returned to the Mother Road and Holbrook resumed its role as an overnight mecca on the high desert. The old highway enters Holbrook on Business Loop 40, which is Navajo Boulevard and Hopi Drive. In the 1970s and the '80s, Holbrook and other small towns all along the old highway were bypassed by the interstate. Holbrook was one of the last to be bypassed, but when this finally happened, several of the "mom and pop" businesses closed and franchise operations grew around the interchanges on I-40. Many others stayed open despite the incursion of the interstate.

The Plainsman Coffee Shop and Dining Room, Joe & Aggie's Cafe, the Cholla Restaurant, Gabriel's Pancake House, and the Hilltop Cafe—all on the old highway— provide a variety of dining choices for travelers who leave the interstate and drive through Holbrook. The Arizona Rancho became a youth hostel, but several independent motels remained in business on the old highway, including the Golden Inn, the Royal, the Sand & Sun, and the Western

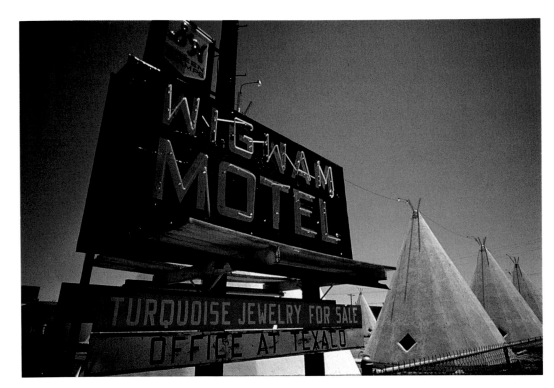

Wigwam Motel, Holbrook, Ariz.

Motel, with its big smiling cowboy sign.

One of the most memorable Route 66 landmarks in Holbrook is Wigwam Village, which first opened for business on June 1, 1950. A semicircle of fifteen concrete wigwams built on the shoulder of Hopi Drive, the motor court draws tourists anxious to sleep in a replica teepee. Chester E. Lewis built the village from blueprints supplied by the firm that had designed and built several wigwam villages across the country. As soon as it opened, Wigwam Village was a hit. Each wigwam has a full bath and air conditioner

and some have double beds. If travelers cannot stop for the night, they at least break out the camera and take a snapshot of their party in front of one of the big cement tents.

All of the wigwams were renovated in 1988, and the following year the Village reopened, complete with a small museum in tribute to old Route 66. A sign says SLEEP IN A WIGWAM and there are big hunks of petrified wood serving as natural decoration. Behind Wigwam Village, near the railroad tracks, sits an abandoned Salvation Army truck that often acts as a temporary home for folks passing through who cannot afford to stay in a wigwam. An old automobile sits in the weeds near the truck. Like so many of the derelict cars along the Mother Road it looks as if it could have been used by Okies trying to get to California. Between Holbrook and Winslow are severed links of the Mother Road, their pavement cracked and smothered with weeds and sand, reaching out a short distance from the interstate.

Just west of Holbrook on Interstate 40 is one of those throwbacks to the days of the Route 66 trading posts. This one is named for Geronimo and is surrounded by stucco teepees and big petrified logs. There are also pennants flapping from the nearby boulders. The place sells all varieties of minerals, including samples of fool's gold, geodes, Apache tears, and slices of petrified wood. There is also a wide sampling of good Indian jewelry and rugs and pottery ashtrays shaped like coiled rattlesnakes. Merle Haggard, the Okie crooner, is singing away on the radio and tourists from Kentucky, Indiana, and Pennsylvania paw through the postcards. In the parking lot is a pink four-door Edsel, another Route 66 veteran that slid off the endangered-species list into total extinction. A short distance down the interstate from the trading post sits the Cholla Power Plant, part of Arizona Public Service's remedy for keeping juice flowing into the large desert cities like Phoenix. Ominous twin stacks with blinking red lights tower above the complex. Power lines stretch toward the horizon from huge towers with legs resembling steel Kachina dolls marching across the landscape.

Close to the power plant is Joseph City, a railroad settlement founded by Mormons in

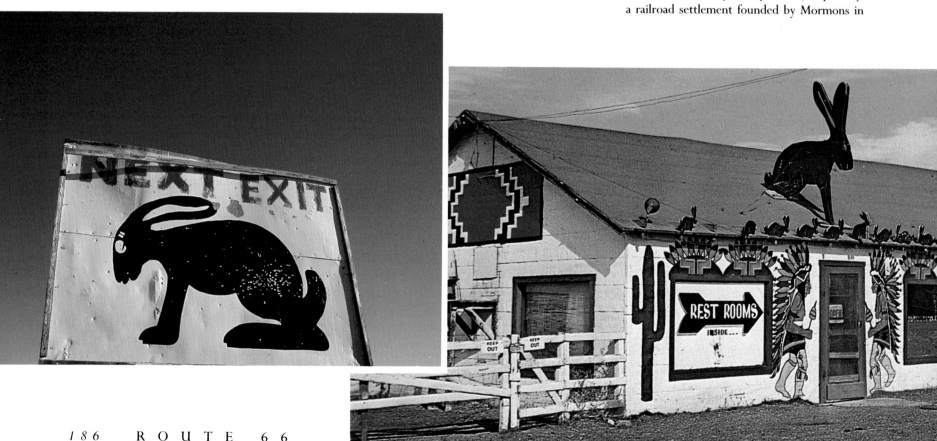

1876 and a Route 66 town of modest brick homes and small businesses. Joseph City has been bleached and tempered by the strong desert sun. Most of the residents make their living from jobs at the power plant. Highway commerce plays second fiddle to the gods of electricity. For every cafe and motel still in operation, two more are out of business. The windows at the Western Hat Cafe are boarded up and the boards are covered with political

posters. But the Cook Shack manages to get by and the blue trim on the Pacific Cafe is bright and fresh.

There is also the Jack Rabbit Trading Post, a cherished Route 66 establishment west of town that is going as strong as ever on a brief expanse of the old highway that became a frontage road for Interstate 40. The trading post was built after World War II on Route 66 across from the railroad tracks that parallel the Mother Road throughout the West. The familiar Jack Rabbit signs—yellow with red letters and black silhouettes of a crouched rabbit—are still highway fixtures. Phil Blansett owns the trading post, as did his father. "This place was started in 1949 by James H. Taylor and he leased it to my father in 1961," says Blansett, who started tending gas pumps and tying on bumper signs at the trading post when he was a kid. "My father finally bought it from Taylor in 1967 when I-40 came through and I bought it from my father in 1969 when he was ready to retire. Someday I plan to retire and then I'll sell the Jack Rabbit." The Jack Rabbit is open every day except Christmas, Thanksgiving, and New Year's Day, and their saying goes, "If you

Far left: Jack Rabbit Trading Post sign near Joseph City, Ariz.

Center: Jack Rabbit Trading Post vintage postcard, "If you haven't stopped at the Jack Rabbit you haven't been in the Southwest," Joseph City, Ariz.

Above: Jack Rabbit Trading Post, Joseph City, Ariz.

A Route 66 Portrait

Angel Delgadillo

Born: April 19, 1927
Occupation: Barber
Residence: Seligman, Arizona

"*I* was born in Seligman, Arizona, before the highway was even officially designated as Route 66 in this part of the country. I was born on the old highway, when it was still just a narrow

Right: Lorenzo Hubbell Co., Winslow, Ariz.

Below: A view from Meteor Crater, Ariz.

haven't stopped at the Jack Rabbit, you haven't been in the Southwest."

An unknown number of tourists have gulped down cups of Jack Rabbit's sweet cherry cider while they contemplated buying a set of cattle horns or the mounted head of a "Jackalope," a whimsical creature, half rabbit– half antelope, that is a popular image on tongue-in-cheek postcards. An old newspaper clipping tacked to the wall near a Jackalope head claims that the "strange specimen can imitate a human voice of a cowboy singing to

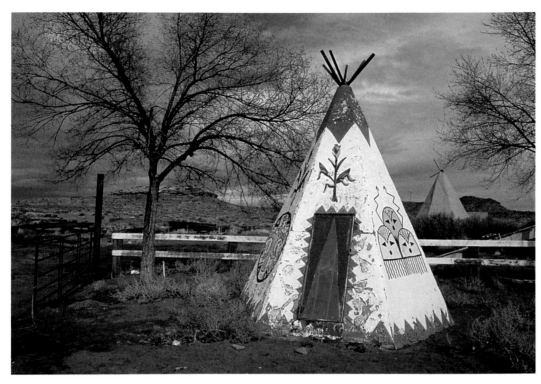

Geronimo Trading Post, west of Holbrook, Ariz., on Interstate 40.

his herds on dark nights." But, the article goes on to say, "Stories that they sometimes sing in chorus have been discounted."

No Jackalope voices, only the whining song of tires on the hot pavement can be heard heading west over Manilla Wash, Cottonwood Wash, and the Little Colorado River on the way into Winslow, an old railroad division terminal settled in the early 1880s and celebrated in the Eagles' song "Take It Easy." Yellow metal signs honor this stretch of the route as the old Beale Wagon Road, and there are also markers commemorating the trails used by Mormon immigrants who journeyed from Utah to Arizona in the 1870s.

Lorenzo Hubbell was one of Winslow's most famous early Indian traders, and his family carried on the name and the business for many years. Winslow was also known as the home of La Posada, a Fred Harvey hotel built in the style of a Spanish rancho from the past. Many cafes, trading posts, motor courts, and garages operated along the old highway in

dirt road carrying traffic east and west. My family's house was right on the edge of the road. In 1917, my father had come to this country from Mexico—the state of Jalisco—and my mother was from Aguascalientes.

"They ended up right here in Seligman. My father was a machinist with the Santa Fe railway, but in 1922 there was a big strike and he never went back to work for the railroad. Instead, he became a barber, and in 1924 he built his own pool hall and barbershop on what became known as Route 66. My mother died in the early 1970s and my dad died in 1978, just about the time that we got bypassed by the interstate highway. My folks raised nine kids—six boys and three girls, and I was the third from the bottom.

"During the Great Depression, times became tough and my dad's business was very poor, and we were just about ready to join the *Grapes of Wrath* people. Our house was boarded up and my dad and brothers got our Model-T Ford ready, and they built a trailer to haul all our things. I was just a little bitty guy and I was real scared about what was going to happen to us. Then my brothers Juan and Joe got jobs playing music and things suddenly got better. They started playing with bands and traveling up and down Route 66, and we didn't have to leave after all. My

Winslow. After the completion of Interstate 40, franchise restaurants began to compete for travelers' dollars, but on Route 66 through the heart of town are a few independent restaurants such as Bud and Irene's, the Two Stars Cafe, and Joe's Cafe.

The highway passes the Tonto Drive-in Theatre as it leaves Winslow and proceeds westward to the site of an old railroad siding called Moqui. It then winds its way past Leupp Corner and the road leading to Meteor Crater, 20 miles west of Winslow and 45 miles east of Flagstaff. Billed as "this planet's most penetrating natural attraction," the giant crater was created 22,000 years ago by a nickel-iron meteor. The hole runs 570 feet deep, 3 miles in circumference, and nearly a mile from rim to rim. When Jack Rittenhouse listed the natural attraction in his 1946 guidebook for Route 66, tourists were able to pull off the highway and see the crater for a nominal charge. Nothing has changed except the price of admission. It has steadily increased and become as steep as the stairs leading from the parking lot to the crater entrance. Tourists who do not wish to pay the entry fee may soak up the sunshine in a stark area called Astronaut Park, dedicated to those who lost their lives in various space accidents. A plaque framed with stainless steel, surrounded by metal picnic tables and some scrub trees and cacti, bears a quote from Ronald Reagan: "The Future Doesn't Belong to the Fainthearted, It Belongs to the Brave!"

Less than 10 miles west of the road leading to Meteor Crater—near the halfway mark between Winslow and Flagstaff—appear the ruins of Two Guns. Here traces of the Mother Road can be seen disappearing into the ranchlands. A nearby service station and camping ground for recreational vehicles perpetuates the name of Two Guns, and the yellow stripe is still visible on the piece of old highway that runs near an unused bridge. There are also deserted gas pumps, wrecked cars, and the remains of a zoo where caged mountain lions and other wild animals were displayed.

Pot shards recovered from the rocky canyons around Two Guns place Indian tribes in this area as early as A.D. 1050 to 1300. These early civilizations were drawn to the fertile farming land of the plateau caused by the disintegration of the volcanic fields of lava and ashes that spewed out of the San Francisco Mountains to the west. Just a short distance west of Two Guns is Diablo Canyon, a great gash in the desert plain several hundred feet wide and more than a hundred feet deep. Early travelers, including settlers in covered wagons, found this canyon difficult to cross.

In 1874, when the route was primarily a military road, a cavalry scouting troop rode through a nearby pass and came upon a wagon train of immigrants headed for Prescott. The pioneer families had just been massacred by hostile Indians. The livestock had been run off, the wagons and their contents were in flames, and the corpses of murdered men, women, and children had been thrown into the fires. The troopers raked the charred bones from the ashes and buried them in a common grave near the road.

father got some odd jobs too and my family stayed right here and we stuck it out.

"We lived on the edge of the old highway going right through the town and when we were kids, we'd play in the yard and wait for the traffic to pass. I can still see the shadows of the big trucks and the automobiles coming by, and those shadows would dance on the walls of our house. Us kids would try to jump on those shadows and ride away with them down the road. That was our game—that was how we traveled. We became shadow chasers.

"As we grew up, we saw more of those people coming from the Dust Bowl states. We'd see people inside the old vehicles with tools and spare tires and water bags and washtubs and chickens and mattresses passing right by our house. It seemed every car had a bunch of children, and there was always a grandpa and grandma, too. They were so drab and tired and to us they were funny-looking and we were kids and sometimes kids can be cruel. We'd laugh at them and point our fingers. We forgot that we almost had to join those people and go west.

"Some of those families broke down in Texas or Gallup or out here in Arizona and they didn't go any farther. Some of them set up housekeeping and got jobs and worked until they had the

Four years later, in 1878, Navajo warriors, stymied by marauding Apaches who stole ponies, raided hogans, and carried off Navajo women as slaves, finally figured out how the Apaches escaped in the desert wastelands. A Navajo scout crawling through the tall grass and sagebrush near Diablo Canyon discovered a deep crack in the earth that gave way to an underground cavern. After finding the Apache hideaway, a band of Navajos blocked all possible means of escape from the cave, gathered dried sagebrush and wood, built a fire, and pushed the flaming mass into the cave opening. The passageway filled with smoke and flames and when the fire burned down, more fuel was added. With what little water they had, the Apaches tried to extinguish the fire. When the water was gone, they cut their ponies' throats and threw the blood on the flames. They also tried to seal off the entrance with rocks and the quarters of the dead ponies.

Negotiations broke down when the Navajos' demand went unheeded that some of their captive women be set free. The Navajos realized the women had already been killed, and in a wild rage they poured gunfire into the cave and built up the fires once more. Navajo scouts listening on the flat stone surface above the cave opening reported that only a few of their enemy were able to sing their final death song. Finally the chanting subsided and only smoke drifted from the cave. The next afternoon, after the great stones had cooled off, the Navajos entered the cave and found the charred bodies of the Apaches twisted into grotesque shapes near the smoldering ponies. After that the hidden cavern came to be known as Apache Cave, or the Apache Death Cave.

For many years, old-timers in the area told another bizarre story about Two Guns. This episode under discussion took place in 1905, and actually started at the Wigwam Saloon on Second Street in Winslow. A pair of young cowboys, John Shaw and Bill Smith, had just strolled into the saloon for a quick drink when they spotted a stack of six hundred shiny silver dollars on a dice table run by Frank Ketchum. The two cowpokes wasted no time. They pulled their guns and stuffed as much money as possible into their pockets and hats before they backed out of the saloon and made their escape.

Sheriff's deputies scoured the countryside looking for the two thieves, and some of the posse rode a train as far as Flagstaff to see if the culprits were hiding there. That evening the lawmen received a tip that Shaw and Smith had been seen hiding near the Diablo Canyon Station. When the deputies arrived, they found the hapless pair inside a warehouse. A gunfight erupted. More than twenty shots were fired. When the smoke cleared, Smith lay wounded and Shaw was sprawled out dead. They buried Shaw that very night not far from Apache Cave and the deep canyon. Then they returned to Winslow and put Smith under a doctor's care at the local hospital.

Meanwhile, a bunch of cowboys had gathered over at the Wigwam Saloon once word got around about the big shootout at Canyon Diablo. One cowboy remembered that Smith and Shaw had been to the saloon earlier in the day and had put down their money for drinks but never even got a sip before they fled the scene with the silver dollars. "Was Shaw given that snort before they planted him?" the cowboy asked his compadres. When he was told that lawmen do not usually go around giving drinks to dead men, the cowboy became concerned. "That fella has a drink

Twin Arrows, Ariz.

comin' to him and he should get what he paid for. We should go to Diablo Canyon and give him one!" The other cowpokes were drunk enough to see the merit of the suggestion and within minutes about twenty inebriated cowhands hopped the freight train headed west. They arrived at the site of Two Guns with a wide assortment of liquor bottles. After borrowing a few shovels, they unearthed Shaw's bullet-riddled body, held it upright, and just as the sun started its slow rise over the horizon, they poured a straight shot of whiskey between his lifeless lips. There was just enough light for someone to snap a photograph of the scene, and for many years a picture of Shaw taking his final drink with the boys was proudly displayed in the Wigwam Saloon.

Passing freight wagons, stagecoaches, and trains were common sights around Two Guns where saloons, gambling dens (called poker flats), whorehouses, and dance pavilions operated on a stretch known as "Hell Street." Some of the more popular drinking establishments were the Colorado Saloon, Texas Saloon, The Last Drink, The Road to Ruin, Bughouse Joe's, and Name Your Pizen. A buxom madam named B. S. Mary ran one of the best houses of ill repute. There were tales of whorehouse fights complete with hair pulling, chair smashing, and, of course, blazing guns. In its wild days, Two Guns would never have been recommended by Duncan Hines nor would it have made an automobile club endorsement list. By the time the old highway was established, Two Guns had settled into a tamer shadow of its former self, a place more

suited to catering to tourists and truckers than mule skinners and cowboys.

During the decades when Route 66 was filled with traffic, people visited Two Guns and some even found the cave tucked away among the brownish-red rocks in the side canyon leading to Diablo Canyon. The unmarked cowboy's grave went unnoticed. Travelers can catch a glimpse of the hidden cave directly behind the wrecked stone buildings and car graveyard that was Two Guns. Few tourists realize that so much violence has taken place at this once busy highway refuge. The ghosts of Apache and Navajo warriors, slain pioneers who never reached their destinations, a foolish young cowboy named John Shaw, and a gaggle of brightly painted whores wait for their next reincarnation at Two Guns and Diablo Canyon.

On the highway again, proceeding west, the route crosses Babbitt Tank Wash and Padre Canyon, a place almost identical in looks to Diablo Canyon, before reaching Twin Arrows, a trading post and truck stop 20 miles east of Flagstaff on I-40. Twin Arrows has the look and feel of the old wayside businesses along the highway. Inside the small eight-stool diner, fry cooks serve up good road grub—steak and eggs and hash browns—despite a joke menu that talks about buzzard eggs, fried pack-rat tail, sagebrush coffee, roasted jack-rabbit ears, meteor crater stew, braised rattlesnake hips,

money to go on or else go back to where they came from. Some stayed right here. My cousins became *Grapes of Wrath* people and they went to California. There were thirteen of them, and as they traveled across the land the police gave them a hard time and made them keep moving. The family had to sleep in cemeteries and under bridges and in camps. But those kids grew up and they ended up building half the freeways in Southern California. The Dust Bowlers made something from their lives. They became architects, engineers, carpenters, plumbers, doctors, and teachers.

"And when the Second World War was going, I remember all the convoys on the old highway. There were cannons and jeeps, and truck after truck. Troops rode the trains, too, and they'd stop here and the soldiers would get off. They'd be in their green uniforms and they'd march on the old highway to stretch their legs and get some fresh air. After the war, the tourists came. We thought they'd never quit coming. The restaurants hummed with business, and the motels were busy. So was the pool hall and the drugstore and the little diner next to the theater. There was so much excitement. There were lots of railroaders back then, too. They may have had families someplace else, but those men lived a lot of their lives right

sautéed centipede legs, prickly-pear pie, and lizard tongue pudding.

Soon after passing Twin Arrows, the desert gives way to pine forests as the pavement starts to climb into the Coconino National Forest. Winona, one of the Arizona place names immortalized in Bobby Troup's song about Route 66, is not easily remembered by too many folks. Located only 14 miles east of Flagstaff, the town was first named Walnut but was changed to Winona in 1886. During the decades when the Mother Road was the only path through this mountainous region, the Winona Trading Post sold plenty of groceries and gasoline. There were also cabins and a cafe, although many travelers preferred camping in the pines near Flagstaff. The Camp Townsend–Winona Road was the original path of U.S. 66 just to the east of Flagstaff—the largest trading center of the northern portion of the state.

Picturesque Flagstaff, the unofficial capital of northern Arizona, is located in a land of deep canyons, roaring streams, endless vistas, snowcapped peaks, and dense pine forests. Flagstaff is the seat of gigantic Coconino County—twice the size of Massachusetts—and the base for tourists interested in seeing the sights. The city is the hub for several points of interest, including the Museum of Northern Arizona, founded in 1928; the Grand Canyon, nature's most extraordinary masterpiece just to the north; the Arizona Snow Bowl, in the nearby San Francisco Mountains; Sunset Crater, an extinct volcano; and Lowell Observatory, where astronomers discovered the planet Pluto in 1930.

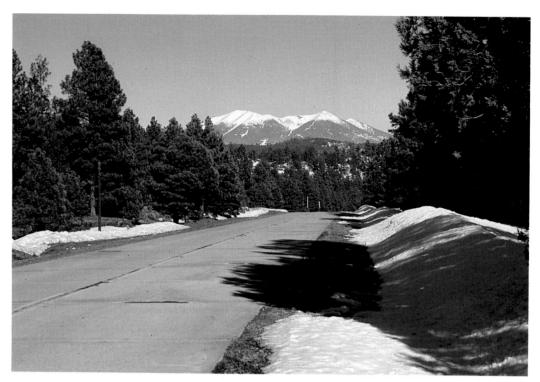

West of San Francisco Peaks near Flagstaff, Ariz.

Settled in 1876, Flagstaff had several names. The one that finally stuck resulted because of a tall pine tree stripped of its branches which was used as a flagpole and a trail marker for wagon trains bound for California. Eventually that trail became U.S. Route 66.

Interstate 40 has replaced the original old highway route, but there are a few tangible remnants of Beale's Road, the old National Highway, and the Mother Road. The course of Route 66 is called Santa Fe Avenue through Flagstaff, and for years scores of motor courts

and cafes had a captive audience thanks to the swarms of vistors. In early July when Flagstaff's annual All-Indian Pow Wow, highlighted by parades, rodeos, and tribal ceremonial dances, got underway, the town was filled with cowboys, Indians, and tourists. Choices of places to find food, drink, souvenirs, or a bed were limitless—Hyatt Chalet Motel with "Refrigerated Air Conditioning," Western Hills Motor Hotel and Restaurant, Twilite Motel, Sage Motel, Nor Star Motel, 66 Motel, Hotel Monte Vista with Ma Zip's Pancake House, The Westerner

("Steam Heated"), Joe's Place serving "Good and Bad Liquor," Black Cat Cafe, which was advertised as "A Good Place to Eat," the Skyline Motel ("In the Pines"), the Grand Canyon Cafe featuring Chinese and American food, Wigwam Curios, Kachina Cafe ("Good Meals and Courteous Service"), the Saga Motel, the Timberline Motel, and the Lumber Jack Cafe, offering "Heavenly Fried Chicken" and "Delicious Pancakes."

Many of these places, and scores of other motels and restuarants on both sides of the highway in Flagstaff, outlasted the coming of the Interstate. In the downtown district along Santa Fe Avenue, across from the brick railroad station, are old highway haunts such as the Grand Canyon Cafe and the Hong Kong Cafe, where silent Indians feast on long, crisp French fries and steak. There are also the trendier vegetarian eateries and markets, which feature natural foods, herbal teas, and organic juices for the skiers and students from the campus of Northern Arizona University. The sidestreets of town support therapeutic massage, Rolfing salons, and New Age bookstores. Shops sell crystals, incense, and Birkenstock sandals, and distribute literature about Gestalt counseling and midwifery.

"Flagstaff is a combination of Taos and Aspen," says a ruddy-faced university student at the Sundance Bakery on San Francisco Street, just a block off the Mother Road. "It's also like Santa Fe but not as artsy. You can buy yogurt or espresso on one corner and then cross the street and get a sack of piñon nuts and go in an old saddle shop and haggle over a Pendleton blanket or a leather rifle scabbard."

Old downtown hotels, including the Weatherford and the Monte Vista, are open and active. So is El Charro Cafe where patrons are treated to live mariachi music while they dine on "authentic Mexican food." Down at the corner of San Francisco Street and Santa Fe Avenue, a watering hole called Joe's Place is still an honest bar. Budweiser and Coors signs glow in the windows and the walls are decorated with the heads of deer, elk, and antelope. Two pool tables are usually busy day and night, and clever saloon signs offer such advice as BE GOOD OR BE GONE, and NEED MONEY? TRY WORKING.

After leaving Flagstaff the old highway moves through more pines in the Kaibab National Forest. The road then passes near a settlement named Parks, because of its location near a number of open areas which the locals referred to as "parks," and an old sawmill and lumbering center on the Santa Fe railroad tracks called Bellemont. Ahead is

"Don't Forget Winona."

here. They slept here and took meals here and they bought ice cream and whiskey and tobacco and chewing gum and got their hair cut here. They came to our kids' baseball games. They were our friends. When the railroad decided not to use Seligman as an overnight stop anymore, we lost hundreds of those railroaders. That hurt. It also hurt when the government decided to bypass us and the other Route 66 towns that depended on the traffic for their livelihoods. But even so, the old road is still alive. It's as strong and important as before. In some ways, it may even be stronger. There's been a revival of interest and people are as excited as ever about Route 66. People say they're tired of driving the interstates, and they want to get off the high-speed roads and see something else. Young people whose parents and grandparents drove Route 66 want to experience the highway. It's a piece of history. The old road has new life."

Williams, the town that shares its name with Bill Williams Mountain, elevation 9,264 feet. Both were named after a colorful trapper and scout, who was generally credited with being the first white American to explore the region in the 1830s.

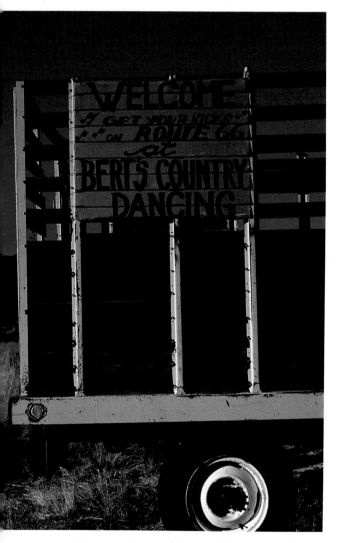

Sign on truck, two miles west of Valentine, Ariz.

Bill Williams, born in 1787 in North Carolina, lived at different times among Osage and Ute Indians. Early in his life, he had been a Baptist circuit rider in Missouri. Williams first visited the site of the town that bears his name as early as 1826. He was said to have spent the winter of 1832–33 in the area and was ambushed and killed by Indians in 1849. In 1954, a group of Williams citizens formed the Bill Williams Mountain Men organization in order "to perpetuate the lore, memory, and romance of the mountain men of old"—and in particular old Bill Williams. For years perfectly sane businessmen have grown beards, dressed up in old buckskins, and ridden horseback to Phoenix, more than 150 trail miles to the south.

Surrounded by the Ponderosa pine forests of the Coconino Plateau, Williams developed into an important railroad, lumbering, and livestock town. Less than 60 miles from the Grand Canyon's south rim, Williams also became known as the "Gateway to the Grand Canyon," a title that was even registered as the town's trademark. South of town a paved road leads to good trout fishing and camping grounds in the Kaibab National Forest. Because of its location, Williams became dependent on the tourists traveling back and forth on Route 66, and the 1½-mile stretch of the Mother Road through the heart of the small mountain town was thick with motels, restaurants, curio shops, and gas stations.

Then during the 1980s, the town was jolted by the coming of Interstate 40 which was going to bypass Williams. The small

business owners realized that the summertime peak of fifteen thousand vehicles that drove down their main street every day would soon diminish. Several businesses closed in anticipation of the bypass. Tales of gloom made the rounds of the cafes and coffee shops for a time, and the town was successful in a legal action that delayed the opening of a final stretch of Interstate 40. In the meantime, many people left town, including several of the Bill Williams Mountain Men.

On October 13, 1984, the inevitable happened. The nearby 6-mile stretch of Interstate 40 was officially opened. Williams had the distinction of being the last Route 66 town to be bypassed. It had taken almost two decades, but the interstates had finally managed to replace the old highway from Chicago all the way to Santa Monica. There was a parade and reporters came from across the country to cover the event. Bobby Troup made an appearance and sang his song about the Mother Road. Politicians gushed speeches and, like a scene from *The Music Man,* there were big crowds on Bill Williams Avenue, eating, drinking, and trying their best to grab the moment. Many of them wanted to freeze time. But that wasn't to be. The clocks never stopped or even slowed down—just the traffic count and the stream of travelers who paused in Williams for a hot meal or a cold drink. A short time after Williams was bypassed, officials from the American Association of

State Highways and Transportation gathered and voted to decertify U.S. Route 66. In their bureaucratic wisdom, they honestly believed this final action would close the book on the Mother Road. It didn't. Only another chapter —albeit a bitter one—was concluded.

"The road is like Elvis Presley," one Route 66 devotee told reporters. "It just won't die." He was right.

Despite the bureaucrats' best efforts to eradicate the old road, this wonderfully preserved stretch of the highway through western Arizona acts as a tribute to Route 66. In fact, it's one of the best preserved fragments of the Mother Road anywhere. It reaches from Seligman on through Peach Springs, Truxton, Crozier Canyon, Valentine, Hackberry, Walapai, Kingman, Oatman, and Topock. This original 156-mile stretch of Route 66 between Seligman and Topock is especially important because of its scenic and historic value. Thanks to the Historic Route 66 Association of Arizona, memorial signs were erected in the late 1980s in honor of the old road.

Seligman, a railroad town founded in 1886, is a true bastion for Route 66, due mainly to the efforts of a quiet barber named Angel Delgadillo and his family and friends. Named after Jesse Seligman of Seligman Brothers, New York bankers connected with the old Atlantic and Pacific Railroad, the town of Seligman guards the eastern end of the historic section of the highway that continues through to Oatman and Topock near the Colorado River.

Slipping into Seligman at nightfall,

visitors pass the deserted Whiting Brothers service station and ferret out rooms at the Navajo, the Aztec, or one of the other motels. More than likely, they grab supper at the Copper Cart, where breakfast is served anytime and trucks may park in the rear. A grim-faced lady, with a beehive hairdo tinted blue and the disposition of a mother superior, puffs on a cigarette, eyeballs the clientele, and counts the day's receipts at the cash register. The skinny dishwasher in a dirty white apron and Buddy Holly glasses takes a break at the counter and waitresses tend to customers weary from a day spent on the road. The

menu warns, "Not Responsible for Any Well Done Steak," and the aroma of sauerkraut, chili, and fried fish permeates the dining room. Plates filled to the brim with either pork chops, ground beef smothered in onions, or pork roast awash in brown gravy, with side dishes of mashed potatoes, string beans, and Jell-O revive every customer who walks through the door. Rhubarb pie à la mode and a big mug of coffee strong enough to bring Bill Williams back to life conclude the feast.

Behind the counter, individual serving boxes of cereal stand in neat pyramids. At the

Downtown neon, Flagstaff, Ariz.

stool next to the dishwasher sits an old man content with his cheeseburger and the news he finds in the two-day-old edition of the *Arizona Republic*. Between handling customers' orders, the waitresses manage to smear on more lipstick, enjoy a smoke, and even put in a little time on a crossword puzzle.

Just a block off the old route on Floyd Street waits a family feline, its eyes glowing like coals and its dusty fur smelling of juniper smoke. It crouches on the porch but disappears in the shadows when strangers show up and the front light comes on. This is the residence of Angel Delgadillo, the town barber, one of the founders of the Historic Route 66 Association of Arizona, one of the most commited Route 66 supporters in the United States. "I graduated from high school in Seligman in 1947 and immediately went to barber college in Pasadena, California," says Angel. "I passed the barber board in Arizona and worked in Avondale and served my apprenticeship in Williams, and then I came back here and opened my own place on May 22, 1950, in my dad's old barber shop right on Route 66."

Angel and his wife, Vilma, a Mexican native, who was working as a maid on a ranch outside of town when she met her future husband, raised four children and nurtured a love for the highway that brought visitors and news of the world outside of Seligman to their kitchen table. "There was so much activity here," says Angel.

Grand Canyon Caverns, east of Peach Springs, Ariz.

"Back in the early years, the town had a big Harvey House and motor courts galore and we accommodated many, many people in this little town. We met all sorts of people —poor folks, soldiers, truckers, railroaders, families on vacation. Every one of them had stories to tell us and we all shared our lives together while they were here.

"When we got bypassed by the interstate in 1978 business shriveled up some and we struggled but the strong ones survived and we waited for the world to rediscover us and remember that Route 66 wasn't all destroyed. We formed our association. We had an early meeting at the Copper Cart. Folks from Kingman and Truxton and Oatman and the other good Route 66 towns on this stretch of the old highway got involved and we organized. Pretty soon we saw the results—many people got off the interstate and came back to our towns and to the real highway. They're still coming. I believe they always will."

In the morning, after a good night's sleep, travelers can get a trim or a shave or even more tonic for their souls down at Angel's barber shop on the Mother Road. Inside the tiny shop the scissors and combs are neatly arranged inside cabinets and there are rows of hair oils and dressings, Osage Rub to cool scalps, and tins of talcum powder. Angel, always smiling, deftly strokes his straight razor back and forth on a leather strop hanging from a barber chair with porcelain arm rests. His father bought the chair in 1929 for $196.50 and had it shipped from St. Louis.

In a back room sunlight seeps through the curtains, revealing two pool tables, a snooker table, and a Wurlitzer jukebox. It is a fine barber shop and Jack Cutberth, the barber from Clinton, Oklahoma, who became known as "Mr. 66," would have been proud to cut hair there and swap stories about the old highway with Señor Delgadillo. Cards from journalists and visitors from around the world adorn Angel's walls and the big mirror, and there are old newspaper clippings about Angel's appearances on network television shows in behalf of preserving Route 66 and about the Delgadillo family band.

"My brothers and I and our sisters played music at all the Route 66 places in Arizona," says Angel. "We played dance music in Flagstaff, Prescott, Winslow, Kingman, and at the Grand Canyon. We liked to play the standards—'Stardust,' 'I'll See You in My Dreams'—and we also turned out some of the smoothest Latin and Mexican music anyone ever heard. I can still get high just from those memories. But it's still like that here today.

On the road through this country is the way America was before TV and fast cars and jet planes. People still have time to sit and visit. People still care."

Next door to Angel's barbershop is a small grocery store owned by Joe, one of the other Delgadillo brothers. On the next corner is the Snow Cap, a drive-in restaurant operated by Angel's big brother, Juan. The Snow Cap serves standard highway food, but with flare and ample doses of Juan's humor for seasoning. For instance, menu choices include "Hamburgers Without Ham," "Cheeseburgers

Top: Delgadillo's Pool Hall, 1924, Seligman, Ariz.

Bottom: The **Snow** Cap, "dead chicken and all the trimmings," Seligman, Ariz.

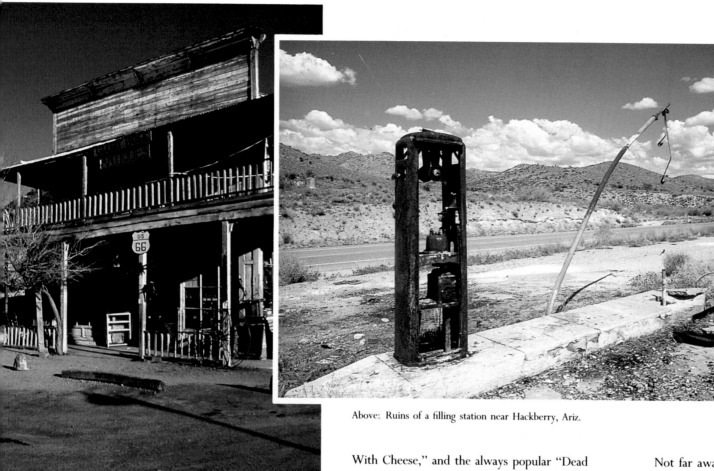

Above: Main Street, Oatman, Ariz.

Above: Ruins of a filling station near Hackberry, Ariz.

With Cheese," and the always popular "Dead Chicken." Sometimes Juan comes outside to show off his white 1936 Chevy with the roof sliced off and decorated with plastic flowers and a Christmas tree mounted in the back. "I treat people the way I want to be treated," smiles Juan. "I like to have as much fun as possible." On the restroom door is a sign that says, "Dishwashing, Laundering, Bathing, and Sleeping in Restrooms Prohibited. Please Conserve Water."

Not far away, close to the building that was once a Harvey House and next to the old Delgadillo family home where Angel and Juan and the others chased shadows on the walls, an old man moves through the weeds. Each day he comes to feed cats descended from the pets of the railroaders who got orders to move out of Seligman and left their cats behind. Later the old man will go to Angel's and get a haircut.

Seligman sets the stage for the rest of

Ray Barker, owner, Frontier Cafe, Truxton, Ariz.

the Mother Road through Arizona. Instead of taking the interstate, which cuts straight across the country, travelers interested in bringing home memories head down the old highway marked by colorful memorial signs. Big sunflowers grow at the base of telegraph poles studded with green glass insulators, flanking the railroad tracks. Freight and passenger trains moving east and west on the nearby tracks seem to play hide and seek with the vehicles on the old highway as the pavement winds through the landscape and enters the Hualapai Indian Reservation. The path gently cuts through sagebrush and over rangeland covered with the dens of prairie dogs, past the remains of a tourist stop called Hyde Park, and then down a grade that allows travelers to catch a glimpse of the lower end

of the Grand Canyon in the far distance to the north. Many tourists pull off the old highway to stop at Grand Canyon Caverns, sometimes called Sipapu Caverns. For a fee, guides take visitors in elevators twenty-one stories underground to see huge rooms where some locals claim Indians used to hide. The ancient cavern was rediscovered in 1927 by Walter Peck, a woodcutter, who stumbled and almost fell into the deep funnel-shaped hole on his way to a poker game.

Fourteen miles to the west of the caverns lies Peach Springs, in the extreme southern part of the Hualapai Reservation and named by early explorers for the peach trees that managed to grow next to a well-used watering hole. Even before 1935, when Route 66 was just a dirt road through this area, Peach Springs supported several cafes, auto lodges, and garages. The appearance of Interstate 40—25 miles to the south—did not help local business, but Peach Springs hung on.

Continuing westward, the old highway comes upon Truxton, a relatively new community that clings to the past. Named for a nearby canyon and spring, this area was visited in 1857 by Lieutenant Edward Beale and his camel caravan. Beale probably came up with the name to honor his mother, Emily Truxton Beale, and his grandfather, Commodore Thomas Truxton. In a journal entry for April 26, 1858, Beale noted, "At Truxton Springs, the Indians stole a mule from us." The spring is located 15 miles south of the Music Mountains and in the early 1870s served as a garrison site for C Troop, Third

A Route 66 Portrait

Billie Jo Moore

Born: December 27, 1924
Occupation: Proprietor, Oatman Hotel
Residence: Oatman, Arizona

"*I* was born in Comanche, Oklahoma. My dad worked in the oil fields until he lost one of his legs and couldn't work anymore. I had just graduated from high school and there wasn't anything for me or my three younger brothers, so in 1943, we all moved to California to get jobs. I eventually got married to a man named Luther Trammel, and we had

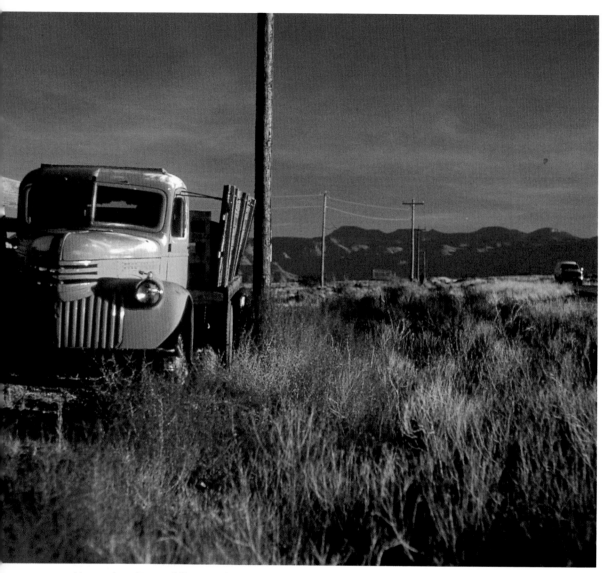

Marooned truck, east of Kingman, Ariz.

U.S. Cavalry. The town of Truxton was established in 1951 by D. J. Dilts, anxious to take advantage of a proposed railhead leading to the Grand Canyon which never materialized. Dilts built a Route 66 service station and restaurant on this site.

When travelers pause at the Frontier Cafe in Truxton, they are transported back to the time when Route 66 traffic was so heavy there were a dozen roadside businesses booming in the little town. "We had people coming here twenty-four hours a day when we first came to Truxton and took over this cafe in 1957," says owner Ray Barker. An Oklahoma native, Barker served a hitch in the marines, did a little farming, and was an iron worker for a while before he and his wife, Mildred, moved to Arizona. They ran a garage at Peach Springs for a few years and then moved to Truxton and bought the cafe and adjoining motel. "The traffic may have slowed down, but things really haven't changed much around here. In fact, our population has actually gained because of folks who came here to retire."

Ray, Mildred, and their daughter, Sue, keep the Frontier Cafe going by turning out some of the finest meals on the highway. From steaks and veal cutlets to burgers and home fries, the food at the Frontier lives up to its reputation. Hunks of shrapnel, from 500-pound bombs exploded by air force planes at a nearby practice range, rest on the mantel over a sweet-smelling juniper fire. Photos of mountain lions and elk are tacked to the walls. Ray's mother and stepfather, Vera and Alvin Beyers, live in a mobile home behind the cafe, and on winter mornings the old man pokes in the cafe fire and entertains guests with tales of the way life used to be.

"I was born in Tahlequah in the Cherokee Nation, in 1907, before Oklahoma became a state," says Alvin Beyers.

"I worked as a logger and in the oil fields and then I came out west in the 1930s to help build the big dams here in Arizona. We came out in a 'thirty-three Chevrolet. My brother and I saw the advantage of this part of the country and this highway. We got two of the best wreckers money could buy. Later I bought a liquor business here in Truxton and the highway department folks accused me of making people drunk so they'd have accidents and have to use my wrecker service.

"That wasn't the case. I was making a living. I'll never forget the time a car turned over in a ditch on the other side of Peach Springs and inside was a lady and two teenagers—a boy and girl. That boy was split right through his face and blood was running everywhere, but I knew he was okay because he was hollerin' so much. I kicked out the windshield and we pulled out the mother and her girl. There was blood all over and the woman knew she was ruined, but I told her she'd be all right. I pulled off the mirror and held it up and said, 'Look honey, see there, you're okay. There ain't nothin' wrong with you.' Then she felt better. She got up and walked off. I got tired of those wrecks. When the interstate came along and traffic slowed down, a

gentleman stopped and asked what I was going to do and I said stand in the middle of the highway and shout 'Glory' at the top of my lungs."

Ray gently interrupts the old man to toss another log on the fire. "Now we have more time for relaxation around here," says Ray. "There's time to sit down and visit with people who stop." On the western edge of town a sign says "You Are Now Leaving Truxton. Thank You, Please Come Again." If travelers are smart, they will do just that.

Continuing on, the old highway winds through Crozier Canyon, named for an early cattle raiser, and dips past Valentine, named after a former Indian commissioner, not the romantic holiday. In Valentine sits a two-story brick Indian school that's all boarded up. The last stretch of Route 66 to be paved in Arizona was completed near here in 1937.

On the road, west of Oatman, Ariz.

two kids and moved up into the high Sierras where we ran a little restaurant for about fifteen years. Then we talked to friends who were in business near here on the Colorado River, and we came out in 1971 and operated a dinner house for almost ten years just outside of Needles on the Arizona side of the border. When my husband became ill, we sold out and moved to Oatman and bought this hotel. My husband died, and several years later I married Harry Moore. We maintain and run the hotel, the bar, and restaurant.

"The Oatman Hotel's an interesting place. It opened in 1924, and it's built from big adobe blocks. These walls are very thick. Originally there were twenty-six guest rooms and the lobby, but over the years different owners converted rooms into the bar and then a kitchen was added. Now we don't rent any of the rooms. Upstairs is a museum. But right until the early fifties, when this town was still on the older version of Route 66, this was a good stopover for travelers. The building went into the National Register in 1983.

"There's history all over this town and these mountains. Down at Goldroad there were service stations and tow trucks. People would hire local men just to drive or tow their cars up over the steep pass and down the other side. This road was very frightening for many

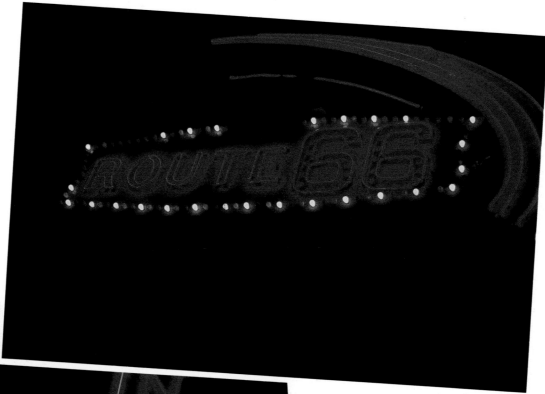

Right: Andy Devine Boulevard, Kingman, Ariz.

Below: Broken neon, Kingman, Ariz.

Only a few miles later the old highway passes by Hackberry, on the east side of the Peacock Mountains, at one time a booming silver mining town and a shipping point for ranchers. Soon the road leaves Crozier Canyon and becomes what was once called the "longest continuous curve on a U.S. highway." The road winds out into a great plain and goes by dirt ranch roads, nut orchards, housing developments, a golf course carved out of the high desert, and a discarded truck that has TOPOCK OR BUST painted on the door. The highway moves beneath more power lines

Twilight at Oatman, Ariz.

hanging from the steel Kachina doll towers. After a sudden spring rain the long drooping cables look like silver spider webs sparkling with dew. By now the Mother Road is perfect for sprinters. The two lanes run straight as a yardstick all the way into Kingman.

ROUTE
US
66

An important mining, business, and tourist center, Kingman was established in 1883 and named after Lewis Kingman, locating engineer for the Santa Fe railroad. In Kingman the old highway goes by the name Andy Devine Boulevard, after the jolly cowboy film star who was born in Flagstaff but grew up in

Kingman where his father once managed the historic Beale Hotel. Named after the adventurous naval officer who camped near Kingman, the Beale Hotel has hosted many Route 66 tourists and notables during the years, including Greta Garbo, and Charles and Anne Morrow Lindbergh, who were greeted by a cheering crowd of more than fifteen hundred on July 8, 1928, when they stopped in Kingman to inaugurate the new forty-eight-hour air mail service between Los Angeles and New York.

Kingman will always be a staunch Route 66 town. There are many motels, cafes, and service stations that reflect the sense of pride and individuality that has forever been a trademark of business establishments on the

folks. It could get boiling hot around here, too. I suppose no place on earth gets as hot as it can get down on that river. It must have been something for the people from back East, or the Dust Bowl refugees who had come all this way looking for comfort. Oatman once had a population of eight thousand. Now we have about a hundred and fifty people living here year-round and then as soon as the wind starts howling up north we get our share of 'snowbirds.'

"Back in the old days, Oatman was quite a gold mining camp and all the supplies were brought in by freight wagons and burro teams, and they used burros in the mines. When the mines closed and the prospectors and miners left, the burros stayed behind and adapted to the desert. Now they're all over these mountains. We have a town herd in Oatman. They wander through the streets, turning over garbage cans and messing in people's yards. Tourists like to see the burros and the shops sell bags of alfalfa pellets to folks who enjoy feeding the burros on the streets. When the sun goes down and the tourists leave, so do the burros. They wander off into the hills and go to their watering holes.

"People also come here and ask if it's true that there are ghosts in the hotel. I haven't seen one yet. But I have heard footsteps in the hallways, and

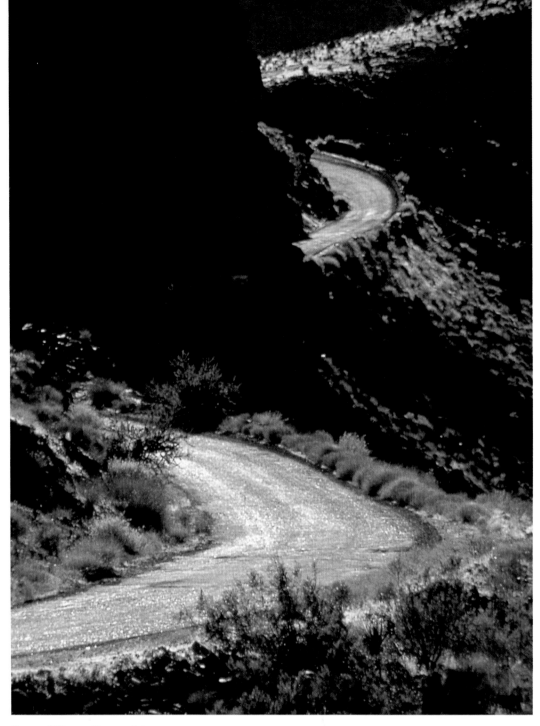

Oatman Hill, near Oatman, Ariz.

old highway. "Once you get Route 66 into your blood and learn some of the history and meet the people who remain so enthused about the road, the more you want to get involved," says Jerry Richard, another primary mover and shaker behind the Historic Route 66 Association of Arizona. "It's truly amazing the support and interest we've received from all over the country and even from abroad."

Richard races back and forth in a bright red 1970 Corvette with Route 66 license plates. He shuttles between the busy Association offices headquartered in an old Packard dealership on Andy Devine Boulevard and the ninety-eight-room Quality Inn he owns and manages a few blocks away. Richard completely redecorated the spacious restaurant and lounge at the big motor hotel and filled it with signs, photographs, and assorted memorabilia from the Mother Road. It is called the Route 66 Distillery and some of the menu items include a line of "Main Street U.S.A. Burgers," such as the Okie Burger, Joads Burger, Bobby Troup Burger, and Grapes of Wrath Burger. "People get a real kick out of coming here," says Richard. "They'll stop and have a drink or a bite to eat and look around. There's so much nostalgia tied to the highway. It was this country's most popular road and was known worldwide, and as far as we're concerned it always will be."

Included in the Distillery decor are canvas water bags, highway shields, hub caps, and neon lights. There is also a copy of the marriage license of Clark Gable and Carole Lombard, dated March 19, 1939, the day the two movie stars were quietly married in a

Methodist church in Kingman. Gable and Lombard wasted no time in getting back on the highway. After the ceremony, they did not even pause at the Beale Hotel or one of the motor courts in Kingman but headed out of town back toward California. They made it only as far as Oatman, a rustic mining burg 28 miles southwest of Kingman tucked away in the Black Mountains. One of the first Route 66 towns ever to be bypassed, Oatman was part of the Mother Road until 1953 when the Ash Fork–Topock stretch was replaced by a newer section of Route 66, now I-40.

There is nothing better than seeing a sunset from the old highway as it heads out of Kingman and begins its arduous ascent to Oatman. There are warnings about flash floods and once travelers start the steady climb toward the dark peaks, it is immediately clear

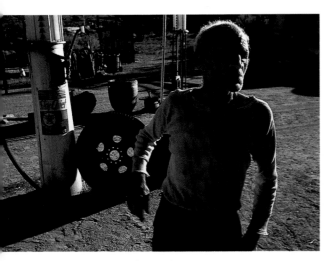

Ed Edgerton, proprietor, Ed's Camp, near Goldroad, Ariz.

why so many lowlanders feared this steep stretch of the highway. Some tourists even paid hard-earned vacation bucks to salty locals to drive the family sedan over the mountains, while the Okies left Kingman at three A.M. to beat the worst of the sun on their perilous drive to the hills. There are stories of travelers freezing behind the wheel on a hairpin curve and trying to back their car to safety. In the past, the charred remains of loaded pickup trucks that lost their bearings could be spied in the mountainous brush. This section of the Mother Road was tailor-made for billy goats and daredevils, and Rhett Butler and his laughing blond bride must have loved zooming over the narrow road on their wedding night.

The road passes through the striking Sacramento Valley, and starts up the Gold Hill grade, considered the steepest part of the entire route. After reaching Ed's Camp, surrounded by thick-armed saguaro cactus and pickups, the road tops the Sitgreaves Pass and descends into the town site of Goldroad, where footings, foundations, and mine shaft entrances can still be seen. It was at this former mining town where Rittenhouse noted: "For eastbound cars which cannot make the Gold Hill grade, a filling station in Goldroad offers a tow truck which will haul your car to the summit." Leaving Goldroad, the old highway continues to descend, twisting and turning around mountains, until it enters historic Oatman, the mining town that would not die, thanks to flea-market addicts and tourists who find pleasure in feeding the semi-wild burros that wander down the main street. Route 66 is not overlooked in Oatman.

when I lived in an apartment a half-block away, I looked out my kitchen window one night and all the lights in the rooms upstairs were on and they shouldn't have been. By the time I got down here the lights were off and it was dark as pitch. We've also had the jukebox come on in the middle of the night, and people claim they've heard giggling and voices, and objects have been moved. We call whatever it is the 'Oatie Ghost.' Some think it's the ghosts of Clark Gable and Carole Lombard. Their honeymoon room is up there, and it's just the way it was when they stayed here in 1939. There's a regular ol' iron bedstead with metal springs, cotton mattress, quilts, and blankets. The sheets are still there too. It wouldn't be a bad place for a ghost or two. Now people stop and look at the room, and they throw coins on the bed and I turn the money over to a children's Christmas fund."

The road to Oatman, Ariz.

Highway shields appear in storefront windows and locals toast the memory of the old highway.

On clear evenings a big wheel of moon lights the path out of town, beyond the bars, cafes, curio shops, and the old part of Oatman, which was a red-light district. Far below, over slopes of mesquite, yucca, and greasewood, tiny lights twinkle in the valley of the Colorado River. The old road south of Oatman goes down a gentle slope, past a spigot where travelers could get water, the site of a burned-out gas station, and worn places ideal for overnight camps. The road to Topock is rough and there are many dips, curves, and hills. Some travelers opt for a detour, down Highway 95 and across a back-door bridge into Needles. Others ride the brake pedal and bounce along through the washes and past feathery tamarisk trees, watching the stars as they drive all the way down to the end of the line.

At the bottom, on the east bank of the river, waits the sleepy little desert settlement called Topock, a Mojave word for "bridge" or "water crossing," and the last Arizona town on the old highway. At this point, Route 66 once crossed the Colorado, the river that carved the Grand Canyon, on an arched steel bridge. The old bridge now supports pipelines, and a newer span, with wide lanes, carries cars and trucks on I-40 across the restless river. It is said that when the Dust Bowl migrants reached this point and first caught sight of the river, they became euphoric. It evoked in many of those wayfarers the same feeling immigrants experience when they see the Statue of Liberty for the first time.

Travelers who stop to hear a fiddler's serenade and knock back a quick jigger of whiskey at the Oatman Hotel high in the mountains still have a warm glow as they approach the border. The feeling sticks with them as they move toward the chocolate-colored river and the golden land called California waiting on the other side.

CHAPTER NINE

California

"California, here I come."
—*Song title*

Left: Freight train, between Amboy
and Ludlow, Calif.

Above: Mormon temple, Santa Monica Blvd.,
Los Angeles, Calif.

*J*uly. Needles, California. Say no more.

Fill the tub with ice, drool over pictures of the North Pole, close the blinds, sleep naked without even a sheet. Try anything to get cool. None of it will help. It's hot enough outside to make a rattlesnake sweat.

Each day starts like an egg hitting a hot skillet greased with butter. The desert sun is hard at work before travelers can recover from the rude bleeps of automated wake-up calls—at desolate motels in a no-man's land between the old highway and the interstate. Droning radio deejays announce that the temperature's already close to triple digits and climbing faster than a cat burglar. Lukewarm trickles from the shower bring no relief; glasses of ice water at a cafe named the Hungry Bear help a little.

"It's so damn hot today, a trip to hell would look good," winks a red-headed waitress, balancing plates of French toast on both arms. She deposits her load at a booth filled with solid polyester gamblers on their way to the casinos at Bullhead City and Laughlin along the steamy Colorado River. Outside, their bonfire-red convertible with ebony upholstery—a real Detroit sled—bakes in the parking lot like an enormous metallic potato. By lunchtime, the thermometer will show 120 degrees.

In the older part of Needles, where Route 66 is called Broadway, there are reminders of the years when the Mother Road carried traffic going east and west through the city. At some motels, truck tires, painted white and lying on their sides to serve as flower planters, now hold only dust and brittle weeds. Bread wrappers and yellowed newspapers lie in the parched gutters along the streets. A grassy plaza bordered by slender palms and pepper trees near the railroad tracks becomes an oasis for customers waiting for stores to unlock their doors. In the shade of an auto repair shop, a young man with a lunch bag and a wine hangover sips carry-out coffee and leans against a Cyclone fence. A heavy woman, accompanied by a barefoot teenage girl in a faded dress and a retarded boy who mumbles to himself, walks down the sidewalk flanking the old route. The trio gazes inside darkened stores. They join hands and cross the road to rest at one of the picnic tables at Irene's, a long-suffering hamburger and taco stand on the corner of "D" Street and Route 66. Handmade signs are taped to the windows.

We Are Seventh Day Adventists
Our Only Closing Day Is the Seventh Day, the
Sabbath (Saturday).
Open Every Sunday Morn Through Friday.

Our Burritos Are Big and Delicious—
Homemade

Do You Know the Answer?
What Was the Last Miracle That Jesus
Performed

Far left: Downtown, Needles, Calif.

Near left: California state decal.

Just Before He Was Crucified?
If You Can Quote the Scripture and Tell Me
Where
It Is In the Bible, You Will Get a Free Taco

Inside, a woman scurries around, trying to get the place open. She flips a switch and instantly orange juice swirls inside a big plastic globe. Soon the smell of coffee and bean burritos drifts outside and reaches the tables under the palms. The large woman and her charges get up, take long drinks from the water fountain at Irene's back door, and continue their stroll down the sidewalk alongside the Mother Road.

"Irene's has been here for years and years," says the large woman. "Lots of folks traveling down Route 66 have stopped here for lunch. Course I recall when this old highway was really busy. There were all kinds of cars and trucks coming through here. On some parts of the highway the police used to park old cars on the shoulder with a dummy inside so folks would slow down. I was driving by one of them one time, and I waved at the dummy and I'll be damned if it didn't wave right back at me." The large woman laughs at her own story, and she and the other two scurry away before they get within camera range of a young woman in a jeep who stops at the corner and hops out to get a quick photo of Irene's. She snaps the shutter and leaves without earning a free taco by answering the question posted on Irene's window. For a moment the streets are deserted, but others soon appear on this section of the old highway in Needles.

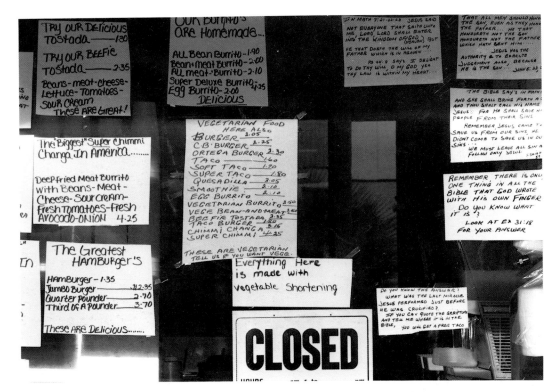

Irene's, Needles, Calif.

A man, his lips moving silently as though he were saying the rosary, counts out a big wad of folding money as he walks calmly by Irene's. He vanishes around a corner. Two landlocked surfers slide down the road on skateboards that leap over the curb to the sidewalk and back to the pavement. A dusty state patrol car pulls in at a coffee shop, and a female officer joins other troopers already draining their third cup of java. Down the road, across from the Palm Motel where rooms now rent by the month, drab sparrows hunt and peck around stately agave plants growing beneath a pioneer wagon. A National Old Trails plaque was placed here in 1923 by the Needles chapter of the Daughters of the American Revolution. Behind the highway memorial, a crew of shirtless men—backs bronzed from lives in the sun—tear apart an old bungalow with crowbars. They work to the accompaniment of Hank Williams blaring from a portable radio. Up the road and around a bend from the 66 Motel are uniformed gas station attendants who actually wash windows, check tire pressure, and peek under the hood without being asked. A

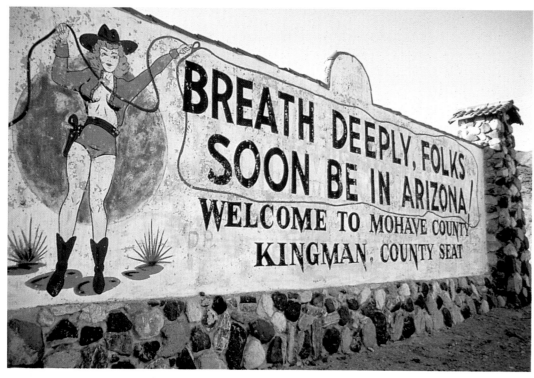

Colorado River crossing on California-Arizona border.

railroaders, ranchers, and hunters, Needles took its name from the group of sharply pointed peaks in the Black Mountains of Arizona, just across the border. But the town always managed to attract people. Most were just passing through on their way to someplace else. Long ago, remnants of the once powerful Mojave tribe sold bows and arrows, beadwork, and trinkets to early motorists or to travelers aboard the Santa Fe Limited. Needles became both a splendid railroad town and a highway trade center.

U.S. Route 66 developed out of a dirt track and a wooden plank trail that ran near the train tracks across the Mojave. Like the Old Trails Highway, the railroad route took advantage of low ground and the few precious places with water. As a result, both the railroad and Route 66 followed a circuitous path from the Colorado River at Needles all the way into the Los Angeles area where the road now ends. The original route crossed the river into California, ran through Needles, climbed steep grades onto a plateau, headed north for a short distance, and turned westward through the small towns of Klinefelter, Homer, Goffs, and Fenner. In 1931, a southern section of the highway was ready, which permitted a straighter route between Needles and Essex. Goffs and the other towns on that loop were bypassed. From Essex, the road ran across the desert to Amboy, Bagdad, Ludlow, Newberry, Daggett, and Barstow. The route then cut south through Lenwood, Hodge, Helendale, Oro Grande, and Victorville, and went through Cajon Pass and more small towns on the way

hitchhiker with inky blond hair washes off several days of road dirt in the unlocked restroom. Tempered by weather and time, the people of Needles emerge from hiding places like swarms of desert creatures. Life goes on as usual along the old highway in California, not just another state but also a state of mind.

When Steinbeck's Joad family crossed the Colorado River and entered California, Tom Joad saw the sunbaked town of Needles, and he called the town and the ragged mountain peaks beyond it "murder country." The Okie family's old car squeaked and

bounced across the border, and Tom told the others that they still had the terrible Mojave to face. At a refugee camp near Needles, they walked through the reeds and willows along the river bank and contemplated the rest of their journey. Tom Joad scanned the tough mountain ranges and the searing hot road snaking across the desert.

"This here's the bones of a country," Tom said. He hit the nail square on the head. The desert hasn't changed. In some ways, neither has Needles. One of the oldest towns in the Mojave and a center for miners,

Junked cars, Essex, Calif.

to San Bernardino. Then the old highway turned due west and shot through many more crossroads and southern California cities, including Claremont, Pomona, and Pasadena, on its way to Los Angeles and the beaches at Santa Monica, its final destination.

Beyond the grade west of Needles, the old road crosses bleak flatlands, where at dusk the temperature starts to become halfway civil and in the winter can get bitter cold. Small owls coast above sand and rock while coyotes hold nightly conversations. Out under the heavens, travelers can see forever. It is not difficult to remember that the region was once covered by a great sea.

During World War II, this was the desert training center for U.S. troops. Tens of thousands of General Patton's best soldiers practiced battling Nazi warriors on the blistering Mojave sands. After the war, motorists, confronting the great expanse of desert that buffers Los Angeles and the Pacific coast, followed the lead of the Okies and limited their Mojave driving to the evening hours. They hung water bags on the bumper, packed coolers with ice, and made sure the gas tank and radiator were topped off.

The long Mojave stretch is still considered one of the most grueling legs of the entire Route 66 journey. After reaching

Above: The Mother Road in the Mojave Desert, near Chambless, Calif.

Right: A couple shows off old Route 66, Chambless, Calif.

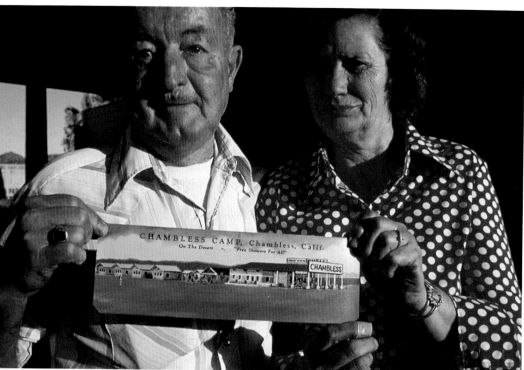

South Pass, high in the mountains, and then Mountain Springs Summit, the old highway moves away from Interstate 40 through heat waves shimmering from the desert floor. Essex shows up at the end of a gentle descent on the two-lane old road marked by 66 signs. In the wash below a narrow highway bridge, tin cans are part of the landscape. A car hood, partially buried in sand, shades a jack rabbit from the high noon sun.

Essex (population 100, elevation 1,775) is a Route 66 town with wrecked cars in a salvage yard, a few trailer houses, and a stone post office where there is an American flag and a poster that says "Loitering and Soliciting in This Building Are Prohibited." There has not been a loiterer or solicitor caught in Essex for years. In front of the post office is a clump of wispy paloverde trees, and up the pavement, near a highway maintenance station, is a water tap. Off in the distance to the northwest, travelers can make out cars and trucks moving like bugs on Interstate 40.

Amboy, where there has always been hot food and gasoline, is only 35 miles ahead. But first the old highway moves by what's left of

Danby, Summit, and Chambless—never really towns, only shady spots on the desert route. Far ahead, in another universe, are the San Gabriel Mountains, and beyond that range, the orange groves and wide Pacific beaches. The land of the Mojave is bleak, and rugged mountains parallel the highway. Travelers stare at deserted garages and gas stations and spy solitary trailers, some of them occupied, parked way off in the desert. It would not be much of a shock to drive over a rise and see one of the lost tribes of Israel stumbling across the sand. This is the part of the Mother Road

Roy's, Amboy, Calif.

Born: September 26, 1909
Occupation: Motel, cafe, and service
**   station owner**
Residence: Amboy, California

where delirious Dust Bowl refugees dreamed of juicy tangerines and figs or a dipper of sweet water.

For many miles before reaching Amboy, the names and initials of passing travelers or young lovers appear on a narrow berm of sand alongside the old highway. The letters and words are usually written with rocks, but some people have used roadside debris—

bottles, hubcaps, and cans—for their messages. There remains a peace symbol from the 1960s, and solitary destinations like *Mexico* or *L.A.* are spelled out with stones and sticks. One amorous messenger used a discarded tire for the letter *o* in the word *love*. Mostly there are first names—*Mary, Ed, Jane, Kelly, Russ, Dave, Pete.* It is as though people want to leave part of themselves in the desert and let others

"*This* spot on the ol' highway, here in Amboy, was as busy as any place in the desert. I should know, I've been working right here since 1938. I was born in Bandera, Texas, but the desert is my home. Highway 66 has moved a little bit over the years, but since about 'thirty-three, it's been out front of this cafe and

know that they have been there.

At Amboy, where Route 66 intersects with the Twentynine Palms Junction, is Roy's Cafe and service station. Next door, stark white tourist cottages with attached "swamp coolers" simmer in the sunshine. Buster Burris runs the complex, and years of desert living show in his dark, creased face. During lunchtime, almost any day of the week, the cafe is busy. Gamblers en route to the crap tables and one-armed bandits on the Colorado River stop for chili and beans, meat loaf, egg salad, or one of the other dishes on a menu that Buster says "was designed with all our old friends in mind."

One gambler, wearing a checkered sport coat and enough cream on his pompadour to oil a diesel truck, looks like he just stepped off a used-car lot. He could stand a touch of strong drink, and his hand shakes as he tries to raise a cup of coffee to his lips. When half of it has spilled, he resorts to slurping the hot brew from a saucer. A few off-duty marines, with bur haircuts and dressed in civilian duds, from the nearby base at Twentynine Palms, occupy some of the tables. There are also authentic tourists at Roy's, having lunch while they study a road map and scribble out "wish you were here" postcards.

Behind the cafe, a worn path leads to restrooms protected by a harmless German shepherd coiled up in the shade like a napping coyote. Buster doesn't miss a chance to turn a buck or even a quarter. The toilets are the pay variety, and require coins for admission. Jagged metal teeth line the top and bottom of the stalls around the commodes to prevent

those without spare change from gaining entry. A sign puts it this way: "Bathroom for Customers Only, All Others Stay the Hell Out." For balance, a more lighthearted message is taped above a smelly porcelain trough—"Please Do Not Throw Cigarette Butts in the Urinal. It Makes Them Harder to Light." Scratched in the mortar between the tiles over the urinal is more desert graffiti and an endless list of hometowns—Chino,

An emerald oasis near Amboy, Calif.

Berkeley, Buffalo, Nacogdoches, Columbus, Santa Fe, Tacoma, North Covina, Salt Lake City, Dallas, Baton Rouge.

Just to the west of Amboy is an extinct volcano known as Amboy Crater. Lava flows that are similar to the bizarre malpais in New Mexico almost touch the edge of Route 66. Some travelers stop to walk up a path leading to the top of the crater so they can brag to neighbors back home in Iowa and Vermont that they have visited a volcano. Continuing west, beyond Bagdad, the old route rejoins the

interstate at Ludlow, passes another ancient volcano, and crosses a dry lakebed before coming to Newberry, Daggett—once the site of a famous weigh station that appears in *The Grapes of Wrath* and now a major supply depot for the marine corps—and finally Barstow.

At one time, Barstow was a busy supply center for miners and prospectors headed to Death Valley. Silver was discovered near the town site in 1881, and, by 1885, Barstow claimed two hotels, one church, thirteen saloons, and even a small Chinatown. The city itself was not officially founded until 1886 as a depot for the AT&SF Railroad. Named after William Barstow Strong, the tenth president of the Santa Fe Railroad, this town on the western edge of the Mojave, along with nearby Daggett, eventually developed into a favorite Route 66 hideout for early Hollywood stars wanting a weekend away from the limelight. That was before Palm Springs became fashionable. Tourists still use Barstow as a base to visit old mines, desert ghost towns, and Indian ruins, or to take Interstate 15 going northeast toward Las Vegas and Lake Mead.

In the 1930s, most Okies, including the Joad family, chose to continue west out of Barstow and go to Bakersfield, on the Kern River at the southern tip of the San Joaquin Valley. That meant leaving the Mother Road behind. It was not necessarily a sad parting. For most, the journey across plains, mountains, and deserts was bittersweet. Other refugees went on to Los Angeles and stuck with Route 66, the highway that got them out of the dust and despair to a land where they hoped to launch a new beginning.

From Barstow, Route 66 veered south to San Bernardino and then turned west once more for the last part—the swan song—of this epic journey to the Pacific Ocean. Once the superhighways were built, traffic drastically slowed on the old road. Many travelers no longer use Route 66 between Barstow and Los Angeles. Instead, they take Interstate 15 south to Interstate 215 into San Bernardino, or hook up with Interstate 10 west all the way to Santa Monica. But not everyone prefers the interstate routes. For these iconoclasts, the old highway offers a sense of the past and is the preferred path to the Pacific. When available, they use the metropolitan version of Route 66 that remains in Southern California.

The old highway curves southwest out of Barstow and continues onto a plateau that rises toward the distant San Gabriel Mountains. Within less than 50 miles after leaving Barstow, the highway passes through five more Route 66 towns—Lenwood, Hodge, Helendale, Oro Grande, and Victorville, the high desert city where many old-time western movies were filmed. Tourists visit the Roy Rogers–Dale Evans Museum in Victorville to see Roy's old parade car decorated with pistols, horns, and silver dollars, as well as Roy's horse, Trigger; Dale's horse, Buttermilk; and their dog, Bullet, all stuffed and mounted for posterity.

Heading west from Victorville on the newer highway, travelers encounter stands of twisted Joshua trees before they climb to the summit of Cajon Pass, the famous gateway to Southern California in the San Bernardino Mountains. Desert Indians, early Spanish explorers and missionaries, and Anglo pioneers, such as Jedediah Strong Smith and Kit Carson, all entered the San Bernardino Valley by way of Cajon Pass.

Before the coming of the interstate, motorists on the old route were forbidden by local ordinance to smoke even in their vehicles during the summer months when the surrounding national forest got as dry as tinder. That was also when most cars had standard transmissions, which meant drivers descending the steep pass relied on second gear as they wound down U.S. 66, threading its way through deep cuts in the rock walls. In the old days, once they reached the bottom of the descent, travelers encountered a fork in the road. City 66 ran directly to San Bernardino, while regular 66 veered to the right, went through an edge of the city, and then turned right again and headed straight west into Los Angeles. Superhighway motorists face a similar decision—Interstate 215 to San Bernardino or take I-15 to Interstate 10, also known as the San Bernardino Freeway, and make the run to L.A. Just before reaching the split a message appears in blue paint on a rock —TRUST JESUS. It is the Christian version of "Have a nice day" and a fitting benediction for the ride into San Bernardino.

Located 60 miles east of Los Angeles, and the seat of the largest county in the nation, San Bernardino's name honors San Bernardino of Siena, an unsuccessful mission

motel. That's where it was when I showed up. My first father-in-law built up the original business. The place is named Roy's, after him. I was only planning on being here for a short time but that fell by the wayside. I got to where I liked it here and decided to stay. Besides the tourist cabins, I opened a repair shop in 1940, and the cafe in 1945.

"We had a lot of military traffic through here during World War II. Patton's boys were on maneuvers all across the desert and many soldiers passed this way in the convoys. Then guys on leave would come through here, too. It all helped the economy. At one time, I had seven wreckers running out of here. I serviced more than my share of head-on wrecks on Route 66. Some of them were pretty mean accidents. Out back is a 1937 Studebaker that was originally a gasoline tanker. It was used to haul gas from Barstow and it only had a top speed of forty-five miles an hour. I put a winch on the back and used it for setting the telephone poles around here.

"The heavy highway business started about 'forty-eight. After the war, my cabins were busy. We kept them rented night and day. Folks pulled over and slept in their cars when they couldn't get a room. That's how busy it was in Amboy. I built the cafe in order

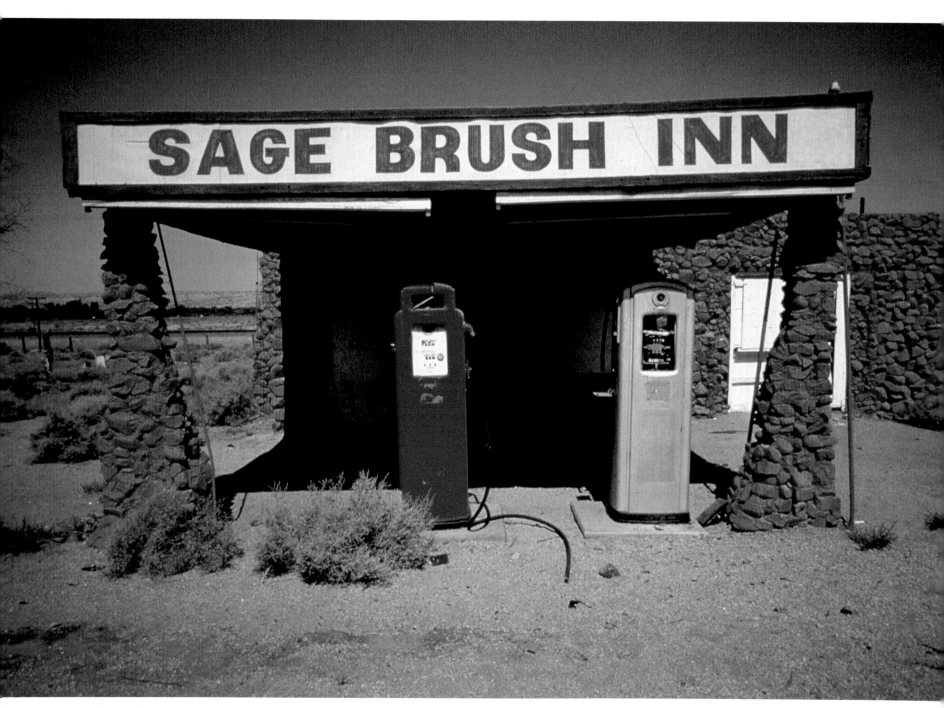

On the road between Barstow and Victorville, Calif.

settlement dating back to 1810. The city itself was founded in 1851 by Mormon immigrants, who purchased the land from Mexican farmers and patterned the town after Salt Lake City. The Mormons stayed a few years until they were recalled to Utah by Brigham Young. The city they left behind became a junction point for several major railroads and the principal eastern highway port for the Los Angeles area.

In the early 1900s, this region carried on a real romance with the navel orange. The orange groves made up what became known as the "Inland Empire," and spread across the foothills of the San Gabriel and San Bernardino Mountains, from Pasadena to Redlands. Times have changed since orange growers planted their first seedlings in the valley. Nature's wind-shaped clouds over the citrus groves and truck farms have given way to a blanket of smog drifting eastward from Los Angeles. On clear mornings the snow-capped San Gabriel Mountains can sometimes be seen and the smell of orange blossoms is still around, but it is harder to detect, thanks to the foul air.

Besides the noble orange, San Bernardino also became associated with one of America's most cherished culinary icons—the hamburger. Los Angeles was given the dubious title "Eat-in-Your-Car Restaurant Capital of the Nation" in the 1930s, but by 1939 in San Bernardino two former New Englanders, Richard and Maurice McDonald, took the wraps off a drive-in burger joint that revolutionized the restaurant industry. Their hamburger stand quickly became a mecca for traveling families and teenagers, but the

McDonald brothers weren't pleased with the slow turnover that occurred when too many customers waited for curb service. For some time the McDonald boys had carefully studied the trend toward self-service at filling stations, groceries, and other businesses. By 1948, they felt their restaurant was ready to follow suit. That year, they fired all the carhops, slashed the menu to the minimum, and turned their San Bernardino location into a prototype for a multitude of other fast-food firms that would emerge over the next half-century.

In the early 1950s, as Howard Johnson's, A&W, and other roadside franchises appeared, the McDonalds expanded their restaurants in California and Arizona. By 1952, they were selling more than a million of their fifteen-cent burgers and twenty-cent malts annually, plus about 160 tons of French fries for a dime per order. Their secret was a standardized operation capable of instant service from assembly-line workers who mass-produced and stockpiled food items for customers. The whole idea was to turn out hot food for a low price. People swarmed to the McDonalds' food factories like ants at a picnic. After Ray Kroc, a former paper cup salesman who was peddling milkshake machines, visited the original San Bernardino restaurant in 1954, he was able to talk the McDonald brothers into franchising their novel approach to food preparation and sales. It was Kroc who took the business nationwide. In 1955, he opened his first McDonald's franchise in Des Plaines, Illinois, near the other end of Route 66. Only six years later Kroc bought out the McDonald brothers lock, stock, and deep frier, but he

to give people a place to eat. We also carried a tremendous amount of auto parts. We had complete motors for most of the makes. It was hard work, but we could change out a motor in a matter of hours and get the people back on the road and on their way.

"From the late 1940s into the early 'seventies, this place was a madhouse. We kept everything open twenty-four hours a day. I had ninety people working for me full-time. During the summer, the number of workers could get as high as a hundred and twenty. There were waitresses, mechanics, maids, and cooks coming in here from Oklahoma, Texas, Arizona, and anyplace else in the country we could find them. People were working so hard they'd fall down in bed exhausted and get a few hours sleep and then come right back to it again. I used to think everybody in the world was driving through Amboy.

"Then everything changed. The interstate was completed. It was just like somebody put up a gate across Route 66. The traffic just plain stopped. That very first day it went from being almost bumper-to-bumper to about a half-dozen cars passing through here. A few years later, there was a big acid spill up on the interstate and they had to reroute the traffic down the old highway. All of a sudden we were reminded of the way things used to be.

Above: Mission Auto Court vintage postcard, "One of the Best in the West," San Bernardino, Calif.

Left: Southern California vintage postcard.

kept their name on the growing empire of look-alike restaurants. More fast-food entrepreneurs copied Kroc and the other franchise food pioneers. Before long the nation's tastebuds and eating habits were changed forever.

By the time the interstate system was fully under construction and the Mother Road was being phased out, fast-food corporations had managed to smother many neighborhood beaneries, highway food stands, and drive-ins owned by individuals. It seemed the nation was determined to clone itself and become uniform when it came to food, drink, lodging, clothing, cologne, shoes, or just about anything else. The age of the diner and hot dog stand was waning. Not everyone threw in the towel. Decades later, even after the franchise drive-ins were overshadowed by "drive-throughs," designed so customers would not have to leave their cars, some of the best cafes and burger stand operators on the Mother Road endured. They thumbed their noses at the chain restaurants and kept right on frying patties the old-fashioned way—with plenty of elbow grease and personal attention.

Although it requires vigilance, travelers who depart San Bernardino on the old route, instead of taking the hectic interstate to Los Angeles, can locate a number of cafes, motels, and other highway businesses that predate the "Golden Arches." They're right there—between the new buildings, franchise restaurants, palms, and eucalyptus trees.

Going west through the many congested towns and suburbs east of Los Angeles, the old highway is called Foothill Boulevard. It is a 50-mile route worth taking. Driving down the boulevard out of San Bernardino into the community of Rialto, it is difficult to miss the Wigwam Village Motel, silhouetted against the mountains. The nineteen stucco teepees provided shelter for exhausted motorists for many years during the prime time of Route 66 and afterward. Like other teepee motor

courts, such as the wigwams of Holbrook, this complex represented a touch of the exotic for tourists, especially those coming to California for the first time. When the neighborhood was more family oriented, the motel marquee suggested, "Sleep in a Wigwam—Get More for Your Wampum." Then business slowed and new owners were not as choosy about clientele. The marquee message changed to the more blunt "Do It in a Teepee." In the fleeting days just before the demise of the Wigwam Village, when uncaring owners decided to tear it all down and start from scratch, there was time for travelers to pause for one more night's sleep in a teepee on Route 66.

Upon entering the office, prospective tenants find a woman desk clerk more surly than the trio of guard dogs snarling and snapping at each other inside the fence around an empty swimming pool. A full moon lights the path to an air-conditioned wigwam, furnished with plenty of mirrors, including one directly over the waterbed covered with a crushed velour spread. The wigwam smells of mildew and the rug is stained, but the bath still has its original tile. Fortunately, the burglar bars over the diamond-shaped windows suggest the possibility of uninterrupted slumber. Back outside, under the rising moon, it is easy to watch a prostitute walking the shoulder of the highway. A Chevy Impala pulls over just ahead and the woman leans in the open window to discuss price with two swarthy gentlemen. An acceptable fee is quickly negotiated. The woman gets in between her escorts for the evening, and the car rumbles down the highway.

"In recent years, business has gotten better—not like the old days but definitely better. Motorcycle groups come through and stop, and tourists on their way to Disneyland who want to get away from the busy interstate. There are the folks on their way to the gambling casinos. They know that there aren't as many state cops on the old road, so they can make better time coming this way. We also have about thirty-five or forty geology students and their professors from Colby College all the way back in Waterville, Maine, who come here for one month every year on a field trip. They stay in the motel and take their meals here. They've been doing that for years.

"My first wife died of cancer, but I remarried and we're staying right here too. This is still a good Route 66 stop and all of those people who still come this way help keep 66 going."

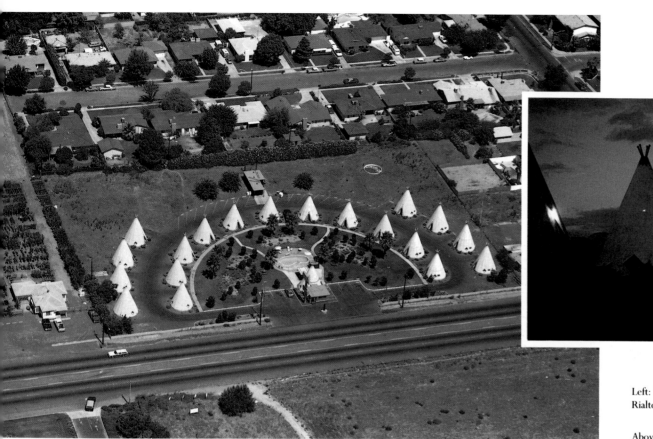

Left: Wigwam Village Motel, "Do It in a Teepee," Rialto, Calif.

Above: Dusk, Wigwam Village, Rialto, Calif.

Across from the Wigwam Village is a shopping center, a mini-storage facility, and a club called Hard Bodies, where patrons come for beer, wine, and good times. Next door to the motel is a small garage for tune-ups and oil changes. It also serves as an "Official Smog Inspection and Repair Station." On the other side of the Wigwam Village is a bowling alley and a plant nursery, selling potted shrubs and bags filled with earth. There is also yet another strip center, featuring California's version of one-stop shopping at its very best—a barber and beauty shop, a tax accountant's office, a gospel record store, a furniture store, a place selling men's hairpieces, a prayer center offering "Eternal life through Jesus Christ," and, last but not least, a tattoo parlor. Neon lights in the parlor window advise, "Yes We Are Open." There's a big easy chair for waiting customers, a whirling ceiling fan, and one of those electric signs with a moving message board like brokers use to flash stock reports. This narrow band of rotating words gets right to the point. "We do not trade tattoos for drugs or merchandise . . . If your homebody can do it cheaper, no problem . . . We will be quite happy to repair your mistake for you . . . You get what you pay for . . . If you want it cheap, it'll look cheap . . . We can help you with all of your tattooing needs, freehand, cover-ups, repairs, touch-ups, cosmetic, whatever . . . We will not work on people with fresh tracks (1 year or less in appearance), severe acne, or open sores that do not appear to be healing . . . You must be 18 years old or older to get a tattoo . . . Think ink."

Back out on the old highway, a pair of bikers—a man and woman dressed from head to toe in black leather and mounted on shiny machines—roar out of the Hard Bodies parking lot. In a flash, they cross the boulevard and check into Wigwam Village for the evening. Later, after the moon's rise is complete, beams of soft lunar light cast shadows on the teepees, scraggly palms, evergreens, and the chrome cycles standing next to the dark wigwam like sleeping Indian ponies. From the swimming pool behind the

Thomas Winery, Cucamonga, Calif.

motel office, the wail of dogs is drowned out by traffic rolling on the Mother Road. By morning the bikers are gone, but a trace of moon lingers over the mountains.

Continuing west on Foothill Boulevard, travelers pass more relics of Route 66— Foothill Drive-in Theatre, El Rey Motel, Fiesta Motel, The Rex Motel. In the city of Fontana where Henry Kaiser constructed the first steel blast furnace west of the Rocky Mountains, one can find motels with names like Sunset, Sand and Sage, Paradise, which offers commercial rates, and the Red Wing, which has weekly terms and kitchenettes. Palm readers are open for business and Bono's Restaurant and Deli lets customers know that it served its first lunch in 1936. At Rancho Cucamonga, a once thriving wine-producing area, is the site of California's oldest winery, established in 1839, where vintners aged their finest wines in redwood vats. This stretch of road is particularly rich with history. Beneath the flimsy buildings that have appeared like weeds along the boulevard, disintegrating adobe bricks made by Indian laborers for early Mexican merchants and ranchers have returned to the soil.

In Upland are more Route 66 road signs and a statue erected by the Daughters of the American Revolution. It is the Madonna of the Trail and commemorates the 1826 journey of Jedediah Smith and his band of hearty trappers—the first white Americans to make the arduous overland trip to California across the Colorado River and the broad Mojave. The statue of a pioneer woman wearing boots and bonnet, and clinging to a rifle and small child,

A Route 66 Portrait

Martin Milner

Born: December 28, 1931
Occupation: Actor
Residence: Del Mar, California

"*I* was born in Michigan, but I was raised out West. I've lived in Seattle, San Francisco, Los Angeles, and San Diego, so I'm actually a westerner at heart. I think that came across in the television show I starred in called *Route*

honors not only the spirit of early settlers but also the many others who moved west, including courageous Dust Bowlers and intrepid travelers, who came to see the bright lights of Hollywood, and ended up making California their home.

Foothill Boulevard continues west to Claremont, a town filled with botanical gardens and several serene college campuses. The old highway then jogs through La Verne and Glendora, where many visitors detour off the original route to see the huge bougainvillea —its parent stalk brought to California by a whaling ship in 1870—and then Azusa, site of one of the early McDonald's.

Top: Santa Monica Pier, Santa Monica, Calif.

Bottom: Foothill Drive In, Azusa, Calif.

Built in 1954, before Ray Kroc took over the fast-food chain, the restaurant at Azusa was one of the few originals that survived modernization. The structure came complete with slanted roof, wall panels decorated with red-and-white-striped tile, and the flanking golden arches. In less than thirty-five years, the burger stand, which was part of a system that caused the ruin of countless independent cafes and diners, has ironically become an endangered highway relic itself. By the close of the 1980s, the McDonald's on Foothill Boulevard in Azusa lay in ruins. The windows were shattered and the red and white tiles were chipped away by souvenir hunters. The rubber trees and shrubs had gone wild, and the planters were crowded with volunteer hollyhocks and empty rum and beer bottles. An official city notice pasted on a wall forbade anyone from entering the empty kitchen. At the top of the sign was the word PELIGROSO— "dangerous." The golden arches had been snapped off and had vanished like rainbows in the eternal California sun. Just a few blocks

The "Blvd" Cafe, "a vanished treasure," Duarte, Calif.

66, which aired from 1960 until 1964 and, I suppose, will always be playing on some channels. My character in *Route 66* was named Tod Stiles. George Maharis played a fellow named Buz Murdock. Later Glenn Corbett took over the other role for a while when Maharis dropped out because of a bout with hepatitis.

"The program was created by Sterling Silliphant and Herbert Leonard, who had cast Maharis in an episode of their hit show *Naked City*. From what I know, Silliphant said, 'Why don't we put together a show about two guys riding around the country in a car?' The idea was for everybody to rediscover the United States through our characters' eyes. Route 66 was very symbolic. It represented the spirit of movement and adventure in the country. It was a natural. From the very beginning the show had a great following and became very popular. I tried to talk them out of using a Corvette in the show. I did my best to convince them to use something really exotic. I said, 'Let's get a Ferrari. A Corvette is too ordinary.' Remember, I'm a Californian and I was used to seeing 'vettes. To me a Ferrari was really something special. But we went with Chevrolet and used Corvettes. It was the perfect vehicle.

"The car we used on the show changed every year. Chevrolet was always very anxious to show their new

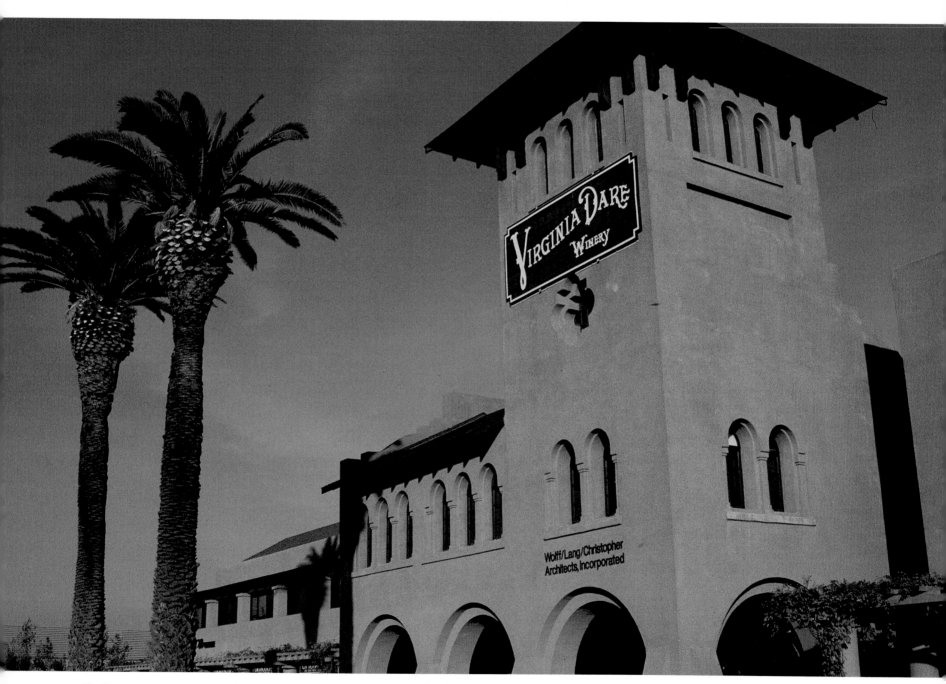

The Virginia Dare Winery, now a shopping center, Rancho Cucamonga, Calif.

Arroyo Seco Bridge vintage postcard, Pasadena, Calif.

up the highway, past tuxedo rental shops and funeral homes, patrons at Volcano Burgers, an old-road veteran, still toast the passing of the McDonald's with glasses of root beer.

A few miles farther west in the town of Duarte, another vintage Route 66 structure managed for several decades to outlive many of the franchise intruders. Operated by the Tomasian family since 1946, the Blvd. Cafe got its name because the complete word "Boulevard" wouldn't fit on the sign. Anyone coming into Los Angeles on Route 66 had to pass this small cafe. Many stopped for a meal and bottle of beer. Tourists, movie stars, and

even anxious gamblers on their way to the Santa Anita race track could not resist the hamburgers and fresh-squeezed orange juice. On Sabbath evenings, the patties and onions frying on the grill lured endless streams of motorists returning to Los Angeles from Las Vegas and Palm Springs. The cafe was even open on Christmas Day.

Like many roadside institutions, it seemed like there would always be the Blvd. Cafe in Duarte. But this wasn't to be. In 1989, the Blvd. served its last meal. The city's redevelopment agency seized the property through eminent domain and bulldozed one of

products. The first year of the show came to an end and we were getting set for the second year, and they didn't want us to use the same 'fifty-nine Corvette. They really wanted us to have a new 1960 model. So Sterling wrote a show where we crashed the car, saving some rich man's life, and the man turned around and replaced our Corvette with a new model, and everybody was happy. Every year after that, we got a brand-new model for the show but there were no more crashes in the scripts. We just changed cars each season and that was it. Nothing was ever said.

"Of the two characters, the one I played, Tod Stiles, was the more intellectual. He came from a well-to-do family and was college educated, optimistic, and a liberal who always believed in doing things the right way. Beneath everything, Tod felt that people could be trusted, and that everything was going to be just fine. He had a great deal of compassion and integrity. Stiles was more carefree. He had inherited some money from his father in order to buy that first Corvette.

"Now Buz, on the other hand, was a real street kid. He was a bad boy from the ghetto—from Hell's Kitchen—and had been involved in crime. His adopted father had died in his arms from an overdose, and Buz had truly seen the worst part of life. He was suspicious and

the finest burger stands on the Mother Road. The building was razed in order to make room for a shopping center. In return, the family received $1.1 million from the city. It was small consolation.

"Money can't buy everything," said a man at the counter, wiping mustard from his beard before the cafe's demise. "Some things are worth too much, and this little place is one of them."

The cafe went out in a final blaze of glory. A hundred regular customers showed up for the occasion. Food and beer were on the house, and continuous jukebox music kept jitterbuggers going for hours. There were plenty of impromptu speeches, stories, laughter, and tears. Someone sent a funeral wreath inscribed "Goodbye, Old Friend." A sign on one of the cafe walls said, "It's the end of an era." By sundown, hundreds of hamburgers and tons of cole slaw had been consumed along with twenty-five cases of beer. It was time to close. People drifted outside, and a hat was passed to buy more beer so the party could go on. Then they all said their last goodbyes to the cafe and left before the wrecking crew arrived to tamper with history.

After Duarte, the original route still goes through Monrovia, where the striking Aztec Hotel was erected in 1926. Then come the suburbs of Arcadia and Sierra Madre. Just to the west, Foothill Boulevard gives way to Colorado Boulevard, the path of the old highway through historic Pasadena. At the foot of the San Gabriel Mountains, the city is known for its Pasadena Playhouse, the Rose Bowl, and the Tournament of Roses, that elaborate floral parade that attracts a mob of sightseers every New Year's Day. On the western edge of Pasadena is the beautiful arched bridge built in 1912, which spans Arroyo Seco.

Far ahead is the "City of Angels" and the conclusion of the Mother Road. Some believe the old highway officially ends at the corner of Arroyo and Colorado in Pasadena. But most of the original path of Route 66 remains in Los Angeles. It winds through Hollywood, Beverly Hills, Westwood, and Santa Monica, and it is eclipsed in many parts by the maze of interstates and freeways crisscrossing the city. An early route went south from Pasadena on Figueroa Street, turned west on Sunset Boulevard through Hollywood, and finally

Will Rogers Highway marker, Palisades Park, Santa Monica, Calif.

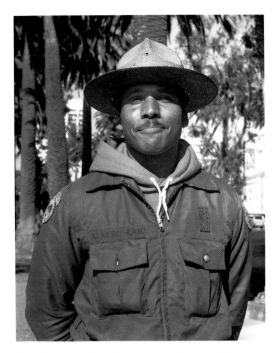

Shai Alkebu-Lan, Park Ranger, Santa Monica, Calif.

veered west on Santa Monica Boulevard. In the 1940s when traffic on Route 66 increased, Californians built their first freeway. Named the Arroyo Seco Parkway, it ran south through ravines and over landscaped hills and became the newest section of Route 66 between Pasadena and downtown Los Angeles.

Time was not especially kind to the old highway or to the city that serves as its western terminus. Los Angeles became shrouded in smog and crime. A concrete jungle of freeways and multi-laned superhighways spread across the metropolis, destroying much of the romance that was Los Angeles in the 1930s. The words

of singer Guy Clark rang truer than most, "If I can just get off of this L.A. freeway without gettin' killed or caught."

Still, portions of these final miles of old highway have never been completely erased. Once travelers find themselves on Santa Monica Boulevard, headed west toward the Pacific, they know they have found a part of the route little changed by time. Visible signs of Route 66 are still there along the avenue, even among chic shops and fashion palaces.

Beyond Hollywood and Beverly Hills lies West Los Angeles, where the boulevard passes the Mormon temple, its 250-foot-tall spire topped by the gold-leafed statue of the Angel Moroni, an ancient Christian prophet who the Mormons believe symbolizes divine truth. When it was completed in 1956, the temple was the second tallest building in Los Angeles. Mockingbirds play on the fence around the temple and thick beds of ivy climb the hillsides. High above, even higher than Moroni, with trumpet raised to his golden lips, a hawk slowly circles in the rich twilight.

Continuing west on the boulevard, travelers pass an Automobile Club of Southern California office, then a hospital, apartment buildings, banks, hotels, and restaurants. There is also, at long last, the smell of the ocean. On the final block of Santa Monica Boulevard, one can visit the American Diner, a restaurant designed to look like an old period piece. At the diner, the waitresses serve Route 66 omelets and lunch specials. Only "goldies"— timeless music—can be played on the jukebox. "Old 66 is still with us," says Tom Snyder, founder of the Route 66 Association,

didn't trust anyone. The characters were very different and that made for a good show. There was balance. Also, there was some awfully good writing. The top-notch writing, direction, and the casting were very critical in that show's success.

"The funny thing is we hardly did any real location work out on Route 66. The show was named after the highway, but we did most of the filming elsewhere. It was nothing against the highway, but we just wanted to keep it neat and clean and convenient, so when the weather was good, we'd be near the East Coast and when the weather was lousy, we'd be in Florida or Texas or Arizona. We did some work up in the Pacific Northwest and we filmed around Chicago and Pittsburgh, too. We cruised the highway in our shiny Corvette and came into everybody's living room every Friday night. Along the way we met Robert Redford, Alan Alda, Robert Duvall, Rod Steiger, Gene Hackman, Lee Marvin, Cloris Leachman, Jean Stapleton, and a lot of other talented folks. For a hundred and sixteen episodes Tod and Buz tooled along Route 66. It was great adventure."

Homeless, end of the road, Santa Monica, Calif.

with twenty-six acres of monuments, statues, and trails shaded by a thousand trees and shrubs. Some of the palms and evergreens are exotic and were brought from across the ocean and planted on the cliffs overlooking the Pacific. There are Canary Island date palms, Mexican fan palms, and New Zealand Christmas trees. The Australian tea trees are twisted and gnarled and a grove of majestic eucalyptuses reach for the heavens.

Twilight is the best time to be at Palisades Park, when the sunlight is scarlet and golden. Joggers appear on the park trail, and tourists, following a park guidebook, pause at a small plaque set in the ground near where Santa Monica Boulevard meets Ocean Avenue.

**WILL ROGERS HIGHWAY
DEDICATED IN 1952 TO WILL ROGERS
HUMORIST, WORLD TRAVELER, GOOD
NEIGHBOR.
THIS MAIN STREET OF AMERICA, HIGHWAY 66,
WAS THE FIRST ROAD HE TRAVELED IN A
CAREER THAT LED HIM STRAIGHT TO THE
HEARTS OF HIS COUNTRYMEN.**

"This is an important monument, maybe the most important in the whole park," says a young man, dressed in a green uniform and wearing a badge and wide-brimmed hat. "Not everyone realizes that this is the ending of the most famous highway that ever existed. It went from this place all the way across the country to Chicago." The park ranger, born in Santa Monica, has taken the ancestral name Shai Alkebu-Lan, which originated in

Zimbabwe and was passed down from his great-great-grandfather.

The sun is disappearing into the sea. Up the coast to the north, lights are coming on at Malibu. A soup kitchen has been set up in the park to feed the homeless. A line forms, mostly men and boys with empty eyes, and they proceed past the tables holding bread and big metal pots of hot soup. The Joads would have felt at home here. One man, who has already finished his simple dinner, sits on the grass and feeds scraps of bread to dozens of pigeons that flutter through the dying light. The birds rest on the grass and some even sit on the man's shoulders and outstretched arms.

Beneath a century plant on the edge of the cliff overlooking the busy coastal highway, another man is wrapped inside a torn sleeping bag. Park rules forbid overnight guests, but the young ranger, with proud African warriors' blood pulsing through his body, does not approach the sleeping man. Instead, he smiles and nods to the others in the soup line and to the man feeding the pigeons. The ranger looks out at the Pacific and turns to see the cars and people making their way down the boulevard. Then he slowly walks away.

Another day has ended on the Mother Road—on Route 66.

Route 66. The name is still magic.

Route 66. It will always mean going somewhere.

as he drains his coffee cup. "Everything people found on this highway is alive and well. All we need to do is offer the public a new opportunity to rediscover it. If that happens, Route 66 will live forever."

After traveling more than 2,400 miles through eight states and three time zones, this is the payoff. For those who have ever made the trip—early adventurers, Okies, homesick servicemen, vacationers—the feeling of completing the journey and seeing the Pacific is incomparable. It's a strong tonic.

One door west of the diner, Santa Monica Boulevard intersects with Ocean Avenue, where the Mother Road ends.

Several blocks away to the south is the historic Santa Monica Pier, and along the avenue for fourteen blocks runs Palisades Park,

Nightfall at the end of Route 66, Santa Monica, Calif.

CHAPTER TEN

Mother Road Revival

"It's not the destination . . . it's the journey."
—*Popular Harley-Davidson adage*

fter making the journey from Chicago to Santa Monica in the preceding chapters, it should be clear that Route 66 truly is America's highway, just as it has been ever since 1926. Other venerable roads, longer or older than Route 66, crisscross the land, but none of them measure up to the Mother Road—not even close. Undeniably this pathway for pilgrims, merchants, drifters, con artists, and travelers remains the ultimate symbol of a restless nation on the move. Through the years this celebrated highway—despite attempts to do away with it—has persevered: Route 66 has become a destination in itself.

If you want to take the pulse of the nation, then go to the most enduring artery and head straight for Route 66. If you want to taste, feel, hear, and experience genuine America—raw and uncensored—then get on the Mother Road. If you believe time is as precious as gold, then you need to exit the turnpikes and freeways and cruise America's Main Street. The old highway winding from the heartland to the edge of the country has new life and meaning. Along the way the necklace of towns, cities, and enticements—some of them funky chic, whimsical, or bizarre—are as alluring as ever.

Left: Restored landmark bridge, Pasadena, California

Above: German bikers' helmets on the Mother Road

Today a curious mix of good, bad, and ugly litters the shoulders of Route 66. Many of the more eclectic attractions are relatively new, but some date back to the origin of the highway or else long before its birth. They include a burlesque museum, a colossal cross, concrete totem poles, a tree filled with pairs of shoes, statues of the Virgin Mary and Jesse James, the oldest house and the oldest church in the United States, the longest pedestrian bridge in the world, a man who can turn his feet around 180 degrees, roaming burros, a round barn, a meteor crater, a smiling whale, the largest catsup bottle in the world, a 140,000-gallon fish tank, ten vintage Cadillacs buried nose down in the earth, a giant spaceman, Trigger stuffed in all his glory, Mickey Mantle's first ballpark, a nudist colony, Clark Gable's ghost, a museum devoted to barbed wire in an old brassiere factory, graves of German soldiers, Elvis Presley's favorite Route 66 motel suite, beds of lava, and so much more.

Although it seems there is something for everyone on Route 66, there are some exceptions. It is not a road for those who like cookie-cutter culture, food in Styrofoam boxes, or sprawling shopping malls filled with indistinguishable people pawing through look-alike merchandise. Even though franchise restaurants, chain stores, and homogenized fast-food joints have invaded the old highway, the true Route 66 crowd does not fully embrace them. They occasionally stop at a Steak n Shake, White Castle, Sonic, or another of the chain drive-ins that suggest the Route 66 style by serving real road chow and often using carhops. Beyond those exceptions, most

travelers much prefer giving their meal order to a human being rather than a talking box.

Route 66ers want kitsch that often is so bad it is good. They go for window decals, refrigerator magnets, salt and pepper shakers, and the other kinds of merchandise sold at the best tourist traps. They crave hash browns, milk shakes, and berry pies made from scratch and on the premises. They like nothing but open road ahead of them. They will stop on a

Phyllis Evans greets highway visitors, Albuquerque, New Mexico

dime to move a box turtle to safety off the pavement and are liable to spend half a day snooping around a deserted road town. They drive with the top down, the radio on, and their minds open. They travel without any reservations.

Traveling Route 66 still promises an adventure, an escapade. For example, ravenous wayfarers do not know what to expect if they have not dined at a particular roadside cafe

before. They step inside and roll the dice, knowing that they could wind up with ptomaine poisoning. On the other hand, they just might find the ultimate feast—a basket of fried chicken or a cheeseburger so juicy that it takes a dozen napkins to wipe the grease off chin and hands. There are still genuine motor courts all along Route 66. Many are just like the ones from the fifties when Mother would invariably ask Father to inspect the room before checking in for the night—just to be sure. Today, as before, nothing about the Mother Road is predictable.

Since 1990, when this book first appeared and the Route 66 resurgence really began, tens of thousands of enthusiasts from around the globe have discovered that this road is not just another American highway. They have also found that neither is Route 66 a romanticized corridor of nostalgia that only allows people to return to the so-called good old days. True, Route 66 serves as the definitive symbol of certain key segments of the nation's past, but it is also very much part of the present as well as of the future.

Travelers may still view distinct layers of history along the various alignments of Route 66 in all eight states. They see palpable examples of the Roaring Twenties, the bittersweet 1930s, the World War II years, and the postwar heyday of the highway. They can also come across the scars and desolation from the limbo years when the interstates threatened the old road with extinction. Finally, they may experience firsthand the highway of the popular revival period—an episode of Route 66 history that appears to have no end in sight.

Those who take to this storied road quickly find it shows them where they have been, where they are today, and where they are going. In some places the old road is more like a street than a highway, coasting through town squares and boldly cutting through the hearts of busy downtowns. Route 66 also takes voyagers past forgotten towns and places that could not resuscitate themselves after the coming of the relentless interstate highways. Still, no matter if it is a span of road crammed with traffic or a desolate stretch surrounded by only time and space, Route 66 continues to attract attention.

During the revival period droves of Europeans, Asians, Canadians, and South Americans have come to the United States hungry for an honest taste of the real America they can only find on the Mother Road. This surge of foreign visitors has been an economic boon to both small towns and individuals. For example, some ingenious Oklahomans make spare cash by obliging travelers from abroad who want bullet holes shot in the replica Route 66 shields they take home as souvenirs.

Many foreign travelers have no interest in the hustle and bustle of big American cities. They have already seen New York and Los

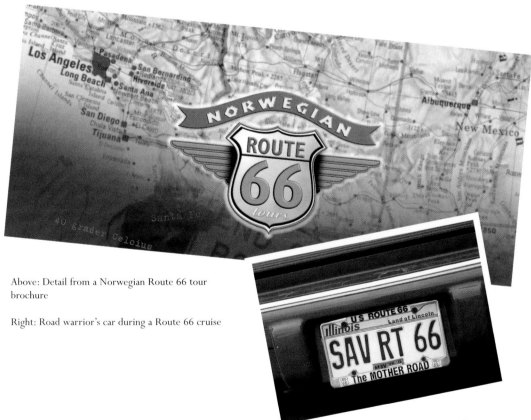

Above: Detail from a Norwegian Route 66 tour brochure

Right: Road warrior's car during a Route 66 cruise

Angels of the Mother Road

Bobby Troup, 1918–1999

"Be not forgetful to entertain strangers: for thereby some have entertained angels unawares."
—Hebrews 13:2

The life span of any highway depends on certain factors—location, materials used in construction, weather, and how much traffic it must carry. Along with those basic components, a highway also must have champions. No highway in history has survived without people willing to fight for its maintenance and preservation. Thankfully, Route 66 has never run short of heroes and heroines.

Action, camera during a Route 66 video shoot

and cruises, and all the other events staged along the highway. Their fascination, even obsession, with the road increases as the Route 66 revival grows stronger and larger in the United States and far beyond.

A 1999 feature story in *People* magazine put it this way: "America's most legendary highway may have been officially decommissioned decades ago, but Route 66 is about to become the comeback trail." That comeback not only took place but continues to gain momentum.

A multitude of changes occurred along Route 66 since 1990. Many are obvious, such as a restored cafe or gas station or a bridge saved from destruction, new historic highway shields, or the rescue of a classic Mother Road business by new owners. Up and down the highway, travelers see reminders that the old road endures. In scores of cities such as Pontiac, Rolla, Baxter Springs, Weatherford, McLean, Grants, Flagstaff, and Needles the evidence is all around. Retail stores, restaurants, motels, service stations, and even car washes, banks, and public schools proudly display Route 66 shields. They want to show their support for this ribbon of history that touches their lives in so many ways.

People also realize that this highway continues because it remains primarily a commercial road. That is what it was all about in 1926, and that is what it is all about today: people trying to turn a buck—rent rooms for the night, serve a rib platter, sell a tank of gas, a handful of postcards, or a peek at the meteor crater. It is about people offering travelers a dream, an illusion.

Angeles. This time they have come to see cowboys and Indians, eat chicken fried steak, and listen to rock 'n' roll. They come for the vast horizons, great spaces, and changing scenery. They come to take the open road—the free road.

On any given day out on the old highway, be prepared to meet travelers from Germany, France, Switzerland, Norway, Great Britain, Japan, Brazil, Luxembourg, Australia, Canada, Portugal, or the Netherlands. They may be traveling alone, in pairs, or as part of a large bus or motorcycle tour. Before they come, they do their homework. They read all the

books, watch all the films and videos, procure the maps and tour guide information, and plot out their trip of a lifetime. Their ranks swell each year, just as do the numbers of domestic travelers from every state of the union.

These "road warriors," as they have proudly dubbed themselves, patronize revitalized diners, curio shops, trading posts, motels, and tourist attractions. Some are university students writing a dissertation on some aspect of Route 66. Others are out to find their past, while still others are looking for a clean start. They pause to pay their respects at the ghost places. They also show up at Route 66 rallies

Many local and state tourism officials finally realized the worth of the old highway. They began to include Route 66 attractions in their promotional literature, guidebooks, and directories. There was also the infusion of investment capital and government funding in businesses and towns. Ironically, the same federal government that tried its damnedest to get rid of the Mother Road came to its senses and pumped millions of dollars into preserving it.

Still, not all the news along the old highway has been good. Sadly, some chambers of commerce, especially in the larger cities, simply do not understand that Route 66 brings vehicular traffic to their city; that it brings people who do not just dash by on the turnpike or interstate but instead stop to eat, buy gas and goods, rent rooms, and visit area attrac-

tions. They have missed an opportunity to reach a broad national and international audience.

One notable exception is the city of Albuquerque, whose civic and business leaders, chamber of commerce, and merchants understand that supporting the Route 66 movement makes good sense. Perhaps larger road cities such as Tulsa, where so much of the old road remains lost or ignored, will follow suit and begin to reap the benefits before it is too late.

Besides oversight and neglect, there has also been serious human loss in all eight states. Major fans and boosters of Route 66 have passed away since 1990.

Also, some of the best-known road attractions vanished from the scene due to closure caused by death, financial strain, or catastrophe. Culturally important businesses along the old road were destroyed to create parking lots or make room for some amorphous convenience store.

Thankfully, the gains greatly outweigh the losses. Individuals and groups have banded together to save and resurrect a host of architectural icons and sites. Each of the eight Mother Road states boasts many more victories than defeats.

There also have been many successes that affect the entire length of the highway. Here is a sampling of just a few Route 66 highlights that have occurred since 1990:

EXPLORE ROUTE 66!

Take the offramp into a bygone era. Discover the 2,400 miles of Route 66 and see how America traveled in the 1920's-60's. Visit the wonderful old trading posts, gas stations, motels, tourist traps, diners and villages along the scenic 'Mother Road'.

Join our nonprofit organization and you'll receive our magazines with access to Route 66 maps, guides, events, memorabilia and more. Get all the details. Send a self-addressed, stamped, business size envelope to:

GIVE A GIFT MEMBERSHIP

NATIONAL HISTORIC ROUTE 66 FEDERATION
P.O. Box 423, Dept. W. Tujunga, CA 91043-0423

Left: First call to arms from the National Historic Route 66 Federation

Go to any village or big city on the old road and you will find folks from every background and demographic category who contribute to the life and well-being of the Mother Road. Some of them make their living from highway commerce. Others concern themselves with historical and cultural preservation issues. Many are in both categories.

Since 1990, when this book was first published, several significant Mother Road guardians have died. Some of these human icons of Route 66 were celebrities whose professional lives tied them to the road. These champions include Yankee slugger Mickey Mantle, a native of Commerce, Oklahoma; the renowned warbler Bobby Troup, creator of the definitive anthem of the highway; Erick, Oklahoma, native Roger Miller, the original "King of the Road"; and Roy Rogers, whose museum at Victorville, California, continues to be a big draw on the old road. Other examples are Gene Autry, the singing cowboy discovered by Will Rogers on Route 66, and Sterling Silliphant, creator of the landmark television series *Route 66*. There is also comedian Sam Kinison, an Oklahoma native who died on a stretch of road in the Mojave Dessert when a drunk driver hit his auto head-on. A signed copy of this original book turned up in the wreckage.

Most of the Route 66 losses, however, came from the ranks of ordinary

- passage and implementation of critical federal legislation including a $10.5 million funding package for preserving historic sites along the route, such as old diners and motor courts
- unprecedented growth of Route 66 associations in all eight Route 66 states and beyond, including the establishment of international organizations in several foreign countries
- establishment by David and Mary Lou Knudson of the National Historic Route 66 Federation, a California-based organization dedicated to promoting and preserving the "Main Street of America"
- opening of several Route 66 museums and information centers along the entire corridor as well as development of Route 66 interpretive sites

- introduction of the Route 66 image within numerous major advertising campaigns, ranging from Ralph Lauren to Kmart lines of clothing
- establishment and posting of historic signage systems and directional guides in the eight Route 66 states
- publication of numerous Route 66 maps and driving guides, especially a definitive series of road maps for each of the eight states created by Jim Ross and Jerry McClanahan
- founding of several national and international touring companies (bus, automobile, bicycle, and motorcycle), including tours that originate in Western Europe and Japan
- inclusion of Route 66 books and other related

materials in school curriculums, as well as in college courses throughout the nation
- launching by Paul and Sandi Taylor of *Route 66 Magazine,* headquartered in Williams, Arizona; as well as the founding of a companion Route 66 radio station
- orchestration of numerous Route 66 events and activities, such as tours sponsored by the Smithsonian Institution, the National Trust for Historic Preservation, and Harley-Davidson.
- creation of a plethora of Route 66 products, including soft drinks, beer, cologne, greeting cards, barbecue sauce, dried jalapeño flakes, and a variety of other goods

Beyond these major developments, there have been scores of significant preservation and restoration efforts in all eight states.

Many travelers start their road trip in Illinois. After all, that is "where the road begins," according to the Route 66 Association of Illinois, one of the most effective organizations on the old road. Illinois is not lacking in folks willing to roll up their sleeves and contribute time and sweat if it means safeguarding some of the old road's best commercial archaeology and historic sites. From Lake Michigan at Chicago to the Mississippi at St. Louis, the highway in Illinois delivers on all its promises. Much of

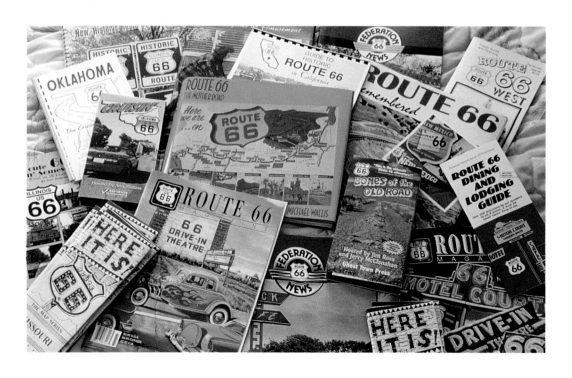

Left: A Mother Road potpourri

the thanks goes to volunteers from throughout the state who help conserve Route 66.

For that reason it is no surprise that many two-lane travelers are eager to launch their Mother Road journey in Chicago. Those who do, often find their bearings at Hit The Road, a travel retail store opened in 1999, just a few miles north of Route 66 and only a short distance from Wrigley Field. The store and its owners epitomize the new Route 66 spirit.

Annice Tatken and Maureen Geoghegan founded Hit The Road in response to the public's insatiable appetite for Route 66 merchandise and creative trip resources. Their busy store offers travel gear, memorabilia, gift items, and features a special line of Route 66 merchandise. Included are sixteen original Route 66 Legends T-shirts designed by the proprietors, both tried-and-true road warriors.

Geoghegan and Tatken read an earlier edition of this book that inspired them to make a 1994 journey down America's Main Street. "That trip changed us forever," explains Geoghegan. The experience also bonded them with the people and places of Route 66. They returned to Chicago, quit their jobs, and launched a business that celebrates the open road. They have not looked back.

On the way out of the Windy City, Route 66 voyagers headed down state have plenty to see before they reach Missouri and points west. They also face—as always—a mixed bag of dining choices to fuel them for the long trek. Some of the old reliable haunts are difficult to ignore, such as Lou Mitchell's on Jackson Boulevard at the start (or end) of Route 66. Lou himself has passed away, but

Above: Entrance to Berwyn, Illinois

the food remains memorable and every female diner still receives a free box of Milk Duds when she walks through the door.

Beyond the Chicago sprawl, other dining opportunities abound all along the old highway in Illinois. In Cicero, some people opt for plump hot dogs and piles of french fries at Henry's Drive-In. Others wait until they reach the nearby Bunyon's, where a huge lumberjack statute cradles an enormous wiener on a bun. Just down the road at Berwyn, a town proud of its highway history, the Skylite Family

men and women with no real claim to fame or any notoriety beyond their hometown or community. Nevertheless, each passing had a profound impact on the highway and the others left behind.

Sadly, many of those who have gone will always remain unknown. Their names and contributions go unrecorded. They worked all their lives on Route 66 as waitresses, fry cooks, mechanics, truck drivers, police officers, clerks, and cashiers and died having neither sought nor found the recognition they so richly deserved.

The list below certainly is not a definitive roll but represents just some high-profile people that the Mother Road lost during the decade since this book was first published. Whether they were writers, actors, athletes, cooks, gas station attendants, or merchants is of no importance. All of them were angels in disguise. All of them heard the poetry in the varicose pavement and patched concrete. All of them deserve to have their names in glowing neon.

- Pearl Aleene Albro *1920–1997*
- Dennis Ast *1932–1993*
- Gene Autry *1907–1998*
- Ray Barker *1925–1990*
- Hillary H. Brightwell *1912–1999*
- Mary E. Brightwell *1918–1998*
- H. B. "Buster" Burris *1909–2000*
- Sheldon "Red" Chaney *1916–1997*
- Glenn Corbett *1934–1993*

Trio of road warriors help Gemini Giant stand guard in Wilmington, Illinois.

Restaurant maintains a Route 66 display for its patrons. In Willowbrook, famished customers flock to Dell Rhea's Chicken Basket hosted by Patrick and Grace Rhea. This palace of fried chicken in an unrivaled meal stop just as it was years ago when the owners flooded the flat roof to create an ice-skating rink as an added lure.

Farther south, the White Fench Farm, a

1920s-era restaurant at Romeoville, displays an impressive collection of antiques and memorabilia in the lobby and maintains a free zoo out back. In Wilmington, at the Launching Pad Drive-In, the towering fiberglass Gemini Giant continues to stand guard outside this famed eatery, owned and operated by the same family who opened the restaurant back in the sixties.

As in all eight Route 66 states, travelers in Illinois will find many of the old standard cafes, motels, and tourist stops not only intact but remodeled and thriving. Some notable stops include the restored Rialto Square Theater and the Route 66 Raceway at Joliet, the remade Polk-a-Dot Drive-In at Braidwood, and the Riviera Restaurant and Bar, known for strong drinks and hot food, in Braceville. Others are the Cozy Dog Drive-In at Springfield, the Sky View Drive In Theater and the Ariston Cafe at Litchfield, and Earnie's, an original roadhouse at Hamel.

At Funk's Grove between Shirley and McLean, another generation of the Funk family is turning out tasty maple sirup [sic] that rivals any in the land. Stephen and Glaida Funk have handed the management torch to son Michael, his wife Debby, and grandson Sean. Just down the highway from the Funk's busy operation, the acclaimed Dixie Truckers Home remains one of the most popular truck stops in the nation. The Dixie—still open twenty-four hours a day, seven days a week—has also become the home for the Illinois Route 66 Hall of Fame, established in 1990.

A key factor in the success of the old road businesses and attractions in Illinois is that the state has the best historic signage system

on the Mother Road. Historic Route 66 markers strategically placed show the way to a host of roadside stops, such as Shea's Historic Route 66 Museum, packed with road collectibles inside an old service station in Springfield, and Henry's Route 66 Emporium, a bustling retail and refreshment rest stop at Stanton.

The new highway shields also help folks find Soulsby's Shell Service Station at Mount Olive. Although Russell Soulsby and his sister, Ola, died after the station closed, there are still plenty of memories at this landmark building that serve a tribute to the old road. More memories await travelers at the nearby Union Miner's Cemetery where the famed union activist Mother Jones—known as "the miner's angel"—lies buried beneath a simple headstone.

Yet well-placed highway shields alone are not enough to keep Route 66 alive. Car shows and road rallies—staple events for some Route 66 groups—may draw big crowds but do not directly help revitalize sagging buildings. The members and leadership of the Route 66 Association of Illinois realize this, and although they enjoy their own annual road trip, they also devote much of their resources and energy to vital preservation projects. Two of their most important contributions came in the late 1990s with the restoration of a 1930s gas station at Odell and a Meramec Caverns sign painted on a barn in Cayuga, just north of Pontiac. Both of these rehabilitated sites, along with other restoration projects, brought more sightseers to the old highway.

"Route 66 in Illinois has seen a real rebirth," explains John Weiss, chair of the state association's preservation committee, the

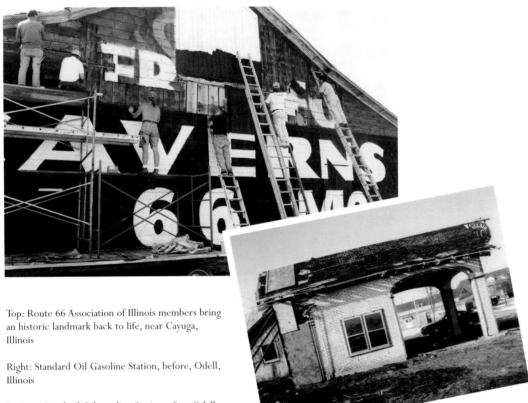

Top: Route 66 Association of Illinois members bring an historic landmark back to life, near Cayuga, Illinois

Right: Standard Oil Gasoline Station, before, Odell, Illinois

Bottom: Standard Oil gasoline Station, after, Odell, Illinois

group that spearheads the restoration efforts. "Our volunteers work extremely hard doing the labor and raising funds. Our efforts help keep the Route 66 nostalgic flavor but the old road is much more than older people and old places. Route 66 is alive and vibrant. We have something here in Illinois for everyone."

Those people leaving Illinois and entering Missouri immediately find that the Show Me State is serious about Route 66 preservation when the Mississippi River and the Chain of

- Gladys Cutberth *1904–2001*
- Norma Lee Hall *1927–2000*
- Lucille Hamons *1915–2000*
- Sam Kinison *1953–1992*
- Howard Litch *1906–1996*
- Miles Marion Mahan *1896–1997*
- Mickey Mantle *1931–1995*
- Roger Miller *1936–1992*
- Lou Mitchell *1909–1999*
- Mary Nichols *1922–1998*
- Lillian Redman *1909–1999*
- Jerry Richard *1950–1997*
- Lyman Riley *1918–1990*
- Jack DeVere Rittenhouse *1912–1991*
- Ronald Bruce Robb *1932–2000*
- Luther Davis "Luke" Robison *1914–1997*
- Helen Olive Rockwell *1912–1995*
- Nyal Rockwell *1913–1998*
- Jim Rogers *1915–2000*
- Roy Rogers *1911–1998*
- Will Rogers Jr. *1911–1993*
- George Rook *1935–1998*
- Mary Scott *1925–2000*
- Sterling Silliphant *1918–1996*
- Ola Soulsby *1912–1996*
- Russell Soulsby *1910–1999*
- Bobby Troup *1918–1999*
- Ed Waldmire *1916–1993*
- Chief Juan Yellowhorse *1930–1999*

Ride on, good friends.
Travel well.

Rocks Bridge come into view. The most famous river crossing on the entire length of Route 66, this bridge closed to traffic in 1968 shortly before the nearby Interstate 270 bridge opened. Through the years the discarded mile-long span sat forlorn and largely forgotten. Except for its use as a movie set, the vine-covered bridge collected graffiti and rust. There was serious talk of dismantling the obsolete landmark.

Then in 1996, Gateway Trailnet, a St. Louis–based nonprofit group dedicated to converting abandoned bridges and rail corridors into recreational trails, took over the old bridge.

Contributions from private and public sources and donations from everyday people poured in to fund the $4 million restoration process. Gateway's extraordinary restoration efforts included extensive structural repairs, deck sealing, and the addition of safety rails and fencing. Trails developed on both sides of the river to provide access to the bridge.

The hard work paid off in big dividends. In 1999, after being closed for thirty years, the Chain of Rocks reopened as the world's longest biking and pedestrian bridge. Some Route 66 aficionados believe the saving of the

Chain of Rocks Bridge is also one of the most important milestones in Mother Road history. Few can disagree.

All along the winding Route 66 corridor in Missouri, more examples of road revival abound. The ongoing struggle to preserve, promote, and develop the old highway in the state results from the efforts of the Route 66 Association of Missouri. Founded by James Powell, the organization's dedicated officers and directors come from the small burgs and big cities scattered on the highway between St. Louis and Joplin.

In Missouri, as elsewhere, Route 66 is never a static highway. There are familiar sites and historic structures on the various alignments and plenty of new ones waiting.

Sometimes, even in a state that relishes its ties to the past, a true relic of the road becomes lost, such as in the sad case of the Coral Court Motel. The venerable Art Deco landmark on the old highway in St. Louis became a true icon of Route 66. It was right up there with the Chain of Rocks Bridge, Ted Drewes Frozen Custard, The Diamonds, Meramec Caverns, Munger Moss Motel, and all the rest.

A favorite stopover for families, traveling salesmen, and amorous couples since 1941, the Coral Court closed all its bungalow doors in 1993. The greater Route 66 family rallied to save the complex, but all their valiant efforts and protests failed to stop real estate developers. Even the motel's listing on the National Register of Historic Places could not halt the Coral Court's demise. A wrecking crew razed the entire motel court in 1995 to make room

May 12, 1995, a gem of the highway goes down in St. Louis, Missouri

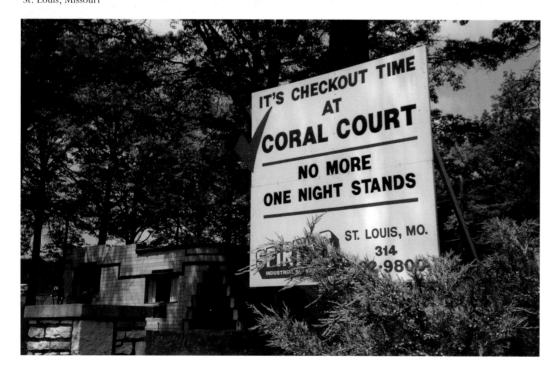

for a housing subdivision. The loss of Coral Court stung Route 66ers. It hurt more than the 1994 demolition of the nearby "66" Park In Theatre, a classic drive-in that gave way to a shopping center.

While the fans of the Coral Court grieved its loss, a photographer named Shellee Graham fought to preserve at least part of the architectural treasure. Before the motor court went down, Shellee documented every aspect of the streamlined architecture, the tile facades, and glass-block windows. Next she joined a posse of volunteers who gathered enough of the wreckage to reconstruct a complete Coral Court unit at the Museum of Transportation in St. Louis. The bungalow of honey-colored, glazed ceramic tiles and glass bricks was unveiled at the museum along with an interactive display of Coral Court and Route 66 memorabilia.

Shellee's devotion to history and hard work, including the publication of a photography and story book about Coral Court, helped salvage a Route 66 relic. Through her book, photographic shows at museums across the nation, and the Museum of Transportation display, future travelers will at least see a piece of a legend that has disappeared.

In the greater St. Louis area, other vestiges of Route 66 not only survive but flourish. For instance, on the original 1920s' alignment of the Mother Road, now called Manchester Road in far west St. Louis County, an entirely new crop of diners has found the Big Chief Dakota Grill. Opened simply as the Big Chief in 1929, the complex then included a cafe, souvenir shop, tourist court, and a filling station where gas sold for a dime a gallon. Tourists and truckers loved dining at the Big Chief, and even Babe Ruth stopped for a meal whenever the New York Yankees came to town.

Reopened in 1995 as the Big Chief Dakota Grill, the restaurant serves hearty fare such as bison burgers and grilled steaks to a steady stream of locals and travelers. In the dining room—decorated with saddles, blankets, and all kinds of Old West paraphernalia—the clientele are serenaded by the tunes of Gene Autry and the Sons of the Pioneers.

After lunch, satisfied diners may cruise a short distance to just east of the town of Eureka and visit a major revival project—the Route 66 State Park. The 1999 opening of this 409-acre park is a prime example of everyday citizens working with the government to transform disaster into triumph. The park is at the site of the abandoned Times Beach where in the early 1980s the discovery of the dangerous toxic chemical dioxin in the soil caused a federal buy out. The entire town was evacuated as residents left behind their furniture, clothing, and personal belongings. The contaminated roads and houses were bulldozed and incinerated. Times Beach was removed from maps and became known as the Three Mile Island of the Mother Road.

Over the years, scientists learned that dioxin was not as lethal as first thought, especially when they could not trace conclusively any illnesses among Times Beach residents to the toxic agent. Nonetheless a massive cleanup, that included burning the soil, continued; and by 1998, state officials announced the town was dioxin free for the first time in twenty-five

Bob Waldmire

Bob Waldmire on the road

Born: April 19, 1945
Occupation: Itinerant artist
Residence: Illinois, Arizona, and the
  open road

"Once upon a time, there was an aging hippie artist who traveled around the country in his old Volkswagen, drawing posters of college towns.

"Then one day, while heading east on a piece of Route 66—back in late 1987—he got the bright idea to draw a

Jim and Louise Gilbert at bridge near Route 66 State Park, Times Beach, Missouri

Robert and Ramona Lehman, proprietors of Munger Moss Motel, Lebanon, Missouri

years. Roadies up and down the old highway cheered the news. They cheered even louder when they learned what happened next.

Once the reclamation effort ended, the state's newest park quickly evolved under the watchful eye of the Missouri Department of Natural Resources. The facility includes hiking, biking, and horseback trails, picnic areas, and a boat launch on the Meramec River. The focal point is a visitors' center, featuring an impressive collection of memorabilia and artifacts donated by the Route 66 Association of Missouri. Crowds of visitors come to the park to hike, bird watch, or reminisce. Like the old road, Times Beach has paid its dues and come out on top.

A visit to the Route 66 State Park at Times Beach sets travelers up for a long string of highway stops in Missouri. Most of the old standards, such as the Gardenway Motel, Tri-County Truck Stop, Meramec Caverns, and the Wagon Wheel Motel, not only endure but have prospered during the revival period. Other examples of renewal, along with reminders of some sad losses, stand on the sides of Route 66 as the old road makes it way through the scenic Ozarks.

One of Missouri's best models of persistence is the Red Cedar Inn. This roadside restaurant in the town of Pacific has become as busy as it was after opening in 1934. Closed

for a spell when folks seemed to prefer Interstate 44, the Red Cedar—a rustic, log building owned and maintained by the third generation of the same family—reopened in 1987. Today growing numbers of Route 66 devotees order chicken and dumplings, catfish, liver and onions, pork chops, real mashed potatoes, and bread pudding so delicious they lick the bowls clean.

More points of interest await down the road. Beyond the highway towns of St. Clair, Stanton, Sullivan, Bourbon, and Cuba is Route 66 Motors, the domain of Wayne and Patricia Bales. The hard-working couple has recycled an old filling station and created one of the better Mother Road gift shops, just five miles west of St. James on a length of Old Highway 66, which acts as the north service road for the interstate. It is also a classic automobile dealership with displays of antique advertising and road signs as well as a sales outlet for every

imaginable sort of highway memorabilia and memento. "We are living our dream," says Wayne, a staunch member of the Route 66 Association of Missouri since its founding in 1990.

At the town of Lebanon, a number of Route 66 enthusiasts check in at the Munger Moss Motel. Many of them do if for no other reason than to find out how this motel got its name. (Author's note: If you want to know, you will have to do the same thing.) The motel has only improved since 1946, when the original Munger-Moss—a sandwich shop on the Big Piney River at Devil's Elbow—left that Route 66 alignment, dropped the hyphen, and moved to the highway town of Lebanon. With the growing resurgence of interest in Route 66, owners Ramona and Bob Lehman welcome guests from around the globe, including adults with vivid memories of staying at the Munger Moss when they were kids.

Road warriors, rested after a peaceful night between the sheets at the Munger Moss, often stop at a small grocery store on the way out of Lebanon to get another Route 66 fix. Much more than a food store, Wrinks—owned and operated since it opened in 1950 by Glenn "Wrink" Wrinkle—has become a certified Route 66 attraction.

Travelers, particularly Europeans, pause to gobble handmade baloney and cheese sandwiches washed down with slugs of cold pop, or buy Route 66 souvenirs. The best part of the experience is listening to Wrink share a story or two about his life and times on America's Main Street. "Old 66 will never die," Wrink is fond of telling his customers. Not one of them disagrees.

The old road is healthy to the west in little Ozark towns and in the lively trade center of Springfield, a jumping off point for Branson, the entertainment mecca of mid-America. As is true in other Route 66 cities and towns, the road stops in Springfield are not just businesses but actual pieces of history.

One of the best is the Gilloiz Theatre, an architectural jewel that opened October 11, 1926, exactly a month to the day before the birth of Route 66. Through the decades the "glorious Gilloiz" attracted large crowds of film fans; but by the 1970s, when downtown businesses began moving to outlying malls, attendance at the 1,100-seat movie palace suffered. By 1980, the once opulent Gilloiz closed and almost immediately began to deteriorate.

In the early 1990s, serious talk started about restoring the downtown Springfield Square. Soon local citizens launched plans to bring back the Gilloiz. The show of strong support helped win the Gilloiz a place on the National Register of Historic Places in 1991. By the following year the Springfield Landmarks Preservation Trust bought the building, and restoration work got underway. Unveiling the first phase of restoration took place in 1994, and more improvements toward full restoration quickly followed. As work continued on the Gilloiz, the city also decided the time had come to reconnect Springfield with its heritage and the legacy of Route 66 by restoring the old traffic routes through the square.

"When traffic was rerouted off the square, they essentially killed business downtown," explains Tommy Pike, a driving force in the Route 66 Association of Missouri. "The city spent so much money to close off the roads and now in a twist of irony we are putting things back the way they were originally."

Another good example of restoring landmarks to their original state in Springfield is the Rail Haven Motor Court. Built in 1938, the original motor court expanded and changed its look through the years. It always

map of the old highway. The rest—as they say in show biz—is history. . . . When the map was finally finished and printed in 1992, the next 'bright idea' was 'incubating.' Already caught up and swept along in this great global phenomenon called Route 66, it seemed so natural to want to end up on 66—to get a place on the side of the road, from which to peddle my maps and other artwork.

"Someone sent me a newspaper story that showed a color photo of the old Hackberry [Arizona] General Store. To make a long story short it was indeed for sale and with the financial backing of my father [Ed Waldmire], the 22-acre property was purchased in January 1993.

"Nine months later, I moved from Illinois to Hackberry and opened the 'Old Route 66 Visitor Center.' Words cannot adequately describe the richness of my five years playing host to the world on the edge of old Route 66. And right up to the end of this five-year-long chapter of my life, they kept coming! They came—these wonderful, happy travelers fulfilling their 66 dreams from all 50 states and over 60 nations."

This introduction of Robert Waldmire comes from the man himself in one of his many Route 66 dispatches. Bob continues to distribute his epistles, replete with sketches of people and places, as he treks up and down Route 66.

Top: Playing on the old road, west of Bourbon, Missouri

Middle: Old Route 66 gas station, six weeks before final demolition in 1994, Springfield, Missouri

Bottom: Grand reopening of 66 Drive-In Theatre, Carthage, Missouri

attracted motorists by advertising itself as a place with "very good beds" and a "popular haven for women and children."

The Rail Haven first became part of the Best Western chain in 1948. Over the years the motor court survived reconstruction, changes of owners, and even the so-called "Wreck of '51," when in 1951 a speeding, out-of-control truck careened into the motel sign in a spectacular collision. Business fluctuated with the times, and the original establishment lost much of its charm. One manager even removed the rail fence that was part of the motor court's name. Then in 1994, Gordon Elliott, owner of Elliott Lodging, bought the Rail Haven and it became a Best Western–member hotel. It also got a badly needed facelift that restored much of its charm and appeal from the old Route 66 days.

The new owner and his family poured more than $1 million into the project. They reinstalled the distinctive split-rail fence that encircles the cottages and renovated the 93-room lodge in a meld of nostalgia and convenience, including special suites with classic chandeliers and old-time radios and telephones. Most importantly, they restored the heritage in a new name—the Route 66 Rail Haven.

Finally, just before Route 66 departs Missouri to briefly scoot through the southeast corner of Kansas, a flurry of both new and restored highway points of interest seduce travelers.

At Carthage, they run the gamut. Some people come to visit the Precious Moments Chapel on the southwest edge of town. At this sprawling complex—complete with theater, museum, and a wedding island—avid collec-

tors end their pilgrimages by buying porcelain figurines, including some wide-eyed angels that represent deceased children.

Many travelers prefer snooping through antique shops that have cropped up around town during the Route 66 revival. Or they check into one of the bed-and-breakfasts created out of the town's large Victorian homes. Some grab a room at the Boots Motel, a road-side refuge since 1939. These days John Ferguson owns and runs the Boots. Since 1991, he has kept the neon lights burning and the pastel, metal lawn chairs in place. Each room is as neat as a pin. All of them look just like they did back in the days when Clark Gable slept like a baby in Room 6 or Gene Autry spent the night while his horse, Champion, snoozed in the attached open garage.

Dining options in Carthage start not far from the Boots at CD's Pancake Hut. This cozy cafe—open twenty-four hours a day, every day of the year—serves breakfast, lunch, or dinner anytime. There is also the Gooseberry Diner, with fifteen varieties of pie baked in the kitchen every morning, or Carthage Deli & Ice Cream, a Route 66 hangout on the town square.

Rested and fed, the main place for road warriors to be on weekend nights in Carthage is the 66 Drive-In Theatre. Completely refurbished in the late 1990s and restored to the original look it had on opening night in 1948, this resurrected "passion pit"—an endangered species for many years—instantly rekindles memories. It also helps create new ones when the patrons pull up to the ticket booth or head for the concession stand to get candy bars, bags of popcorn, and icy drinks.

Jim Ross and Jerry McClannahan, champions of Route 66

After absorbing the sights of Carthage, people headed west still have plenty to see. Old signs and some worthwhile architecture from the various incarnations of the highway remain in Webb City and Joplin, the last stop on the western end of Route 66 in Missouri. The city has lost several heirloom businesses and stops from the days when Route 66 was the only path to take. Yet enough of them still exist on or at least near the old roadalignment through Joplin to give folks a taste of those times.

The R & M Restaurant remains a favorite, as does the upscale Wilders Fine Foods, now owned by Michael and Susan Golis. On Main Street since 1929, making it Joplin's oldest eatery, Wilders underwent a transformation and is one of the most elegant restaurants in town. Observant diners may spy a bullet hole in the solid Art Deco mahogany bar. It is a

souvenir from prohibition when Wilder's hosted a continuous high-stakes poker game and a bordello on the second floor did a booming business.

Bootleggers no longer use Route 66 to exit Joplin and carry their contraband booze into neighboring Kansas and Oklahoma. Times have changed some things. The Mother Road entering Kansas looks different. It is a much quieter place. The highway is no longer thick with traffic as it was long ago when the state's grand total of 13.2 miles of Route 66 was as busy as an L.A. freeway is today. Nonetheless, a Mother Road journey today is not complete without spending quality time in Galena, Riverton, and Baxter Springs—the trio of towns lining Route 66 across the corner of Kansas.

Jim Ross and Jerry McClannahan, creators of the invaluable *Here It Is!* series of Route 66 maps, put it this way: "Kansas Route 66 . . . can be driven in thirty minutes, bicycled in about an hour, and walked in half a day. Yet those 13.2 miles of the Mother Road musn't be missed, for they are as representative of the entire route as any stretch between chilly Lake Michigan and the warm Pacific."

Despite the good news in Kansas, a few old road personalities have slipped away. For example, travelers no longer receive pearls of road wisdom from the affable Howard Litch. The masterful storyteller and director of the Galena Mining Museum died in 1996 at ninety years of age. The best tribute to Howard, however, are the devoted volunteers who lovingly maintain the museum inside a restored railroad depot and greet visitors fresh off the Mother Road.

Often he makes the journey in a 1972 Volkswagen van but sometimes he travels in a 1966 Chevrolet school bus he bought long ago in Gallup, New Mexico. No matter how he makes the trip, each journey is memorable for Bob and all those he meets along the way.

If any one person most typifies the spirit and determination that keeps Route 66 alive and has put the famous highway back on so many maps, it has to be Bob Waldmire.

He has not written books about the old road, nor has he composed any songs or produced films that have helped folks understand why Route 66 still has value. He has no web site. Bob contributes in other important ways.

He is a poet with a sketch pad. His constant outpouring of artwork—pen-and-ink portraits of endangered, destroyed, and hidden places along the Mother Road—has helped inform travelers about the importance of this ribbon of concrete and asphalt.

Bob is the conscience of all road warriors out on the old road.

This unassuming sojourner lives outside of time and without the slightest worry about material wealth. He has learned how to take his creativity and use it, not for exploiting the Mother Road, as some have done, but for saving the highway.

Those travelers who come across

Top: Eisler Brothers Store, a Route 66 haven, Riverton, Kansas

Above: Spring River Inn after the fire, October 1999, Riverton, Kansas

Cruising out of Galena just four miles to the west comes the crossing over the Spring River and the town of Riverton. The Spring River Inn, a restaurant known up and down the highway for turning out top-notch food, burned to the ground in 1999, but this little Kansas burg remains a Route 66 stronghold.

Since 1990, the town of Riverton has emerged as the nerve center for the highway's revival movement in this region. Headquarters for the ardent Mother Road fans of Kansas is Eisler Brothers Old Riverton Store. A focal point on the road since 1925, a year before Route 66 became official, the store sells groceries, freshly made sandwiches, bottles of icy cold pop kept in an old soda cooler, and seasonal potted flowers. It is also famous for its broad selection of Route 66 books, merchandise, and collectibles—some of the best on the road.

Scott Nelson, president of the Kansas Historic Route 66 Association, runs the old store with lots of help from his family. On days when he is not teaching music, Scott is there, stocking shelves and visiting with travelers from around the world. Sometimes Scott's faithful associates show up for a chat, such as Darrell Ray, a tireless Missourian with strong Kansas ties, or Dean Walker, a Kansan steeped in the best local yarns and gossip of the old road.

"We may not have much actual Route 66 roadway," says Scott, smiling, "but what Route 66 we do have we sure make the most of."

One of the strongest of all the Mother Road organizations, the Kansas Historic Route 66 Associa-tion has members from several states and foreign nations. Since the early 1990s, the association has sponsored an annual "Race Across Kansas," a half-marathon run that starts on the issouri-Kansas border, follows the old road through Kansas, and concludes on the Oklahoma state line.

The Kansas association also has promoted tourism and local businesses along the old road and led the fight to save key sites, such as the Rainbow Bridge built over Brush Creek in 1923. The successful battle for this graffiti-covered bridge threatened with destruction came after lengthy negotiations. Finally, in 1996, the association and local government officials joined to refurbish the structure and save it for posterity. Today the bone-white bridge is one of the favorite photo stops on Route 66.

A short way beyond the bridge is Baxter Springs. Known in the distant past as the "First Cow Town in Kansas," Baxter Springs is the last of the Kansas towns on the Mother Road for those westbound. Rich in history and folklore, the town preserves much of its past through the efforts of the Baxter Springs Historical Society. Besides an exceptionally good museum that is constantly improving, Baxter Springs sports many points of interest and more than a dozen restaurants and cafes.

One of the most frequented since the late 1990s, is the Cafe On the Route, located in a bank building robbed by Jesse James in 1876. For many years this building housed Murphy's Restaurant, since moved to another old bank building on the other side of Route 66. At the Cafe On the Route, dishes such as cowboy steak smothered in tobacco onions, pork spareribs, and nut-crusted catfish keep all the tables filled. Some contented diners

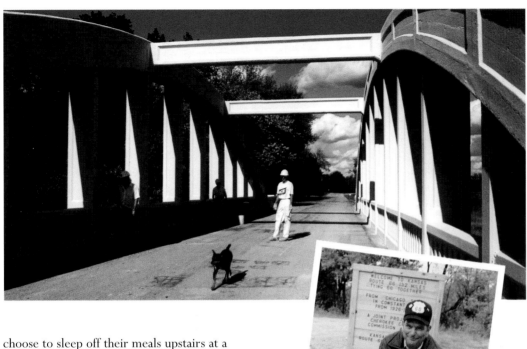

choose to sleep off their meals upstairs at a bed-and-breakfast named The Little Brick Inn.

Westbound travelers departing Kansas only have a few miles to go before reaching the border of Oklahoma, home to almost four hundred miles of Route 66, more than any of the other states. From Quapaw in the far northeastern corner of the state all the way to tiny Texola on the Texas state line, Oklahoma has fully embraced the tremendous Route 66 revival.

The state has also paid a price. There have been losses since 1990, including the deaths of several leading Oklahoma Route 66 figures. All are missed but their love of the old road continues with a new generation. Then there were the losses of businesses and even actual roadway. Some examples include: the

Top: Newly repainted Rainbow Bridge, near Baxter Springs, Kansas

Inset: Dean Walker does his feet trick on old road in Kansas

Bob often compare him to Henry David Thoreau, the poet-philosopher who tried to find a spiritual awakening by returning to a simple life in the woodlands. Still others see in Bob traces of three other spiritual allies—John Muir, Aldo Leopold, and Ed Abbey. Then there is the comparison to the legendary Johnny Appleseed. This eccentric folk hero, whose true name was John Chapman, roamed the American frontier in the early 1800s spreading his apple seeds and the word of Swedish mystic Emanuel Swedenborg. Indians considered him a medicine man, and settlers liked his gentle ways and respected his love of nature.

Instead of apple seeds, Bob leaves behind his magical artwork. He does not spread the word of any mystics, but through his example Bob quietly offers the gospel of the Mother Road.

He no longer lives in Hackberry, Arizona. Others have taken his place there. The gypsy-footed artist has since created a place of solitude far south of Route 66 in the remote Chiricahua Mountains of Arizona. The road is still his home, and he spends much of his time driving back roads, forgotten trails, and his beloved Route 66.

Look for Bob out on the old road.

He is at Glenrio, on the Texas–New Mexico border, cradling a turtle and laughing at the sun. See him

Buffalo Ranch near Afton; Pop Hicks Restaurant, a Clinton institution since 1936; Harvey's Barber Shop and Linda's Route 66 Cafe in Afton; a stretch of original Portland Cement roadway between El Reno and Weatherford; the original Route 66 Diner in Tulsa; and The Browsery, a revered road building in Tulsa.

Still, through the hard work of the Oklahoma Route 66 Association, the Oklahoma Historical Society, and hundreds of individuals, Route 66 in the Sooner State has spawned a new breed of roadside attractions. This state that was home to Cyrus Avery, Will Rogers, Woody Guthrie, Andy Payne, Jack Cutberth, and the fictional Joads has led the way in preserving much of the best of the Mother Road. The roadside highlights alone that have either reappeared or been created in Oklahoma since 1990 are staggering.

In the far northeastern Oklahoma city of Miami, restoration work on the Coleman Theatre Beautiful—as this landmark structure has become known—continues to bring the well-known Spanish revival–style structure back to its original 1929 grandeur. Due to the combined efforts of state and local entities and the contributions of volunteers and donors, the Coleman is again a busy place hosting concerts, ballets, films, and many other events.

One of the many highlights was the 1996 reinstallation of the original pipe organ, the "Mighty Wurlitzer." The money used to buy the organ and restore and refurbish it came from the donations of local citizens. That year the Oklahoma Historical Society also established a Route 66 Mini-Museum on the Coleman's mezzanine.

Right: Andy Payne statue, Foyil, Oklahoma

Continuing west in Oklahoma are more examples of the Route 66 renaissance. At Foyil, the hometown of Andy Payne, winner of the 1928 "Bunion Derby," a handsome granite monument honors his memory. On the eastern edge of town a bronze statue of Payne stands frozen in an eternal stride on the highway he helped make famous.

Just a few miles east of Foyil, the magnificent Ed Galloway's Totem Pole Park draws travelers like a magnet. On the National Register of Historic Places since 1999, the

park complex has been fully restored thanks to the Kansas Grass Roots Association, the Rogers County Historical Society, and the Galloway family. Restoration of the native stone home on the property ended in 1996 and repainting of the various totems and buildings in 1998. Route 66ers enjoy gawking at "the World's Largest Totem Pole" and visiting the museum and gift shop inside Galloway's old fiddle house. They also like picnicking on the shady, nine-acre park grounds, some of which the artist's family donated and the rest the historical society bought.

In Claremore, a good-sized Route 66 town, the Will Rogers Memorial and the J. M. Davis Arms & Historical Museum are still important draws but the list of local road attractions has grown. Visitors now also admire the fully restored Will Rogers Hotel, saved from demolition by the Rogers County Historical Society and reopened in 1998 as the Will Rogers Center. Renovated at a cost of more than $2.5 million, the center contains senior apartments, offices, and, in the lobby, an imposing statue of Will Rogers.

Between Claremore and Tulsa, near the highway town of Catoosa, the Blue Whale— one of the most well-known fixtures on Route 66 since the early 1970s—has returned to its former glory. In 1997, the Catoosa Chamber of Commerce and a volunteer work force spruced up the picnic grounds, cut back brush and weeds, and slapped a new coat of vivid blue paint on the friendly whale. Road warriors who pass him in review claim the Blue Whale's smile seems even wider.

Preservationists have very little to smile

about in Tulsa, a city that somehow cannot commit itself to the Route 66 revival movement. Since 1990, many of the buildings lining the old road through the city vanished, several of them needlessly. One of the few highlights include the saving of the brick-and-terra-cotta facade of the Warehouse Market, an Art Deco edifice located on the business route not far from the heart of downtown Tulsa. The main tenant in this recycled building is Lyons Indian Store, with roots deep in the past. Owned by Larry and Janie Lyons, the third generation of the family to operate the business, this combination trading company and Route 66 gift shop caters to all sorts of people. They include connoisseurs seeking genuine Indian artifacts,

Native Americans hoping to find costume materials for traditional dances and ceremonies, and tourists after souvenirs from America's Main Street.

Across the Arkansas River, just beyond Tulsa proper, in the bedroom community of Red Fork, travelers often pause at Ollies Station Restaurant on the shoulder of the old highway. Patrons regularly say the food at Ollies tastes like the food they grew up with made by their mom or grandma, the highest compliment for any down-home cafe.

Even a horrific fire in 1999 did not put a damper on Ollies. John and Lin Gray, husband and wife proprietors, wasted no time in rebuilding their restaurant to continue serving their

in Texas, that radiant grin melted on his face, tracking the journey of a busy wasp in the hot grasslands. Look for him in Illinois, at his family's famed Cozy Dog Drive-In. Watch as Bob hands out one of his coveted certificates of merit to a Route 66 cafe that provides salad bars for vegetarian travelers. Listen to him gently explain to a stranger why rattlesnakes are just as important as people.

"I will not abandon Route 66. I plan to stay involved as an artist, advocate for preservation, and fellow traveler-explorer. So you may find me along the road from time to time, perhaps at a Route 66 event. Till then, may your lives and travels be safe and joyous.
For the earth,
Bob Waldmire"

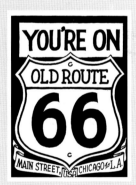

Route 66 seed

Left: Fully restored Totem Pole Park, Foyil, Oklahoma

Right: Blue Whale with a fresh look, Catoosa, Oklahoma

loyal following of locals and people of the old road. On a network of miniature railroad tracks overhead and throughout the dining room, John's model trains chug and snort while folks work on bowls of peach bread pudding straight out of the oven. It is comfort food for the drive ahead.

Between Tulsa and Oklahoma City, the Rock Cafe in the town of Stroud also understands the value of comfort food. This cafe has survived highway bypasses, oil busts, and killer tornadoes to emerge as one of the most resilient businesses on Route 66. Built of large sandstone rocks removed from the earth when highway workers carved the Route 66 roadbed, the cafe opened in 1939 and was an instant success. It soon became a bus stop for Greyhound and during World War II many young men took their sweethearts to the cafe before departing for military service.

Old-timers recall ice storms and trucks sliding down the highway like hockey pucks. They speak of power failures when cooks had to use the open fireplace to prepare meals and heat the restaurant. Others remember pushing the jukebox to an open window so local kids could dance outside under the moonlight. There are bitter memories as well, such as during the years of racial segregation when black customers had to order their food at the back door and sit outside to eat.

Through the years, the Rock's business plummeted with the coming of the turnpike that left Stroud and many other towns without much of a living. The Rock went through different owners, including some who had no regard for the cafe's place on the highway or

Above: The Round Barn, ready to stand forever, Arcadia, Oklahoma

in the hearts of so many people. That began to change in the early 1990s when a young woman named Dawn Herr took over the Rock. There were ups and downs—divorces, absences, and twisters—but Dawn and her second husband, Fred Welch, became secure at the Rock. They serve everything from buffalo burgers and Cajun dishes to German and Swiss cuisine to people who drive from far away to eat there. Bikers riding in packs or solo park their gleaming cycles out front or beneath the tall tree loaded with mistletoe. They consider the Rock their home. So does everyone else who walks through the front door.

The body and soul nourishment at the Rock Cafe sticks with folks continuing west. In Chandler, another staunch highway town,

citizens have banded together to save and restore an abandoned 1937 National Guard armory. They plan on converting the sandstone building into an Oklahoma Route 66 Welcome Center. The good folks of Chandler had plenty of role models to follow, including one just to the west at the town of Arcadia.

It would be a mistake to drive the old road in Oklahoma and not visit Arcadia, home of the Round Barn. Built in 1898, this perfectly round building with a great domed roof has become a true pearl in the long necklace of Route 66 attractions. Thanks to a gang of mostly elderly volunteers from the Arcadia Historical & Preservation Society led by the late Luke Robison, his wife Anna Robison, Eula "Toodie" Teuscher, Nellie Ottinger, and others, the dilapidated barn underwent a complete restoration. Contributions raised in the community and other generous donations paid for all the work.

Countless travelers have stopped to see the Round Barn since it opened to the public in 1992. They marvel at the expert carpentry used to create the curved arches. They listen to their voices echo in the cavernous upper story loft, tailor-made for fiddle music and the ideal setting for parties or weddings. Most of those who stop scribble their name in a guest book and buy a Mother Road keepsake from Butch Breger, manager of the gift shop that generates funds for upkeep.

A different sort of monument in Oklahoma City has become a stopping place not only for those using Route 66 but also large numbers of other visitors. Unveiled in 2000, the Oklahoma City National Memorial honors the victims killed on April 19, 1995, when a bomb exploded at the Alfred P. Murrah Federal Building. The bomb took 168 lives, making it the worst act of terrorism in the nation's history.

"I come here whenever I can," says a lone motorcyclist clad in leather and denim. "I pull off old Route 66 going through Oklahoma City and find my way here. This is part of the reality of my trip, just like the other places I visit. This is a very important stop."

Another memorial traces its origin to the old Mother Road alignment to the west of Oklahoma City between the highway towns of El Reno and Weatherford. In 2000, an actual section of Oklahoma Route 66—a dozen slabs of Portland cement roadway weighing forty

thousand pounds—ended up at the Smithsonian Institution.

The unusual contribution to the prestigious museum resulted from the Oklahoma Department of Transportation tearing up sections of old alignment despite spirited objections from Route 66 preservationists. Once work crews removed the roadway, however, most of the protesters agreed that at least the discarded portion of highway—original road dating from 1932 when Route 66 was first paved in Oklahoma—would live on as part of "America on the Move," a major exhibit at the Smithsonian.

Other pieces of Route 66 history from Oklahoma also found their way to the Smith-

sonian. A prime example is the time-worn Hamons Court sign from Lucille Hamons's old gas station and motel near the town of Hydro. Owned and operated by the so-called "Mother of the Mother Road" since 1941, Lucille's was a top-priority stop long before the Route 66 revival. In later years any road warrior looking for a cold drink and some conversation with a true Route 66 veteran paused at Lucille's.

Although Lucille died in 2000, her presence remains on the highway she loved. The sign from her business and the other remnants of Route 66 at the Smithsonian will ensure that a valuable part of the nation's history will last for many years to come.

Left: Lucille Hammons, less than a year before her death, at Oklahoma Route 66 Hall of Fame ceremony, 1999, Clinton, Oklahoma

Above: Pop Hicks burns, 1999, Clinton, Oklahoma

Beyond Hydro and Weatherford in the Mother Road strongholds of Clinton and Elk City, two other museums established in the 1990s also honor America's Main Street.

Clinton may have lost the landmark Pop Hicks Restaurant to fire in 2000, but the town remains one of the most stalwart on Route 66. One of the main reasons is the Oklahoma Route 66 Museum. A shining star of the revitalized highway, the museum—a creation of the Oklahoma Historical Society—opened in 1995. Almost overnight it became one of the real revival sensations on the Mother Road.

Made possible by a combination of state and local funding sources, the museum, trimmed in bright neon and filled with colorful displays, is a showcase offering a broad selection of important highway memorabilia and artifacts. Visitors to the museum take a decade-by-decade journey down America's Main Street, moving through exhibit areas and video displays that evoke strong emotions and accentuate the experience of open road travel.

Besides the Oklahoma Route 66 Museum, Clinton offers visitors several other choice highway stops. One of the best is the Mohawk Lodge and Indian Store with its authentic handmade Indian merchandise. Another is the nearby Cheyenne Cultural Center, featuring Indian arts and crafts exhibitions and dance demonstrations. Even with Pop Hicks gone, Clinton's dining options remain excellent. They include Jiggs Smoke House offering an assortment of meats ranging from beef jerky to succulent barbecue sandwiches so big truckers need both hands to lift them to their mouths.

For savory sit-down meals, roadies like to slide into a booth or pull up a chair at the Route 66 Restaurant, part of the Best Western Trade Winds Courtyard Inn. The free-standing dining facility and neighboring motor lodge are just across the road from the Oklahoma Route 66 Museum. The restaurant features steaks, catfish, and German sausage. They serve apple pie fit for a queen or a king. Speaking of kings, "The King" himself—Elvis Presley—spent the night at the Trade Winds on at least four different occasions. Those overnights came in the 1960s when he and his entourage traveled in Cadillac caravans from Memphis to Las Vegas or Los Angeles.

Restored to its original condition by Dr. Walter S. "Doc" Mason Jr., the "Elvis Presley Suite," or Room 215, still has many of the original furnishings, including the bed, vanity, divan, and bathroom fixtures. "He was always a very satisfied customer" recalls Doc Mason, himself a Route 66 legend. The Tradewinds also is the home of one of at least six Michael Wallis suites, named for the author of this book, scattered along Route 66.

West of Clinton at Elk City, another outstanding display of relics related to the road wait at the National Route 66 Museum. This outstanding 6,500-square-foot complex focuses on the people of the Mother Road and offers visitors a stroll through the eight states, highlighted with murals and historic vignettes. Outside the museum travelers are greeted by restored giant kachinas fashioned from welded oil drums and pipes. For many years these colorful figures greeted folks at the Queenan Trading Post, a Route 66 treasure that once prospered on the western edge of Elk City.

"We did not get rich but that trading post was something we really loved," explains Wanda Queenan, who owned and managed the business with her late husband, Reese. During the Route 66 revival of the 1990s, Wanda came out of retirement and became a curator at the

Oklahoma Route 66 Museum, Clinton, Oklahoma

National Route 66 Museum. "I cannot think of anywhere else on earth I would rather be than right here," says Wanda, smiling. "This town, this countryside, this old highway is my home."

Wanda Queenan's quiet eloquence sums up the feelings of many people in Oklahoma. That reaction resonates in Mickey Mantle's boyhood stomping grounds in the state's northeast corner. It also resounds across the land to the far western towns of Erick and Sayre—home of the Owl Drug Store, the Old Hotel Bed & Breakfast, and the RS&K Railroad Museum. Finally, Wanda's words ring true in Texola, the tiny last town in Oklahoma squatted right on the Texas line.

In Oklahoma the old highway—the Mother Road—is still home.

Those taking the long stretches of surviving old road who slip across the border find the same thing holds true in the Lone Star State. Across the Texas panhandle, the Route 66 revival has spread quicker than poison ivy at a nudist camp picnic.

The original Texas Route 66 totaled only 178 miles. At least 92 percent of the old road in Texas remains available for public travel. Due to the continued strong support from the Texas Old Route 66 Association, founded in 1991, the road revival has steadily progressed. Like the other seven states, each of the highway communities in Texas has something unique and interesting that cannot be found elsewhere.

Thanks to Richard Smith, one of the state's most vocal Route 66 supporters, and several other local citizens, the highway's past lives on in Shamrock. A prime example is the

Tower Station and U-Drop Inn, an Art Deco building complex that continues to attract photographers and architectural fans from around the world. In 1999, the First National Bank bought the Tower Station property from James Ray Tindall, son of the original owner. The bank then gifted the property to the city of Shamrock to restore and furnish as a tourist welcome and information center.

Leaving Shamrock, westbound journeyers cruising the old highway—mostly frontage road—reach McLean, a town that provides places to eat, drink, and sleep, as well as plenty of other diversions. They run from wall murals painted in the 1990s depicting some of the best Route 66 sites in Texas to the restored Phillips 66 gas station.

McLean also is the home of the Devil's Rope Museum, with its large collection of barbed wire, and a permanent Route 66 exhibit, featuring highway artifacts, commercial signage, and, of course, gifts. Lucky travelers stopping at the museum may run into Delbert and Ruth Trew, area ranchers and two hardworking supporters of the Route 66 movement in Texas.

"When people travel this old highway across the panhandle today, I tell them to remember those who went before them," says Delbert. "A bunch of them came looking for an easier life down the road. Sometimes we still see folks doing the same thing."

Continuing on, travelers reach Alanreed, with both the oldest cemetery and oldest Baptist Church on the Mother Road in Texas, and the fading remains of several gas stations and an old reptile ranch. The state's excellent

Tribute to a Texas Panhandle town

Route 66 signage system keeps everyone on the right path to Groom with its leaning water tower. Groom also boasts one the most popular attractions on the old road—a gigantic cross. Built of tubular white steel in 1995, the cross rises from a farmer's field west of town between old Route 66 and Interstate 40.

Officially named "The Cross of Our Lord Jesus Christ," it looms 190 feet tall, contains 75 tons of steel, and can withstand fierce panhandle winds up to 140 miles per hour. It ranks as the second largest cross in the world, the tallest in the western hemisphere. At night travelers can see the big cross for miles thanks to blazing floodlights. A guard house provides twenty-four-hour protection. Since it went up,

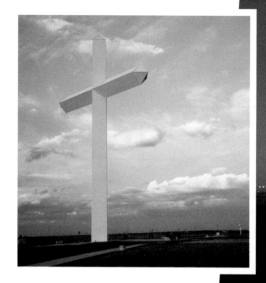

Above: Steel cross, west of Groom, Texas

Right: Twilight at the Cadillac Ranch, west of Amarillo, Texas

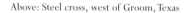

life-size bronze statues of the stations of the cross appeared around the base. In keeping with the best tradition of the ultraconservative "Bible Belt," followers built a monument to all aborted fetuses.

Many people, especially truckers, stop along the road to be married beneath the huge cross. The cross is both comforting to some travelers and controversial to others. This is in keeping with the reception of earlier Route 66 landmarks such as the wigwam motels and the Cadillac Ranch that have long since become standard Route 66 fare.

After Conway to the west, the old road enters Amarillo—the biggest city in the region and an important Route 66 revival market-

place. Amarillo Boulevard and the historic old San Jacinto District along Sixth Street, once the busy city route for the Mother Road, are not to be missed. Antique shops, galleries, cafes, bars, and other attractions popped up all along Sixth Street throughout the 1990s. In 1994, the San Jacinto area with its brick-paved streets gained a place on the National Register of Historic Places.

Out on Interstate 40, as elsewhere in the city, many of the restaurants and motels wisely have adopted a Route 66 theme. One of the pioneers—the Big Texan Steak Ranch, which started on Route 66 in 1959—continues to bring the true Mother Road flavor to both travelers of the old road and the superslab.

"I believe the future of Route 66 lives in the youth of today," says Becky Ransom, a former Amarillo schoolteacher and the personnel director for the Big Texan. "The kids are searching for who they are and where they came from and those answers and much more are found in the journey they take down Route 66. That journey can be in a car, on the Internet, watching a video, perusing the pages of a book, or in chance encounters. That is how I started my journey and I do not see it ending anytime soon."

On the western edge of Amarillo, near where old Route 66 rejoins the interstate, people still pause for a closer look at the hulks of ten classic Cadillacs buried nose down in the dirt. In 1974, Stanley Marsh III, the wealthy and eccentric Texan, unveiled his unorthodox shrine to America's passion for the open road. Since then, the Cadillac Ranch has become one of the most famous roadside attractions in the world.

In 1997, the Cadillac Ranch was back in the headlines when Marsh decided to dig up the cars and replant them a mile west to escape the expanding Amarillo sprawl. Within no time, another well-worn path led from the frontage road to the Cadillacs. Bikers, tourists, and open-road pilgrims continue to stop. They take photos and some leave friendly graffiti. They may scribble their names and the date, a message, or perhaps some kind of tribute to the Mother Road.

Along the western portions of Route 66 in the panhandle, there is ample evidence of restoration and revival on the old road. In the town of Vega, an original tourist court appropriately named the Vega Motel and located at the intersection of U.S. 385 and Old Route 66, usually has every carport filled at night. Other area motels, including the newer ones that appeared since the revival sparked, also get a healthy share of road business. So does Dot's Mini Museum, with displays of Route 66 and cowboy collectibles, and the scattering of cafes and fast-food joints geared up for both interstate and old road trade.

Unfortunately the Neon Soda Saloon—the once bustling roadside cafe and Route 66 haven George and Melba Rook created at Landergin—faded and died following George's death in 1998. Still, both George and the glory times of Landergin live on in stories told of the 1996 "Run to the Heartland." Hosted by the

Rooks in honor of the old road's seventieth anniversary, the event ranks as one of the most important gatherings in the highway's history. Many leading Route 66 champions appeared, and it marked the first Steinbeck Award ceremony sponsored by the National Historic Route 66 Federation.

Just down the old road from the remains of Landergin, life continues for a handful of highway businesses at the town of Adrian. One with particular drawing power is the Mid-Point Cafe & Gift Shop, one of the oldest eateries on Route 66. Originally only one room with a dirt floor when it opened in 1928, the cafe has added importance other than its continuous service and some superior burgers and pie. A monument acknowledges that Adrian is the official midpoint of Route 66, equidistant between Chicago and Santa Monica.

Then there is Glenrio, a wind-swept town straddling the border of Texas and New Mexico. Once a bustling railroad settlement and later a noteworthy stopping place on America's Main Street, Glenrio's downfall started when Interstate 40 bypassed the place. This forced business to close and people to move on and make a new start. It is a ghost town in the making, just as it was in 1990, but more ghosts have moved in and taken up residence. The Route 66 revival came too late for Glenrio and many other towns.

Yet these sites are as important as the multitude of Route 66 towns that are still serving up hospitality to generations of new travelers. Ghost places remind travelers of another time.

West of Glenrio, the old highway slithers

by the skeletal remains and weathered remnants of the empty hamlets of Endee and Bard. Travelers find no trace of human life until they reach San Jon. This once active trade center for ranchers only endures thanks to its proximity to the interstate highway. East- and west-bound traffic pull in for fuel, instant grub, or a few minutes of browsing in a curio shop that was once a church. The best Mother Road lures have gone and a vacant lot has replaced a block-long building covered with a mural of scenes from the Old West.

Although the old road alignment in the eastern part of New Mexico is picturesque, evidence of the Route 66 revival is not apparent until Tucumcari, forever a Mother Road bastion. In Tucumcari, road warriors can take the pulse of Route 66 at such respected high-

German travelers at Thomas Coffin's Route 66 sculpture, Tucumcari, New Mexico

way icons as Dels Restaurant, Tee Pee Curios, and the Blue Swallow Motel. Just a few minutes in Tucumcari confirms that the beat of the old highway is strong and steady and the revival of interest in Route 66 is as real as the road itself.

Those who require additional proof need only look into the eyes of Mike and Betty Callens. They have been the steadfast proprietors of The Tee Pee since 1985, four years after I-40 bypassed Tucumcari. The Callens and other Tucumcari citizens pitched in and went to work instead of allowing the highway bypass to cripple their town. As a result, they helped build an economy based on a combination of tourism and local trade. Mike and Betty are survivors. They are also inspiring role models for some Mother Road newcomers who have taken over the Blue Swallow Motel, a Route 66 fixture since 1939.

Many who stop there still feel the presence of Lillian Redman, the former Harvey Girl and an authentic road angel who owned and operated the historic property for so many years. Miss Lillian passed away in 1999 just shy of her ninetieth birthday. Before she left, Lillian and her magical cat, Smoky, moved into a small house not too far from the Blue Swallow. Sometimes she returned to visit and greet guests. She died knowing her beloved motel ended up in caring hands.

Hilda and Dale Bakke own and operate the Blue Swallow. The Bakkes and their daughter moved to Tucumcari from Colorado and took over the declining motel property in 1998. That was right after Dale spotted a newspaper advertisement offering what the seller described as "The Deal of the Century."

Hilda and Dale Bakke, owners of the Blue Swallow Motel, Tucumcari, New Mexico

Neither of the Bakkes knew much about Tucumcari, motel management, or Route 66. They became quick studies.

Hilda, a native of Brazil, and Dale, born and raised in Minnesota, went right to work. They scrubbed and painted, stripped the wooden floors, updated the plumbing and electricity, and always "tried to repair rather than replace." Dale, a skilled electrician by trade, rebuilt the neon blue birds outside the rooms. He also restored the Blue Swallow's blinking signature sign that has acted as the old road's night-light and attracted weary voyagers for decades. The Bakke's cat, Frances, naps curled up on a lobby chair, where guests often mistake her for Smoky. Two fine photo portraits of a smiling Miss Lillian have places of honor on the lobby wall.

After Tucumcari, most Route 66ers pick up the old road at Las Palomas after a Stuckeys stop. Ahead, the towns of Montoya, Newkirk, and Cuervo greet travelers hopscotching the

old road and interstate across plains and fenced pastures studded with yucca, mesquite, and juniper. At this point the two-lane becomes the best place for playing tag with the long lines of freight rolling east and west.

Before too long, Santa Rosa comes into view. The legendary Club Cafe, a Route 66 mainstay for years, is history. Nonetheless, Santa Rosa is still the hometown for several worthwhile eateries. If anyone leaves this town hungry, then they have no one but themselves to blame. One of the most popular stops in town since opening in 1996 is the Lake City Diner. Located in the heart of Santa Rosa in a stone building that once housed a bank, this exquisite diner attracts growing numbers of highway voyagers.

"Some folks tell us that a stop at our place is an important part of their trip. That makes us feel very special," says Frances Marquez, owner of the diner.

Other dependable Santa Rosa eating

Frances Marquez launched her Lake City Diner in an old bank building, Santa Rosa, New Mexico

houses include the Comet II Drive in & Restaurant, Silver Moon Restaurant, Route 66 Restaurant, and Sand & Sun Restaurant. Yet another is Joseph's Bar and Grille, founded in 1956 as La Fiesta by Joe Campos. Renamed Joseph's Restaurant, this reasonably priced old road fixture now belongs to the founder's son, Joseph Campos II, who also became the forward-thinking mayor of Santa Rosa in 1998. Within two years, the town had a new Route 66 Auto Museum and a lengthy list of civic improvements in the works. Most of these projects, including new road and directional signage, tree plantings, and historic renovation directly related to the active business loop of Route 66 in Santa Rosa.

"Even after I stop being the mayor, I will be a citizen of this town," says Campos. "Anything we can do to help preserve and protect Route 66 is positive for this town and for all who live here. That old highway is still our cultural corridor. It deserves saving and nurturing."

The place that most epitomizes the positive outlook voiced by the passionate Campos, is Albuquerque—largest city in the state and one of the largest on Route 66.

Travelers can either take the original Mother Road routing to Albuquerque by way of Santa Fe or else continue due west on the interstate highway. The Santa Fe route offers some interesting dining options along the original alignment, such as Bobcat Bite, a rustic restaurant just a few miles southeast of the Ancient City. At the Bobcat, patrons usually choose to devour possibly the best green-chile cheeseburger in the world.

Those who bypass Santa Fe for the more

Above: The Aztec Motel on Route 66 since 1931, Albuquerque, New Mexico

Right: Albuquerque veteran in last days

direct approach to Albuquerque can gas up and peruse the wares at Clines Corners, still a major souvenir depository. From there westward motorists reach the thriving highway town of Moriarty and then head into shadowy canyons. They drive through Edgewood, Barton, Sedillo, Zuzax, Tijeras, and Carnuel. After cruising through so many small towns and cities, most old road travelers notice Albuquerque's size. They also notice the city still pays plenty of attention to the Mother Road.

When some Route 66 adventurers reach Alburqueque, they think they have died and gone to heaven. The old highway was always good to this city; and during the years of the Route 66 revival, Albuquerque has taken the lead in tending to the needs of the old road

corridor, Central Avenue—eighteen miles of flashing neon lights, timeless motels, curio shops, and exceptionally good diners and restaurants. This choice segment of urban roadway runs out of the rugged canyons past the state fairgrounds and trendy Nob Hill district. It flanks the University of New Mexico and then slices through downtown before whizzing by Old Town, crossing the Rio Grande and ascending Nine-Mill Hill. All along the Albuquerque route are pristine examples of architectural renewal, such as the restored KiMo Theatre, as well as first-rate pie palaces and dining rooms to tempt famished road warriors.

One fuel stop that corrals its share of customers is the Route 66 Diner, not far from the university campus. Established in the late

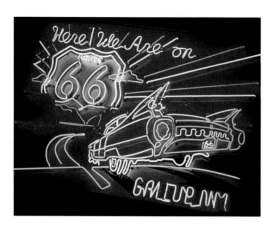

Monument to the open road, Gallup, New Mexico

1980s in an old Phillips 66 gas station, the diner burned to the ground in 1995. The following year, the owners resurrected the diner to its former glory. It continues to cater to a variety of folks—students, office workers, and, of course, tourists.

Examples of Mother Road revival stand out all along the city route. During the late 1990s, community and local authorities joined forces and set out to reclaim Central Avenue. Together they made a concerted effort to clean up derelict motor courts that for many years had become havens for prostitutes and drug dealers.

By 2000, at least nineteen old buildings in Albuquerque were placed on the National Register of Historic Places. "We've [New Mexico] been so poor that we don't rebuild, so we don't tear down," explains Rich Williams, the energetic president of the New Mexico Route 66 Association. "This road is part of Americana and we aim to save it."

This positive attitude surfaces along all 376 miles of Route 66 in New Mexico. It prevailed west of Albuquerque where preservationists successfully saved the steel truss Route 66 bridge over the Rio Puerco. The historic bridge that dates back to 1933 still stands next to the newer I-40 span. That attitude has also helped the winding lengths of Mother Road through Laguna, Budville, Villa de Cubero, and in all the other towns where people chose to not forget their roots.

At Grants, the largest stop between Albuquerque and Gallup, the former uranium boom town still draws visitors to the New Mexico Mining Museum with its Route 66 display. Dining choices include the Monte Carlo Restaurant, Grants Station Restaurant, and the Uranium Cafe. Always a strong railroad and highway town, Grants still acts as a travel center for motorists on the interstate and those people who choose to take the more scenic Route 66.

More and more people do pick the old highway out of Grants. They motor through Milan, Bluewater, Prewitt, Thoreau, and slide onto the interstate for a spell after the Continental Divide, the backbone of the nation. Then, at last, they come to Gallup, one of the matchless towns on the Mother Road.

Gallup is a guardian of many Route 66 landmarks and traditions. The city also makes room for additional ingredients in the savory mix, such as a handsome adobe mosque or the public sculpture garden filled with bronze statues. Along the city's nine-mile stretch of Route 66 are cafes, hotels, motor courts, and trading posts that appear much as they did long ago.

After making all the rounds in Gallup, those folks taking the final sixteen miles of old road west to Arizona may feel as if they are in a time warp. The road skirts rock walls tattooed with ancient advertisements and vintage curio stands tucked into the base of the steep bluffs.

They glide over the border into Arizona where "Historic Route 66" markers help guide Mother Road traffic. The signs show the way to Lupton, Holbrook, Joseph City, Winslow, Flagstaff, Williams, Seligman, Kingman, and all the other towns and places of interest waiting if only travelers will leave the four-lane Interstate 40. More than two hundred miles of original Route 66 remains in Arizona. The membership of the Historic Route 66 Association of Arizona, with headquarters in Kingman, makes sure that both the actual roadway and memories of the Mother Road survive for future generations.

Virtually every settlement and city on Route 66 in Arizona has experienced a positive impact from the highway's renaissance. Old road Arizona towns, including even tiny Winona—the place Bobby Troup warned everyone not to forget—are back in business.

Although a large part of the old road in Arizona lies buried beneath the four-lane interstate, such Route 66 landmarks as the Petrified Forest National Park and the Painted Desert Inn endure. A number of long-established old road businesses—such as the famed Jack Rabbit Trading Post near Joseph

Right: Golden carpeted road, east of Winslow, Arizona

City, or Joe & Aggies Cafe in Holbrook—flourish thanks to new family members at the helm.

At the wind-swept highway town of Winslow, citizens have much to be thankful for when it comes to the Mother Road revival. Likewise, all those people who care about Route 66 are indebted to Winslow for what the town has given back to the highway.

As much as any revival project, the restoration of La Posada Hotel in Winslow best exemplifies the tie between Route 66 and those who travel the old road. Opened in 1930, the spacious inn was just steps from the Santa Fe railroad tracks as well as Route 66. Designed by Mary Colter, lead architect for the Fred Harvey Company, the magnificent hotel resembled a Spanish hacienda complete with courtyards, graceful arcades, fountains, and lavish gardens. Colter considered La Posada her masterpiece. It soon became known as "The Most Beautiful Hotel on the Most Scenic Approach to the Grand Canyon." The guest book contained the signatures of Franklin D. Roosevelt, Will Rogers, Harry Truman, Charles Lindbergh, Albert Einstein, Amelia Earhart, and dozens of other celebrities.

La Posada closed to the public in 1957 after only twenty-seven years of operation. By the early 1960s, the Santa Fe Railway auctioned most of the furnishings, gutted the buildings, and transformed them into office space for their employees. Several times over the next forty years, plans to demolish the entire complex almost came to pass. Caring people in Winslow would not let that happen. Due to the continued efforts of Janice Griffith, director of the Old Trails Museum, and her loyal volunteers the hotel remained standing.

When the railway announced plans to vacate the old hotel, the future of the property again became doubtful. By 1994, the National Trust for Historic Preservation placed La Posada on its endangered list and the plight of the old hotel came to the attention of Allan Affeldt. In 1997, after three years of intense negotiation, Affeldt and his wife, Tina Mion, bought La Posada. They immediately set about to restore the hotel to its original grandeur.

Under the guidance of the new owners,

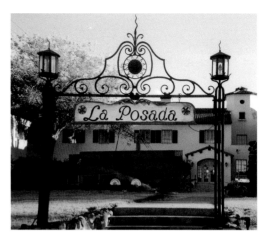

La Posada Hotel back in business, Winslow, Arizona

this national treasure reopened for the public in late 1997 in the midst of a $5 million renovation program. Today, guests—including many straight off the Mother Road—check into one of the restored guest rooms or dine in the Turquoise Room and Martini Lounge.

In 1999, Winslow again made news when the volunteer group that first focused on La Posada turned to revitalizing the downtown

area. Members of La Posada Foundation put a bronze statue of a man toting his guitar on the corner of an empty store lot. They dubbed it "Standin' on the Corner Park," in tribute to "Take It Easy," the hit road tune by The Eagles that made Winslow famous. No telling how many Route 66ers have stopped to have their picture taken beside the mute guitar player who gazes down the road looking for that girl in the flatbed Ford.

"Winslow is rocking again just like when I was a little girl," exclaims Diane Patterson, who runs a Route 66 souvenir mail-order business. "The Mother Road has returned to life and in a big way!"

Taking it easy in Winslow, Arizona

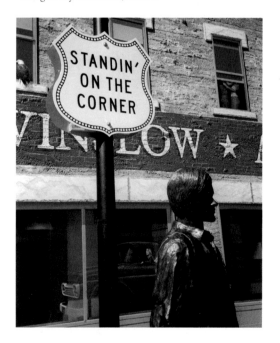

This holds true farther west in picturesque Flagstaff, home of Northern Arizona University and the largest old road town in the state. "Flag," as most roadies call it, fully embraced the Route 66 revival. Annual celebrations and fund-raisers help feed the coffers of local organizations whose main efforts involve the preservation and enhancement of Route 66.

Besides a glut of motels and cafes, Flag is also where Route 66ers flock to what many swear is the best roadhouse on the Mother Road—the Museum Club, better known as "The Zoo." Built on America's Main Street in 1931, this bar got its moniker when the original owner, a taxidermist by trade, erected the log building to house his stuffed wild critters and Indian artifacts.

By 1936, the museum became a nightclub but, to this day, many of the glassy-eyed animals and birds still dwell in the tree branches above the dance floor. Owned by Martin Zanzucchi, a leader in the northern Arizona Route 66 movement, The Museum Club draws large crowds of Mother Road enthusiasts. They show up to have drinks at the old mahogany bar and hear the rising stars of country music sing their hearts out on America's Main Street.

Westbound on Route 66, the town of Williams, gateway to the Grand Canyon, beckons to wayfarers on the old highway like never before. Ironically, the last of the towns to be bypassed by Interstate 40 back in 1984, Williams has not only rebounded but become a true leader among Route 66 communities.

It is not difficult to see how this has happened. The Grand Canyon Railway once again steams its way from Williams to the south rim

of the Grand Canyon every day from March to December. Landmarks such as Rod's Steak House, in business since 1946, and The Route 66 Place, pull in waves of customers. New souvenir shops with the latest Route 66 merchandise pop up along the crowded road through the heart of town.

Credit for much of the town's comeback success goes to Paul and Sandi Taylor. The couple launched the *Route 66 Magazine* in the early 1990s and then moved the entire operation from Laughlin, Nevada, to Williams in 1996. Along with their daughter, Jessi, and veteran writer and editor Bob Moore, the Taylors have consistently published a quarterly magazine that appeals to tens of thousands of domestic and overseas readers. Out of the Taylor's magazine has grown a bustling gift shop and a radio station formatted to the open road audience. A London office handles the constantly growing European market.

"This old highway is an endless avenue of stories," says Paul Taylor. "As far as this whole road revival goes, we see no end in sight."

Taylor's fellow highway boosters in towns stretching west from Ash Fork to Oatman feel the same way. That includes individuals such as Mildred Barker and her kin still running the Frontier Motel & Cafe in Truxton, or John and Kerry Pritchard, the couple who took over the restored Hackberry General Store from Bob Waldmire, the original gypsy of the road. It includes the many friends of the Mother Road in downtown Kingman involved with the construction of the Powerhouse Visitor Center.

Across northern Arizona—at ancient ruins and neon lodges—the old highway is not a mirage after all but a ribbon of motion and energy. This is the road that tumbles down the hard western slope of Arizona. It then leaps tepid river waters into California, a land that has always promised new beginnings for so many.

For some people, just the mere mention of Needles—the California border town that greets Route 66 wanderers—causes them to break out in sweats and heat rashes. In truth, this old railroad and highway town has much more going for it than record-setting temperatures. Needles has always been near the vanguard of the Route 66 revival movement in California.

Except for a brief interruption, Needles boasts more than ten continuous miles of driveable Mother Road between two outlying Interstate 40 off-ramps. The good folks of Needles have made the most of their section of the old highway as the popularity of Route 66 has increased. More visitors take time to stop and look around town instead of circumventing Needles on the interstate highway.

Old motels and well-established cafes abound, and visitors enjoy slow city drives to see turn-of-the-century homes or stop at the Needles Regional Museum. Directly across the street from the museum stands the stately El Garces, a Harvey House from 1908 until it closed in 1949. The hotel served as offices for the railroad until they moved to new quarters in 1988. Since that time, this magnificent hotel has become the pet project of a band of local citizens, including preservation proponent Maggie McShan. She has led the long-term renovation effort to convert El Garces into a historical museum.

Paul and Sandi Taylor, founders and publishers of *Route 66 Magazine*, Williams, Arizona

A visit to Needles is the ideal tonic for travelers before they make the long drive across the Mojave Desert. Along the way are familiar haunts and, as always, new ones to remind road warriors that Route 66 is fluid and alive and constantly changing.

For instance, Dennis Casebier has founded the Goffs Historic Cultural Center at the desert hamlet of Goffs about a half-hour cruise west of Needles. A retired navy physicist with an abiding interest in the historic Mojave Road, Casebier moved to Goffs in 1992 and set up headquarters in the mission-style schoolhouse that closed in 1937. Casebier and his Friends of the Mojave Road/Mojave Desert Heritage & Cultural Association, or MDHCA, established a research library, publish a news-letter, and collect oral histories from desert old-timers.

Visitors can still see the rock streets built during World War II by some of the sixteen thousand army troops stationed at Goffs.

At Amboy, another well-known Route 66 desert crossroads, Buster Burris, the long-time operator of Roys Cafe Garage & Motel, died in 2000, but the property he maintained for a half-century remains. In 1995, photographer Timothy White and his partner, Walt Wilson, glided into Amboy on their Harleys. They were after gas but came away owning the town after shelling out $146,000 for the diner, motel, abandoned school, church, and a handful of other old buildings.

White and Wilson immediately set about to turn their town of Amboy—which they call a "magical place"—into a desert oasis. At the same time, the former New Yorkers have tried to retain and preserve Amboy's colorful charm that made it "the crustiest, dustiest gas stop on all of Route 66." Besides Mother Road traffic, other frequent visitors to Amboy include some of White's celebrity pals such as Clint Black, Anthony Hopkins, and Harrison Ford.

"When the sun goes down," White told reporters in 1999, "there are millions of visible stars. It's like being on the deck of a spaceship."

To the west of Amboy at Newberry Springs, where the filming of the cult movie *Bagdad Cafe* took place, the old Sidewinder Cafe has assumed the name of the motion picture. Streams of tourists, particularly Euro-peans, come to the cafe to eat and visit with local characters whose numbers seem to steadily increase.

To the west at Barstow, the midway point between Los Angeles and Las Vegas, an impressive Route 66 museum has breathed new life into an old highway town. Hundreds of excited friends and fans of the old highway showed up on July 4, 2000, for the grand opening of the Route 66 Mother Road Museum. Located in the renovated Casa del Desierto, an early Harvey House, the museum immediately became known as one of the finest on the old highway.

Completed in 1911, the Casa del Desierto, or "House of the Desert," not only served railroad passengers but also catered to Route 66 travelers. Highlights of the museum include vintage automobiles and motorcycles, a collection of historic photographs, and artifacts related to the area's Route 66 history.

For a change of pace, a growing number of Route 66ers head to Helendale, situated between Lenwood and Oro Grande on the old Route 66 loop. They divert from the beaten path to take in the nearby Exotic World. This museum, devoted to famous burlesque performers, is the ideal spot to shake off some trail dust. Those in the more traditional museum mood hold out for Victorville, home of the impressive California Route 66 Museum. Another option at Victorville is the Roy Rogers–Dale Evans Museum, a memorial to the nation's favorite cowboy and cowgirl.

Next comes the Cajon Pass, the most important gateway to southern California, long before Interstate 15 replaced the old Mother Road alignment in 1969. The Summit Inn Cafe, built in 1952 and one of few survivors on this portion of the old highway, remains a favorite pit stop.

Motorists, refreshed for their downhill jaunt, head to San Bernardino. They can take in the fully restored California Theater of Perform-

Fine art—Route 66 style

ing Arts now being used as a playhouse and the California Historic Route 66 Museum located at the site of the original McDonald's, before moseying to Foothill Boulevard (aka Route 66) for the final leg of the Mother Road journey.

Many businesses tied to highway trade have vanished on this long stretch through what is called "the Inland Empire" and beyond through greater Los Angeles. Yet enough remain to provide a flavor of past times.

The Wigwam Village, the teepee-shaped motel units on Foothill, has enjoyed an increase in tourist trade with the Route 66 revival. The once notorious and often rundown operation also cleaned up its act and spruced up the entire complex. Moving westward toward the Mother Road's ultimate stop, several of the more historic buildings have disappeared. In some instances, a battered sign remains as a sad reminder.

There are holdouts that will probably never vanish. One is Sycamore Inn in Rancho Cucamonga, supposedly the oldest restaurant

in operation on Route 66. The first Sycamore served as a Butterfield Stagecoach stop. The current restaurant, the fourth building on the site, dates to 1915, and continues as an upscale dining establishment. More worthwhile stops on Foothill Boulevard include the Azuza Foothill Drive-in, the Claremont Inn and Griswold's Old School House at Claremont, and the well-preserved Aztec Hotel with its 1920s Mayan motif in Monrovia.

Foothill—Route 66—turns into Colorado Boulevard at Pasadena, where one of the finest restorations on the Mother Road proudly stands as an example of historic preservation at its best. Built in 1913, the soaring Colorado Street Bridge across the Arroyo Seco closed to traffic in 1989 due to concerns over its ability to withstand earthquakes. During the early 1990s, at a cost of $27 million, teams of workers carefully restored the bridge. Today it remains the symbolic entrance to Los Angeles and one of the highlights for any road warrior navigating the final section of the old road before it reaches the Pacific at Santa Monica.

There, overlooking the broad beach and distant ocean surf, Route 66 voyagers stoop to read the brass Will Rogers Highway plaque. Beneath the tall palms they pause to pay their respects to the road behind them and to all those who have traveled America's Main Street. They usually linger for a while. Then they leave. It is a ritual repeated over and over again. For traveling Route 66—America's road—is a never-ending journey.

Route 66 Logbook

1912
- National Old Trails Association forms in Kansas City, MO, to promote a national transcontinental highway. Route 66 will later follow this same path from Romeroville, NM, to Los Angeles, California.

1913
- First drive-in gas station opens in Pittsburgh.

1914
- American Association of State Highway Officials, AASHO (later named American Association of State Highway and Transportation Officials, or AASHTO) is established to assure uniformity of highway construction.

1916
- President Woodrow Wilson signs the first Federal-Aid Road Act providing $75 million to states in matching road project funds.

1917
- Ozark Trails Association maps the "Ozark Trails" at a meeting in Springfield, MO. one branch follows the path of what will become Route 66 from St. Louis to Romeroville, NM, where it links with the Santa Fe Trail and the National Old Trail Road.

1920
- Harley-Davidson, founded in 1903, becomes the largest motorcycle manufacturer in the world.

1921
- Congress passes the second federal-Aid Road Act or the Federal-Aid highway Act of 1921, providing for the establishment of an integrated system of roads so states will be eligible to receive federal funds.
- Nation's first drive-in restaurant opens in Dallas, TX.
- Cyrus S. Avery, a business and civil leader from Tulsa, OK, is elected president of the Associated Highways Association of America.

1922
- St. Louis, MO, becomes the site of the first suburban shopping center.

1923
- More than 15 million automobiles are registered in the United Sates.

1924
- Avery is selected to head a joint board charged with designing and numbering a new system of federal highways during an American Association of State Highway Officials (AASHO) meeting in San Francisco.

1925
- Federal-Aid Highway Act passed by Congress, creating the Federal Aid Highway System and the highway numbering system.
- Allan Odell conceives the idea of using consecutive signs along roadsides to advertise Burma-Shave.

1926
- U.S. Route 66 is commissioned thanks to the efforts of Cyrus Avery—who becomes known as the "Father of Route 66"—John Woodruff, and other highway officials.

1927
- U.S. 66 Highway Association forms in Tulsa, OK. John Woodruff is elected the first president.
- Ford Motor Company introduces the Model A.
- Phillips Petroleum introduces Phillips 66 fuel.

1928
- C. C. Pyle's first annual International Trans-Continental Foot Race. Popularly known as the "Bunion Derby," the event puts Route 66 on everyone's map when an Oklahoma farm boy named Andy Payne wins the race.
- First automobile radios are installed.

1929
- Stock market crashes, marking the start of the Depression.
- Chain of Rocks Bridge spanning the Mississippi between Illinois and Missouri opens and by 1935 becomes a Route 66 crossing.
- Coleman Theater opens on Route 66 in Miami, OK.

1930
- La Posada, designed by Mary Colter, opens for business in Winslow, AZ.
- At the Lowell Observatory in the Route 66 city of Flagstaff, AZ, astronomers discover a new planet they name Pluto.

1931
- Thousands of well-wishers gather at Rolla, MO, to mark the completion of Route 66 paving in the state.
- The first cloverleaf exchange west of the Mississippi River is completed in St. Louis, and by 1936 becomes the junction of U.S. 66 and City 66.

1932
- Franklin Roosevelt elected thirty-second president.
- Thousands of motorists take Route 66—advertised as "The Great Diagonal Highway"—to the Olympic Games staged in Los Angeles.

1933
- World's Fair is held in Chicago.
- First drive-in movie theater opens in Camden, NJ.
- First billboards announcing mileage appear on roadways due to concern for fuel economy.

1934
- Drought and sandstorms drive thousands of tenant farmers and others from the Dust Bowl states down Route 66 to California.
- Andy Payne, the "Bunion Derby" winner, elected clerk of the Supreme Court of Oklahoma, a post he will hold for the next thirty-eight years.

1935
- Will Rogers and Wiley Post killed in airplane crash. Both are buried near Route 66.
- Route 66 is extended from downtown Los Angeles to its famous termination point overlooking the Pacific Ocean in Santa Monica.

1936
- U-Drop Inn, destined to become a famous Route 66 landmark, is constructed in Shamrock, TX.

1937
- Nine striking miners are shot and killed on Route 66 during labor unrest in Galena, KS.
- Route 66 is almost completely paved in all eight states.

1938
- Route 66 bypasses the ancient city of Santa Fe, NM, and is rerouted directly west from Santa Rosa to Albuquerque.
- Amarillo, TX, hosts a gala celebration to salute the completion of the paving of Route 66 from Chicago to Santa Monica and the formal dedication of Route 66 as the Will Rogers Highway.

1939
- John Steinbeck calls Route 66 "the mother road" in his Pulitzer Prize–winning novel, *The Grapes of Wrath*.
- Clark Gable and Carole Lombard wed in the highway town of Kingman, AZ, then speed up Route 66 to spend their honeymoon night in the mountain town of Oatman, AZ.
- Air-conditioning for cars is introduced.

1940
- Premier of the motion picture adaptation of *The Grapes of Wrath*, directed by John Ford.

1941
- General George Patton trains his armored troops throughout the Mojave Desert just off Route 66.

1942
- New car and truck sales are banned as civilian auto industry gears up for the war effort. Gasoline and tire rationing ordered for all civilians.

1943
- Automobile production in U.S. falls from 3.7 million in 1941 to 610 in 1943.
- German prisoner of war camps open throughout the nation, including several on or near Route 66.
- Dust Bowl folk singer Woody Guthrie publishes his autobiographical *Bound for Glory*.
- Broadway show *Oklahoma!* premiers, based on the play *Green Grow the Lilacs,* by Lynn Riggs, a writer-poet from Claremore, OK.

1944
- Congress approves a "National System of Interstate Highways," but no funding is allotted for road construction.

1945
- Ed Waldmire, an Illinois native, invents the "crusty cur," a battered hot dog on a stick.
- World War II ends. Civilian passenger car production resumes and gas rationing ends.

1946
- Bobby Troup writes "(Get Your Kicks on) Route 66" and sells the song to Nat King Cole.
- Jack Rittenhouse publishes *A Guide Book to Highway 66,* the standard guide for many years.
- The world's first drive-through window opens at Springfield, MO.
- First drive-in banking service in America instituted by a Chicago bank.

1947
- The U.S. 66 Highway Association is reestablished during a meeting in Oklahoma City.

1948
- Original McDonald's Restaurant featuring fifteen-cent hamburgers and ten-cent fries opens in San Bernardino, CA.
- Approximately thirty thousand motor courts (motels) in operation across the U.S.

1950
- Uranium boom underway in Grants, NM, after Paddy Martinez makes discovery on Haystack Mountain.

1951
- Ernest Hemingway writes a portion of *The Old Man and the Sea* while staying at Villa de Cubero in New Mexico.
- The George Washington Carver National Monument near Joplin, MO, becomes the first national park honoring an African American.

1952
- The U.S. 66 Highway Association sponsors a caravan down Route 66 to dedicate the road as the Will Rogers Highway.

1953
- Chevrolet begins production of the Corvette, a car that becomes closely associated with Route 66.
- First Holiday Inn opens.

1954
- Ford Motor Company introduces the Thunderbird.

1955
- Ray Kroc opens his first McDonald's franchise store in Des Plaines, IL.
- Jack Kerouac's novel *On the Road* is published.
- Disneyland opens in Anaheim, CA.

1956
- Passage of the Federal-Aid Highway Act, calling for construction of an interstate highway system, including five highways to replace Route 66.

1957
- La Posada closes its doors.
- The numbering system and shields for the proposed interstate highway system are confirmed and construction begins.

1959
- Our Lady of the Highways shrine erected by Francis Marten on Route 66 in Illinois.

1960
- First of four consecutive seasons for the popular television series *Route 66* debuts on CBS.

1961
- Ray Kroc buys out the McDonald brothers for $2.7 million.

1962
- AASHTO turns down Missouri's petition to renumber Interstate 44 as Interstate 66.

1963
- Burma-Shave signs are taken down along roadways.

1964
- Studies reveal that 90 percent of the American public travel by private automobile.

1965
- President Lynden B. Johnson signs the Highway Beautification Act, outlawing billboards on the new interstates.
- Nat King Cole dies.
- Major fire shuts down the Dixie Truckers Home in Illinois for a day.
- The Gateway Arch completed in St. Louis, MO.

1966
- U.S. Department of Transportation is established.

1967
- Woody Guthrie dies.

1968
- John Steinbeck dies.
- Chain of Rocks Bridge is closed to vehicular traffic and by 1970 is bypassed by a new interstate bridge.
- The big Tesan Steak Ranch moves from Amarillo Boulevard (Route 66) to a site along Interstate 40 on the east side of Amarillo, TX.

1969
- Jack Kerouac dies.
- Premier of *Easy Rider,* filmed in part on Route 66 that helped to define and capture the feelings of the time.

1972
- The Eagles record "Take it Easy." The hit song about a fellow "standing on a corner in Winslow, Arizona," becomes one of the favorite tunes for Route 66 travelers.

1974
- Stanley Marsh 3 erects the Cadillac Ranch just west of Amarillo, TX.

1976
- The U.S. 66 Highway Association formally disbands.

1977
- Route 66 is decertified in Illinois and Missouri, and the highway shields are removed and replaced with interstate highway signage.
- Andy Payne, winner of the 1928 Bunion Derby, dies.

- The Society for Commercial Archeology, a confederation of aficionados of roadside architecture, is founded.

1980
- Onondaga Cave becomes a Missouri state park.

1981
- Chain of Rocks Bridge is used as a location for the final scene of the motion picture *Escape from New York.*

1982
- Federal government recommends residents of Times Beach, MO, abandon their homes because of contamination from dioxin spraying.

1983
- Federal government buys out the highway town of Times Beach, MO.

1984
- Final section of original Route 66 is replaced by four-lane interstate highway at Williams, AZ.

1985
- Route 66 is officially decommissioned.

1988
- First annual Arizona Route 66 Fun Run is staged.

1990
- Congress passes the Route 66 Study Act of 1990, recognizing the highway's importance and value and identifying options for preservation.
- Several states establish Route 66 associations in order to preserve and protect the highway.

1992
- Club Cafe closes in Santa Rosa, NM.

1993
- *Route 66 Magazine* founded by Paul and Sandi Taylor.
- The Federal Highway Administration celebrates a century of service to the nation.

1994
- The American Society of Civil Engineers declares the interstate highway system one of the "Seven Wonders of the United States."

1995
- A car bomb destroys the Alfred P. Murrah Federal Building in Oklahoma City, OK, killing 168 persons.
- Oklahoma Route 66 Museum, a creation of the Oklahoma Historical Society, opens in Clinton, OK.
- National Park Service completes its Route 66 survey and issues Special Resources Study.

1996
- Route 66 turns seventy years old.
- Thousands of Harley-Davidson riders from around the world flock to the Mother Road for the first Harley Owners Group (H.O.G.) tour of Route 66.
- Run to the Heartland, Landergin, TX, draws one of the largest gatherings of Mother Road fans and notables in history.
- The original McDonald's Restaurant is inducted into the San Bernadino Cruisin' Hall of Fame.

1998
- The National Route 66 Museum opens in Elk City, OK.

1999
- Congress passes legislation authorizing a program to conserve the cultural heritage of Route 66. President Clinton signs the landmark bill into law.
- Pop Hicks Restaurant burns to the ground in Clinton, OK.
- La Posada hotel, closed since 1957, is restored and re-opens in Winslow, AZ.
- Restored Chain of Rocks Bridge is dedicated as a recreational trail.
- The Route 66 State Park opens at the site of Times Beach, MO.

2000
- KRTE–FM Radio, "The Voice of Route 66," takes to the airwaves in Williams, AZ.

2001
- Seventy-fifth anniversary of Route 66; major anniversary celebrations and commemorations are staged all along the old highway.
- The second Harley Owners Group (H.O.G.) Route 66 tour attracts motorcycle riders from around the world.

Resource List

BOOKS (FICTION)

Cobb, James H. *West on 66.* New York: Thomas Dunne/St. Martin's Minotaur, 1999.

Fortes, Jack. *The Band Leader.* Philadelphia: Xlibris Corporation, 2000.

Kerouac, Jack. *On the Road.* New York: The Viking Press, 1955.

Kirby, Susan E. *Main Street: Home for Christmas.* New York: Avon Books, 1994.

Kirby, Susan E. *Main Street: Lemonade Days.* New York: Avon Books, 1994.

Nichols, Chet. *The Last Riders on Route 66.* N.p.: 1st Books Library, December, 1998.

Sanders, William. *A Death on 66.* New York: St. Martin's Press, 1994.

Steinbeck, John. *The Grapes of Wrath.* New York: The Viking Press, 1939.

Wheat, Carolyn. *Murder on Route 66.* Prime Crime, July, 1999.

BOOKS (NONFICTION)

Anderson, Warren H. *Vanishing Roadside America.* Tucson: University of Arizona Press, 1981.

Andrews, J. J. C. *The Well-Built Elephant and Other Roadside Attractions: A Tribute to American Eccentricity.* New York: Congdon & Weed, 1984.

Ansaldi, Richard. *Gas, Food and Lodging: A Postcard Odyssey Through the Great American Roadside.* New York: Harmony Books, 1978.

Baeder, John. *Gas, Food, and Lodging: A Postcard Odyssey Through the Great American Roadside.* New York: Abbeville Press, 1982.

Baeder, John. *Diners: Revised and Updated.* New York: Harry N. Abrams, 1995.

Baker, Kent. *66/99: An American Road Trip on Route 66.* Ipso Facto, October, 1999.

Belasco, Warren James. *Americans on the Road: From the Autocamp to Motel, 1910–1945.* Cambridge, Massachusetts: MIT Press, 1979.

Blake, Peter. *God's Own Junkyard: The Planned Deterioration of America's Landscape.* New York: Holt, Rinehart and Winston, 1964.

Boyne, Walter J. *Power Behind the Wheel: Creativity and Evolution of the Automobile.* New York: Stewart, Tabori & Chang, 1988.

Buckley, Patricia R. *Route 66: Remnants.* Arizona: Historic Route 66 Association of Arizona, 1989.

Butler, John L. *First Highways of America.* Iola, Wisconsin: Krause Publications, 1994.

Casebier, Dennis G. *Goffs & Its Schoolhouse: The Historic Cultural Center of the East Mojave Desert.* Essex, California: Tales of the Mojave Road Publishing Company, 1995.

Clark, Marian. Introduction by Michael Wallis. *The Route 66 Cookbook: Comfort Food from the Mother Road, Deluxe 75th Anniversary Edition.* Tulsa, Oklahoma: Council Oak Books, 2000.

Crump, Spencer. *Route 66: America's First Main Street.* Corona Del Mar, California: Zeta Publishers, 1994.

Curtis, Spencer. *The Missouri U.S. 66 Tour Book.* St. Louis, Missouri: Curtis Enterprises, 1994.

Davies, Vivian, and Darin Kuna. *Guide to Historic Route 66 in California,* 3rd ed. LaVerne, California: The California Historic Route 66 Association, April 1994.

Finch, Christopher. *Highways to Heaven: The Auto Biography of America.* New York: HarperCollins Publishers, 1992.

Flink, James J. *The Automobile Age.* Cambridge, Massachusetts: MIT

Press, 1988.

Graham, Shellee. *Return to Route 66: Route 66 Postcards.* Tulsa, Oklahoma: Council Oak Books, 1998.

Gregory, James N. *American Exodus: The Dust Bowl Migration and Okie Culture in California.* New York: Oxford Press, 1989.

Guthrie, Woody. *Bound for Glory.* New York: E. P. Dutton, 1943.

Hart, Virginia. *The Story of American Roads.* New York: William Sloan Association, 1950.

Least Heat Moon, William. *Blue Highways: A Journey into America.* Boston: Atlantic Monthly Press, 1982.

Heimann, Jim, and Rip Georges. *California Crazy: Roadside Vernacular Architecture.* San Francisco: Chronicle Books, 1980.

Hess, Alan. *Googie: 1950's Coffee Shop Architecture.* San Francisco: Chronicle Books, 1985.

Hilleson, K., and D. Nakii. *Route 66 Revisited: A Wanderer's Guide to New Mexico, Vol. 1, Albuquerque to the Arizona Border.* Albuquerque, New Mexico: D. Nakii Enterprises, 1988.

Hilleson, K., and D. Nakii. *A Wanderer's Guide to New Mexico, Vol. 2.* Albuquerque: D. Nakii Enterprises (P.O. Box 7639, NM 87194), 1985.

Hoekstra, Dave. *Ticket to Everywhere: The Best of Detours Travel Column.* Chicago, Illinois: Lake Claremont Press, 2000.

Keller, Ulrich. *The Highway as Habitat: A Roy Stryker Documentation, 1943–1955.* Santa Barbara, California: University Art Museum, 1986.

Kurtz, Stephen A. *Wasteland: Building the American Dream.* New York: Praeger Publishers, 1973.

Langdon, Philip. *Orange Roofs, Golden Arches: The Architecture of American Chain Restaurants.* New York: Alfred A. Knopf, 1986.

Lange, Dorothea. *American Exodus: A Record of Human Erosion in the Thirties.* New Haven: Yale University Press, 1969.

Leavitt, Helen. *Superhighways Superhoax.* New York: Doubleday, 1970.

Leibs, Chester. *Main Streets to Miracle Mile: American Roadside Architecture.* Boston: Little, Brown, 1985.

Leverton, Bill. *On the Arizona Road.* Phoenix, Arizona: Golden West Publishers, 1986.

Lewis, David L., and Lawrence Goldstein. *The Automobile and American Culture.* Ann Arbor: The University of Michigan Press, 1980.

Lewis, Lucinda. *Roadside America: The Automobile and the American Dream.* New York: Abrams, 2000.

Lund, Michael. *Growing Up on Route 66.* Chesterfield, Missouri: Beachhouse Books, 2000.

Mahnke, Dan. *Antique Roads of America, Bicycle Guide for Route 66.* Self-Published, 1992.

Margolies, John. *The End of the Road: Vanishing Highway Architecture in America.* New York: Penguin Books, 1981.

Margolies, John. *Home Away from Home: Motels in America.* Bullfinch Press, 1995.

Marling, Karal Ann. *The Collossus of Roads: Myth and Symbol Along the American Highway.* Minneapolis: University of Minneapolis Press, 1984.

Moore, Bob, and Patrick Grauwels. *Route 66: The Illustrated Guidebook to the Mother Road.* Del Mar, California: USDC, 1994.

Morgan, Dan. *Rising in the West.* New York: Alfred A. Knopf, 1992.

Noe, Sally. *Greetings from Gallup—Six Decades of Route 66.* Gallup, New Mexico: Gallup Convention & Visitors Bureau, 1991.

Noe, Sally. *66 Sights on Route 66.* Gallup, New Mexico: Gallup Downtown Development Group, 1992.

Patton, Phil. *Open Road: A Celebration of the American Highway.* New York: Simon & Schuster, 1986.

Rayburn-LaMonte, Terri. *Route 66: Goin' Somewhere.* Bloomington, Illinois: McLean County Historical Society.

Repp, Thomas Arthur. *Route 66: The Empires of Amusement.* Lynnwood, Washington: Mock Turtle Press, 1999.

Rittenhouse, Jack D. *A Guide Book to Highway 66.* Albuquerque, New Mexico: University of New Mexico Press, 1946.

Rittenhouse, Jack D. *A Guide Book to Highway 66 (a facsimile of the 1946 first edition).* Albuquerque: University of New Mexico Press, 1989.

Robson, Ellen, and Dianne Halicki. *Haunted Highway: The Spirits of Route 66.* Golden West Publishing, 1999.

Rose, Albert C. *Historic American Roads: From Frontier Trails to Superhighways.* New York: Crown Publishers, 1976.

Ross, Jim. *Oklahoma Route 66: The Cruiser's Companion.* Bethany, Oklahoma: Ghost Town Press, 1992.

Rowsome, Frank Jr. *The Verse by the Side of the Road.* New York: The Stephen Greene Press/Pelham Books, 1990.

Schneider, Jill, and D. Nakii. *Route 66 Across New Mexico: A Wanderer's Guide.* Albuquerque, New Mexico: University of New Mexico Press, 1991.

Scott, Quinta, and Susan Croce Kelly. *Route 66: The Highway and Its People.* Norman, Oklahoma: University of Oklahoma Press, 1988.

Scott, Quinta. *Along Route 66.* Norman, Oklahoma: University of Oklahoma Press, September, 2000.

Silk, Gerald, Angelo Anselmi, Henry Roberts Jr., and Strother MacMinn. *Automobile and Culture.* New York: Harry N. Abrams, Inc., 1984.

Snyder, Tom. *A Route 66 Traveler's Guide and Roadside Companion,* 2nd ed. New York: St. Martin's Press, 1990/1995.

Society for Commercial Archeology. Edited by Jan Jennings. *The Automobile in Design and Culture.* Ames, Iowa: Iowa State University Press, 1990.

Stern, Jane, and Michael Stern. *Roadfood.* New York: HarperCollins Publishers, 1992.

Suttle, Howard. *Behind the Wheel . . . on Route 66.* Red Oak Enterprises, October, 1996.

Teague, Thomas. *Searching for 66.* Springfield, Illinois: Samizdat House, 1991.

Thomas, James H. *The Bunion Derby: Andy Payne and the Great Transcontinental Footrace.* Oklahoma City, Oklahoma: Southwestern Heritage Books, 1980.

Wallis, Michael, and Suzanne Wallis. *Route 66 Postcards: Greetings from the Mother Road.* New York: St. Martin's Press, 1993.

Wallis, Michael, and Suzanne Wallis. *Songdog Diary: 66 Stories from the Road.* Tulsa, Oklahoma: Council Oak Books, 1996.

Weiss, John. *New, Historic Route 66 of Illinois.* A.O. Motiva-tion Programs, 1997.

Wilkins, Mike, Ken Smith, and Doug Kirby. *The New Roadside America.* New York: Simon & Schuster, 1992.

Witzel, Michael. *The American Gas Station: History and Folklore of the Gas Station in American Car Culture.* Osceola, Wisconsin: Motorbooks International, 1992.

Witzel, Michael. *The American Drive-In: History and Folklore of the Drive-In Restaurant in American Car Culture.* Oceola, Wisconsin: Motorbooks International, 1994.

Witzel, Michael. *Gas Station Memories.* Osceola, Wisconsin: Motorbooks International, 1994.

Witzel, Michael Karl. *Route 66 Remembered.* Motorbooks International, 1996.

Woodward, Kirk. *Motorcycle Guide to Historic Route 66.* Self-Published, 1995, 1996, 1997.

U.S. ORGANIZATIONS

Historic Route 66 Association of Arizona, P.O. Box 66, Kingman, AZ 86402.

California Historic Route 66 Association, 2127 Foothill Boulevard, N66, LaVerne, CA 91750.

Route 66 Association of Illinois, 2743 Veterans Parkway, #166, Springfield, IL 62704.

Kansas Route 66 Association, P.O. Box 169, Riverton, KS 66770.

Missouri Route 66 Association, P.O. Box 8117, St. Louis, MO 63156.

New Mexico Route 66 Association, 1415 Central NE, Albuquerque, NM 87601.

Oklahoma Route 66 Association, P.O. Box 21382, Oklahoma City, OK 73156.

The Texas Old Route 66 Association, P.O. Box 66, McLean, TX 79057.

National Historic Route 66 Federation, P.O. Box 423, Dept. WS, Tujunga, CA 91043-0423.

INTERNATIONAL ORGANIZATIONS

Canada Route 66 Association, P.O. Box 31061, #8-2929 St. Johns Street, Port Moody, BC, V3H 4T4.

Route 66 Association of Belgium, Georges Moreai Street 172, 1070 Brussels, Belgium.

Route 66 Association of Germany, Kallstadter StraBe 8, 67098 Bad Durkheim, Germany 06322/8634.

Friends of Route 66, Germany, Im Lettemacker 1/4, 79588 Efringen-Kirchen Germany.

Friends of Route 66, UK, The Drum Inn, Cockington Village, Torquay, Devon TQ2 6XA UK.

Friends of Route 66, Norway, Smorasveien 22, 5238 Radal, Norway.

Dutch 66 World Association, Postbus 2012, 1620 EA Hoorn, the Netherlands, 02290-18318.

Association Française Route 66, 88 rue de Chateau, F,92600 Asnières, France.

The U.S. Route 66 Club (Japan), Kei Hirano, Marketing, 4-1-3, Kyutaro-machi, Chuo-ku, Osaka 541, Japan.

Acknowledgments

Word spread very quickly up and down Route 66 that I was preparing a new edition of this book. In no time, I received offers of assistance, cartons of photographs, personal information, and letters of encouragement from hundreds of people. Many of them are dear friends; all of them share with me a passion for the Mother Road.

Some deserve special mention, especially my wife and constant companion, Suzanne Fitzgerald Wallis, and our faithful muse Beatrice. Others in this category include Tim Bent and Julia Pastore, my guiding lights at St. Martin's Press; Linda Adams, Debra Silkman, and the entire crew at The Wallis Group; Jim Fitzgerald and Carol Mann; Michael Carlisle; Zigy Kaluzny; and Terrence Moore.

Here are the rest in alphabetical order.

Gary A. Adkins; Albuquerque Convention and Visitors Bureau; Kathy Anderson; Bob Audette; David Bahm; Tom Baird; Hilda and Dale Bakke; Wayne and Patricia Bales; Mildred Barker; Baxter Springs Historical Society; Butch Breger; Mike and Betty Callens; Joseph Campos II; Teri A. Cleeland; Isabell and Joe Eisler; Glaida and Steve Funk; Michael and Debby Funk; Robert Gehl; Maureen Geoghegan; Jim Gilbert; Susan and Michael Golis; Shellee Graham; Grants Mainstreet Project, Inc.; Janice Griffith, Old Trails Museum; Hiroshi Hanamura; Dan Harlow; David and Mary Lou Knudson, National Historic Route 66 Federation; Ramona and Bob Lehman; Linda and Christopher Lewis; Frances Marquez; Dr. Walter S. "Doc" Mason; Jerry McClanahan; Jeff Meyer; Billie Jo Moore; Bob Moore; Scott Nelson; Howard Nichols; Norwegian Route 66 Association; Dan Oberle; Jane Osborn, Friends of the Coleman Theatre Beautiful; John Paget; Diane Patterson; Glenda and Tommy Pike; Tonya Pike; Scott Piotrowski; James Powell; Wanda Queenan, The National Route 66 Museum; Rebecca Ransom; Darrell Ray; Steven N. Rider; George Rockwell; Jim Ross; Route 66 Mother Road Museum; Pat Smith, Oklahoma Route 66 Museum; Richard Smith; Annice Taken; Paul and Sandi Taylor, *Route 66 Magazine;* Tom Teaque; Eula "Toodie" Teuscher; Trailnet, Inc.; Delbert and Ruth Trew; Bob Waldmire; Buzz Waldmire; Dean and Paula Walker; Robert Weil; John and Lenore Weiss; Dawn and Fred Welch; Timothy White; Rich Williams; Martin Zanzucchi.

Photo Credits

66: Wallis Collection
67: Courtesy Anne Remington
68: Suzanne Fitzgerald Wallis, 1989
69: Courtesy Kim Corder and James Memorial Library
70: Courtesy Kim Corder and Pat Terrill
70–71: Calvin E. Hazlewood/Courtesy Dan Otis
72: Terrence Moore, 1984
74: above left, Courtesy Museum of Ozarks' History; above right, Courtesy Anne Remington; below, Suzanne Fitzgerald Wallis, 1989
75: Courtesy Anne Remington
76: Wallis Collection
77: Tom Snyder, 1986
78: Suzanne Fitzgerald Wallis, 1989
79: Suzanne Fitzgerald Wallis, 1989
80: Wallis Collection
81: Suzanne Fitzgerald Wallis, 1989
82: Tom Snyder, 1986
83: Suzanne Fitzgerald Wallis, 1989
85: Laura Meyer, 1988
86: Tom Snyder, 1983
87: Suzanne Fitzgerald Wallis, 1985
88: above left, Terrence Moore, 1984; above right, Wallis Collection; below, Don Wheeler, 1989
89: Fred W. Marvel, 1984/Courtesy Oklahoma Tourism and Recreation Department
90: Suzanne Fitzgerald Wallis, 1989
91: above, Courtesy Phillips Petroleum Company; below, Courtesy Phillips Petroleum Company
93: Courtesy Will Rogers, Jr., 1951
94: Orrick Sparlin, 1951/Courtesy Coleman Renovation Committee
95: Wallis Collection
96: above, Jeff and Laura Meyer Collection; below, Wallis Collection
98: left, Joy Galloway Collection/Courtesy Kansas Grassroots Art Association, Inc.; right, Joy Galloway Collection/Courtesy Kansas Grassroots Art Association, Inc.
100: above, Don Wheeler, 1989; below, Hugh S. Davis/Courtesy Betty Turner, The Browsery, Tulsa, Okla.
102: Terrence Moore, 1984
103: above, Wallis Collection; below, Don Wheeler, 1988
104: Don Wheeler, 1989
105: Suzanne Fitzgerald Wallis, 1988
106: left, Suzanne Fitzgerald Wallis, 1988; right, Suzanne Fitzgerald Wallis, 1988
107: Suzanne Fitzgerald Wallis, 1988
108: Terrence Moore, 1980
112: above left, Terrence Moore, 1976; above right, Suzanne Fitzgerald Wallis, 1989; below, Suzanne Fitzgerald Wallis, 1989
114: Richard Smith, 1988
115: Tom Snyder, 1989
116: above, Suzanne Fitzgerald Wallis, 1989; below, Wallis Collection
117: Suzanne Fitzgerald Wallis, 1988
118: left, Suzanne Fitzgerald Wallis, 1989; right, Tom Snyder, 1989
119: above, Tom Snyder, 1989; below, Suzanne Fitzgerald Wallis, 1988
120: Suzanne Fitzgerald Wallis, 1988

121: Tom Snyder, 1989
122: Terrence Moore, 1976
123: Tom Snyder, 1984
124: left, Wallis Collection; right, Wallis Collection
125: Wallis Collection
127: Terrence Moore, 1976
128: above, Suzanne Fitzgerald Wallis, 1988; below, Suzanne Fitzgerald Wallis, 1988
129: Wyatt McSpadden, 1989
130: Suzanne Fitzgerald Wallis, 1988
132: Suzanne Fitzgerald Wallis, 1988
134: above, Wallis Collection; below, Suzanne Fitzgerald Wallis, 1989
137: Tom Snyder, 1983
138: Courtesy Texas State Department of Highways and Public Transportation
139: Suzanne Fitzgerald Wallis
140: Terrence Moore, 1970
141: Terrence Moore, 1988
142: Suzanne Fitzgerald Wallis, 1988
143: above left, Wallis Collection; right, Wallis Collection/ Courtesy Clark Kimball; below left, Suzanne Fitzgerald Wallis, 1989
144: Courtesy Lyman Riley
145: Courtesy Ron Chavez
146–147: Terrence Moore, 1976
149: Suzanne Fitzgerald Wallis, 1988
150: left, Courtesy Phillips Petroleum Company, 1982; right, Suzanne Fitzgerald Wallis, 1988
152: above, Terrence Moore, 1976; below left, Terrence Moore, 1988; below right, Terrence Moore, 1984
153: Suzanne Fitzgerald Wallis, 1989
154: left, Suzanne Fitzgerald Wallis, 1989; center, Terrence Moore, 1989; right, Terrence Moore, 1984
155: Terrence Moore, 1984
156: Courtesy Ron Chavez
157: Terrence Moore, 1976
158: Courtesy Ron Chavez
159: above, Suzanne Fitzgerald Wallis, 1989; below, Jeff and Laura Meyer Collection
160–161: Suzanne Fitzgerald Wallis, 1988
162: DOD Collection/Courtesy State of New Mexico, State Records Center & Archives
163: Mary Murphey, 1989
164: left, Tom Snyder, 1983; right, Wallis Collection
166: Tom Snyder, 1983
168: Terrence Moore, 1970
169: above, Suzanne Fitzgerald Wallis, 1988; below, Suzanne Fitzgerald Wallis, 1989
170: above, Suzanne Fitzgerald Wallis, 1989; below, Terrence Moore, 1970
172: Suzanne Fitzgerald Wallis, 1989
173: above, Tom Snyder, 1989; below, McNitt Collection/ Courtesy State of New Mexico, State Records Center & Archives
174: left, Suzanne Fitzgerald Wallis, 1989; right, Suzanne Fitzgerald Wallis, 1989
175: Suzanne Fitzgerald Wallis, 1989
176: above, Courtesy Armand Ortega; below, Suzanne Fitzgerald Wallis, 1988
177: Tom Snyder, 1983

178: Courtesy Phillips Petroleum Company, 1982
179: Terrence Moore, 1980
180: Suzanne Fitzgerald Wallis, 1988
181: above left, Wallis Collection; above center, Suzanne Fitzgerald Wallis, 1988; above right, Wallis Collection; below right, Wallis Collection
182: Terrence Moore, 1980
184: Terrence Moore, 1971
185: Terrence Moore, 1976
186: left, Terrence Moore, 1980; right, Courtesy Phillip Blansett
187: left, Terrence Moore, 1980; right, Terrence Moore, 1988
188: above, Suzanne Fitzgerald Wallis, 1988; below, Suzanne Fitzgerald Wallis, 1988
189: Suzanne Fitzgerald Wallis, 1988
190: Tom Snyder, 1983
192: Terrence Moore, 1976
194: Tom Snyder, 1984
195: Terrence Moore, 1980
196: Suzanne Fitzgerald Wallis, 1988
197: Terrence Moore, 1971
198: Suzanne Fitzgerald Wallis, 1988
199: above, Courtesy Mrs. L. V. Moore; below, Suzanne Fitzgerald Wallis, 1988
200: left, Terrence Moore, 1988; right, Courtesy Phillips Petroleum Company, 1982
201: left, Suzanne Fitzgerald Wallis, 1988; right, Suzanne Fitzgerald Wallis, 1988
202: Suzanne Fitzgerald Wallis, 1988
203: Suzanne Fitzgerald Wallis, 1988
204: above, Suzanne Fitzgerald Wallis, 1988; below, Tom Snyder, 1989
205: Suzanne Fitzgerald Wallis, 1988
206: Terrence Moore, 1976
207: Terrence Moore, 1976
208: Suzanne Fitzgerald Wallis, 1988
210: Terrence Moore, 1976
211: Suzanne Fitzgerald Wallis, 1988
212: left, Suzanne Fitzgerald Wallis, 1988; right, Wallis Collection
213: Suzanne Fitzgerald Wallis, 1988
214: Terrence Moore, 1976
215: Suzanne Fitzgerald Wallis, 1988
216: left, Terrence Moore, 1976; right, Terrence Moore, 1976
217: left, Suzanne Fitzgerald Wallis, 1988; right, Suzanne Fitzgerald Wallis, 1988
218: Suzanne Fitzgerald Wallis, 1988
220: Terrence Moore, 1976
222: above, Courtesy James Powell; below, Wallis Collection
224: left, Wallis Collection/Courtesy Wigwam Village Motel; right, Suzanne Fitzgerald Wallis, 1988
225: left, Suzanne Fitzgerald Wallis, 1988; right, Courtesy Martin Milner, 1989
226: above, Suzanne Fitzgerald Wallis, 1988; below, Suzanne Fitzgerald Wallis, 1988
227: Courtesy Richard Tomasian, 1989
228: Tom Snyder, 1990
229: Jeff and Laura Meyer Collection
230: Suzanne Fitzgerald Wallis, 1988
231: Suzanne Fitzgerald Wallis, 1988
232: Suzanne Fitzgerald Wallis, 1988
233: Terrence Moore, 1976

234: Hiroshi Hanamura, 2000
235: Zigy Kaluzny, 2000
236: Zigy Kaluzny, 2000
237: top left, Norwegian Route 66 Association; bottom left, Shellee
   Graham, 1997; right, John Paget, 1998
238: John Paget, 1998
239: David Knudson, 1996
240: Jerry McClannahan, 2000
241: Steve Ryder, 1998
242: Shellee Graham, 2000
243: top, John and Lenore Weiss, 1998; center, John and Lenore
   Weiss; bottom, John and Lenore Weiss
244: Shellee Graham, 1995
245: Dan Oberle, 1996

246: top, Shellee Graham, 1998; bottom Hiroshi Hanamura, 1999
248: top, Hiroshi Hanamura, 1993; middle, Tonya Pike, 1994;
   bottom, Jim Ross, 1998
249: Kathy Anderson, 1998
250: top, Jerry McClannahan, 1999; bottom, Tonya Pike, 1999
251: top, Shellee Graham, 1996; bottom, Suzanne Fitzgerald Wallis,
   1997
252: Dan Oberle, 2000
253: left, Shellee Graham, 1996; right, Shellee Graham, 2000
254: Jim Ross, 1995
255: left, Jim Ross, 1999; above, Suzanne Fitzgerald Wallis, 1999
256: Hiroshi Hanamura, 1999
257: Bob Waldmire, 1994
258: above, Jeff Meyer, 1997; right, Hiroshi Hanamura, 1999

259: Zigy Kaluzny, 2000
260: top, Zigy Kaluzny, 2000; bottom, Zigy Kaluzny, 2000
261: left, Zigy Kaluzny, 2000; right, Zigy Kaluzny, 2000
262: Zigy Kaluzny, 2000
263: top, Dan Oberle, 1999; bottom, Hiroshi Hanamura, 2000
264: Diane Patterson, 2000
265: Terrence Moore, 2000
266: Jerry McClannahan

About the Author

Michael Wallis
www.michaelwallis.com

Michael Wallis is a historian and biographer of the American West. An award-winning reporter, his work has been published in more than one hundred national and international magazines and newspapers including *TIME, Life, People, Smithsonian,* and the *New York Times.*

Wallis is the author of ten best-selling books, including *The Real Wild West: The 101 Ranch and the Creation of the American West, Mankiller: A Chief and Her People, Way Down Yonder in the Indian Nation,* and *Pretty Boy: The Life and Times of Charles Arthur Floyd.*

He has won several prestigious awards and honors, including the Western Heritage Award from the National Cowboy Hall of Fame, the Oklahoma Book Award from Oklahoma Center for the Book, and the Best Western Nonfiction Award from the Western Writers of America, Inc. In 1999, he was inducted into the Missouri Writers Hall of Fame and received the Arrell Gibson Lifetime Achievement Award from the Oklahoma Center for the Book. Michael received the coveted Steinbeck Award in 1996 and was inducted into the Oklahoma Professional Writers Hall of Fame. In 1994, Michael received the Lynn Riggs Award from Rogers State College in Claremore, Oklahoma, and he was the first inductee into the Oklahoma Route 66 Hall of Fame.

Since 1982, Michael and his wife, Suzanne Fitzgerald Wallis, have made their home in Tulsa, Oklahoma. They also maintain a hideout in New Mexico.